FIRE IN A CANEBRAKE

The Last Mass Lynching in America

LAURA WEXLER

SCRIBNER

NEW YORK LONDON TORONTO SYDNEY SINGAPORE

SCRIBNER
1230 Avenue of the Americas
New York, NY 10020

SCRIBNER and design are trademarks of
Macmillan Library Reference USA, Inc., used under license
by Simon & Schuster, the publisher of this work.

For information about special discounts for bulk
purchases, please contact Simon & Schuster
Special Sales: 1-800-456-6798 or
business@simonandschuster.com

Designed by Colin Joh
Text set in Janson

Manufactured in the United States of America

1   3   5   7   9   10   8   6   4   2

Library of Congress Cataloging-in-Publication Data
Wexler, Laura, 1971–
Fire in canebrake : the last mass lynching in America / Laura Wexler.
p. cm.
1. Lynching—Georgia—Walton County—Case studies. 2. Mass murder—
Georgia—Walton County—Case studies. 3. African Americans—Crimes
against—Georgia—Walton County—Case studies. 4. Walton
County (Ga.)—Race relations. Title.

HV6465.G4 W49 2003
364.1'34—dc21
2002075814

ISBN 0-684-86816-4

FOR R.L.W. AND M.E.R.,

AND FOR MY PARENTS

$12,500.00 REWARD!

Rewards totaling $12,500.00 have been offered for information leading to the arrest and conviction of persons involved in the killing of 4 Negroes in Walton County on July 25, 1946.

All Information Will Be Kept Confidential

— CONTACT —

FEDERAL BUREAU OF INVESTIGATION
Telephone WAlnut 3605   Atlanta, Ga.

— OR —

GEORGIA BUREAU OF INVESTIGATION
Telephone WAlnut 5333   Atlanta, Ga.

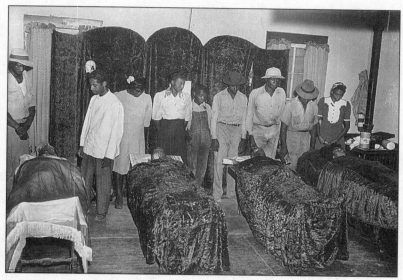

In Young Funeral Home in Walton County, Georgia, friends and relatives view the bodies of the four victims of the Moore's Ford lynching: *(left to right)* Roger Malcom, age twenty-four; Dorothy Malcom, age twenty; George Dorsey, age twenty-eight; and Mae Murray Dorsey, age twenty-three. (© Bettmann/Corbis)

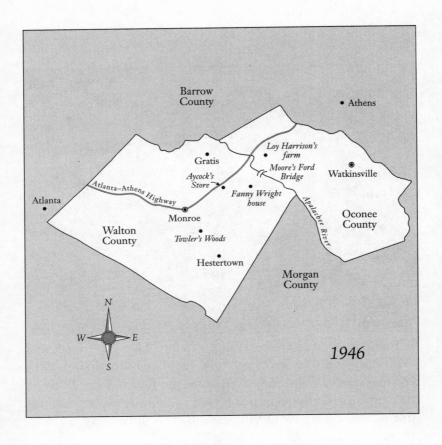

And how do you reach the truth if lying has become a habit?

—ARIEL DORFMAN, AFTERWORD TO *DEATH AND THE MAIDEN*

FIRE IN A CANEBRAKE

CHAPTER ONE

I don't want any trouble," said the white man, Barnette Hester.

He stood on one side of the dirt road, and his two black tenants, Roger and Dorothy Malcom, stood on the other side. They were shouting and cursing, their voices echoing through the Sunday-evening quiet. The noise had reached Barnette Hester in the barn. He'd stopped in the middle of milking, run out to the road, and issued his warning.

At twenty-nine, Barnette Hester was tall and thin, so thin he appeared boyish, as though his body hadn't yet filled out. His three older brothers were broad-shouldered men who spoke in booming voices, but he, the youngest, was shy to the point of silence—except on Saturday nights, when he drank liquor and talked and laughed a little. He'd been born in the modest house across the road. When the other men his age went off to the war, he stayed home to help his parents, and his father made him overseer of the family farm. They owned one hundred acres: a few behind the house, and the rest beyond the barn. That afternoon, after returning from church, Barnette had walked through the rows of cotton and corn and reached the same conclusion as many of Walton County's farmers: it was the beginning of lay-by time. The crops were nearly full grown, and fieldwork would be light for the next month or so, until the harvest.

When it was harvesttime, Barnette would work in the fields from sunup to sundown, snatching the cotton from the bolls and stuffing it into burlap croker sacks. And Roger and Dorothy Malcom would work alongside him. As children, Barnette and Roger had been playmates. But in January, when Roger and Dorothy moved onto the Hester farm, they'd become Barnette's tenants. Once, earlier in the spring, he'd found them fighting in the road in front of his family's house and told them to go home—and they'd obeyed. They'd walked to the fork in the road, taken the path down a small hill, and disappeared inside their tenant house. Barnette issued the same warning this evening, and he expected the same reaction.

Instead, across the road Roger Malcom charged at Dorothy. She dodged him, then ran down the road, into the front yard of the Hesters' house. As she passed, Barnette heard her say, "Roger's gonna kill me."

Roger went after Dorothy. He followed her into the Hesters' yard, and to the big fig tree, where he lunged at her again. Just then, Barnette's wife, Margaret, stepped out the front door of the house onto the porch. She watched Roger and Dorothy in the yard for a moment. Then she looked up and called to Barnette, "He's got a knife, and he's going to cut her."

Barnette crossed the road and entered the front yard. When he neared the fig tree, Dorothy darted onto the porch and she and Margaret rushed inside, leaving only Barnette's seventy-year-old father on the porch. Roger started up the porch stairs, and Barnette hurried to catch up with him. He stepped close, smelling the liquor on Roger's breath. He put his hand on Roger's arm and tried to turn him back toward the road. "Get out of the yard," Barnette said. And then, for the second time: "I don't want any trouble."

Roger Malcom shrugged off Barnette's hand and hunched over. Then he spun around and charged, his arm outstretched.

The blade of the pocketknife entered the left side of Barnette's chest, just below his heart.

After Roger Malcom pulled out his knife, he threw his hat on the ground. From the porch, Barnette's father heard him say, "Call me *Mister* Roger Malcom after this." Then he ran away.

When Barnette clutched his side and began stumbling toward the house, his father, Bob, assumed Roger Malcom had hit him hard in the stomach. Neither he, nor anyone else in the Hester family, realized that Roger Malcom had cut Barnette—not until Barnette collapsed onto the porch. Then Margaret saw the blood and cried out, "Take my husband to the hospital. He's bleeding to death."

With the help of Barnette's eldest brother, who was visiting from next door, Bob Hester carried Barnette out to the car and laid him across the backseat. Pulling out of the driveway, they turned toward the hospital, located nine miles away in the Walton County seat of Monroe.

By then, the white people who lived near the Hesters had heard the commotion. These neighbors—whose surnames were Peters, Adcock, Malcom, and also Hester—were related to Barnette's family and each other by blood or marriage, or both. Their ancestors had claimed farms in this section of the county during the land lottery of 1820, and they'd set their modest frame houses close to each other and to the road, preserving every inch of dirt for cotton and corn. The settlement had been dubbed Hestertown in the early days, and the name stuck because the families stayed. In 1946, roughly thirty Peters, Malcom, Adcock, and Hester families still lived along Hestertown Road. Some of the young men drove fifty miles each day to work at factories in Atlanta, and other men and women worked at the cotton mills in Monroe—but they remained in Hestertown and remained tied to the land and the community. On this July evening, some had been gathering vegetables in their gardens, preparing for the evening meal, when they heard the disturbance at the Hester house. Now they walked out from their farms to see if they could help.

Barnette's cousin Grady Malcom had already reached the road when the Hesters' car passed by. "Get Roger," Bob Hester called out the car window, "because Roger stabbed Barnette."

Grady Malcom, in turn, called to his brother, and together the two men, both in their fifties, ran toward the Hesters' house. When they saw Roger Malcom dart into a nearby cornfield, they followed him to the edge and yelled, "Throw down your knife and come out."

From deep in the cornstalks came the muffled sound of Roger Malcom's voice: "Who are you?"

When the brothers shouted their names, Roger Malcom said he wouldn't come out. But then, after a few minutes, he stood, tossed his knife to them, and surrendered.

By the time the brothers took Roger back to the Hesters' front yard, a crowd of neighbors had gathered. One man drove to the closest store to telephone the sheriff. Another man held Roger down while several others bound his hands and feet. Like Barnette, they'd known Roger Malcom for years, and they knew he was a fast runner—fast as a rabbit, everybody said.

It was nearly dark when Walton County deputy sheriffs Lewis Howard and Doc Sorrells pulled into the yard. They untied Roger Malcom, handcuffed him, put him in the backseat of their patrol car, and drove off in a cloud of dust.

The sheriffs retraced the route Barnette Hester's father had taken one hour earlier, driving roughly a mile to the end of Hestertown Road, and turning onto Pannell Road. Heading northeast, they traveled through the heart of Blasingame district, which lay near the southern point of diamond-shaped Walton County and contained the county's richest farmland. In Blasingame, as in the rest of the county, farmers planted corn, small grains, and timber—but their livelihood depended almost entirely on cotton. Since the beginning of agriculture in Walton County, cotton had been the major cash crop, comprising roughly 85 percent of the county's total agricultural profits each year. Under the guidance of the local extension agent, farmers planted only certain varieties of cottonseed and used only certain fertilizers, and their care paid off. Year after year, Walton County ranked at the top of Georgia's cotton-producing counties. In 1945, the county's farmers had averaged more than a bale per acre, shattering every cotton record in state history.

By 1946, farmers farther south and west had begun to employ mechanical cotton pickers, which did the work of forty farmhands, more quickly and more cheaply. But the rolling hills of Walton County, which was perched on the midland slope between the flat fields of middle Georgia and the mountains of north Georgia, made mechanical cotton pickers unusable. And so, despite the innovations— electricity, automobiles, radios—that had modernized much of rural life in Walton and its surrounding counties, farmers still depended on human labor to pick their cotton. In that respect, the harvest of 1946 would be no different from the harvest of 1846.

Within fifteen minutes of leaving the Hester house, the sheriffs had left the fields of Blasingame behind, passed a small forest known as Towler's Woods, and were entering the outskirts of town. They crossed over the railroad tracks—where several trains daily made the roughly forty-mile trip between Monroe and Atlanta— and drove by the town's two cotton mills, hulking brick structures that employed eight hundred white people. At times the mills ran day and night, but it was Sunday evening, and they were still.

A few blocks west, the sheriffs entered Monroe's downtown, a grid of paved streets containing banks, a department store, a hardware store, a pharmacy, and several restaurants. These were the standard establishments found in every county seat or trading center of the day, but Monroe had more to offer than most. It had two public libraries and two public swimming pools—one for Colored—as well as a city-owned ice plant, meat locker, and power and light system. Though a small town, with a population just under five thousand, Monroe boasted ten lawyers, fifteen doctors, and more than one hundred teachers. It was known throughout Georgia as a wealthy and progressive community, the first in the state to offer a groundbreaking public health-care program for both white and black citizens. And, as the birthplace of no fewer than six of the state's former chief executives, it had earned the nickname Mother of Governors.

Monroe's prosperity was partly due to the continued success of Walton County's farmers, who drove into town weekly to do their banking and buying. But it was also a result of its location as a midpoint on the highway that connected Atlanta, to the west, with Athens, to the northeast. Since its completion in 1939, the Atlanta–Athens highway had funneled tourists and businessmen through downtown Monroe, where they mingled with locals in the shadow of the town leaders' pride and joy: a stately brick courthouse topped by an elegant four-sided clock tower. Recently, Monroe had also earned bragging rights with its new electric streetlamps, which were aglow as the sheriffs drove through town with Roger Malcom.

Earlier in the day, men, women, and children dressed in their Sunday best had filled the pews of Monroe's thirty-six churches; the town fathers were proud to report that 95 percent of their citizens belonged to a church. After morning services, the streets emptied, and Sunday evenings, as a rule, were quiet. But on this Sunday evening, downtown was bustling. Groups of white men stood on the street corners and clustered around the Confederate memorial on the courthouse square. Some passed out pamphlets, signs, and bumper stickers; others gave impromptu speeches in support of Eugene Talmadge or James Carmichael. These were the two names on most Georgians' tongues that summer, the two lead candidates in the most hotly contested governor's race in state history. It was July 14. The election would take place in just three days.

The sheriffs turned onto Washington Street, drove two blocks north of the courthouse, and parked in back of the two-story cinderblock jail. Deputy Sheriff Lewis Howard, who served as the county jailer, took Roger Malcom from the car and led him into the group cell on the jail's first floor. After locking him in with two white prisoners—the county jail wasn't segregated by race—he walked down the hallway leading to the adjoining brick house where he lived with his family and secured the heavy metal door behind him.

Across town late that Sunday night, two doctors left the operating room and met Barnette Hester's father and brothers in a corridor of the Walton County Hospital. They didn't have good news. The blade of Roger Malcom's pocketknife had sliced through the upper region of Barnette's stomach, lacerating his intestine and puncturing his lung. The doctors had washed the protruding section of intestine and reconnected it. Then they'd inserted a tube to drain the fluid in the lung.

The risk of infection was grave, the doctors said. They weren't sure Barnette would live out the week.

CHAPTER TWO

Earlier that Sunday, Roger Malcom had set off with Dorothy and his seventy-four-year-old grandmother, Dora Malcom, for the trip from their tenant house on the Hester farm to Brown's Hill Baptist Church. The tiny frame church sat in a ravine at the edge of Hestertown, down from Union Chapel Methodist Church, where many of Hestertown's white families worshiped. On their way to Brown's Hill, the black people had to pass Union Chapel. As they did, their white landlords often yelled at them, saying they ought to be working in the fields instead of going to church. But it was just talk. No one, white or black, worked on Sunday.

Roger, Dorothy, and Dora Malcom—whom Roger called Mama Dora—had only been walking for a few minutes that morning when Mama Dora's feet began to ache. She continued on along the path that led up the hill from the tenant house, but when she reached Hestertown Road, she stopped and said she couldn't go any farther.

As Mama Dora started back home, Dorothy left Roger's side and ran to join her. Roger asked Dorothy to stay with him. When she said no, he yelled at her. When she still refused, he turned and continued walking. "I'm going on without you," he said. "I was going to leave you in the fall anyway."

Roger Malcom was twenty-four years old and had lived in Hestertown since the day in 1924 when he and his parents moved onto the Malcom farm, which lay roughly a mile from the Hesters' place. Soon after they arrived, Roger's father ran off with another woman. A year after that, his mother died. Mama Dora took two-year-old Roger and his sister on as her own children, and the Malcom family gave them their surname. Roger Malcom's name at birth had been Roger Patterson, but few people in Hestertown—black or white—knew that.

As a child, Roger had been treated kindly by his white landlords. In fact, some white people in Hestertown said the landlord's wife had spoiled him by treating him too much like her own son. He'd had to work in the cotton fields as soon as he could hold a croker sack, but he'd been allowed to play with the other black and white children in Hestertown, including Barnette Hester. That changed in 1931, when Barnette's older brother, Weldon, became the overseer at the Malcom farm and introduced nine-year-old Roger to the beatings and floggings that would be a regular feature of his life for the next fifteen years. One particularly brutal beating occurred on a day in 1937 when Weldon Hester threatened to whip Mama Dora for slacking in the fields. After Roger picked up a hoe to protect her, Weldon Hester attacked him instead. That day Roger fled to the town of Mansfield, in the next county south, but Weldon Hester found him and forced him to return to the farm. A few years later, Weldon Hester threw Coca-Cola bottles at Roger in the Hestertown store after he refused to haul wheat on a Sunday. He'd have beaten Roger further if a few white men hadn't restrained him.

In 1943, at the age of twenty-one, Roger married Mattie Louise Mack, a young black woman he'd met one Sunday at Brown's Hill Church. She left the farm in Hestertown where she'd been working and moved in with him and Mama Dora on the Malcom place. In January 1944, she gave birth to a son named Roger Jr. Eighteen months later, when she ran off to Atlanta, Roger had already met Dorothy Dorsey. She moved in with him and Mama Dora and, despite the fact that Roger and Mattie Louise were still legally married, began calling herself Mrs. Roger Malcom.

Then, in December 1945, Weldon Hester informed Roger and Dorothy that they'd have to move off the Malcom place; he'd rented out the farmland and no longer required their labor in the fields. Luckily, Barnette Hester needed hands on the Hester family farm down the road. So Roger and Dorothy loaded up a wagon with furniture and moved into the tenant house that sat down the hill from Hestertown Road. Since January, Barnette Hester had paid Roger by the day for his fieldwork and paid Dorothy by the week for cleaning, cooking, and helping to care for his two young children. Roger and Dorothy also had a cotton patch on the Hester place. They'd planned to use the proceeds from the sale of that cotton—minus what they owed Barnette Hester for rent, seeds, and fertilizer—to get to Chicago, where Roger's sister had moved. But lately Roger had begun to consider going to Chicago alone. And after Dorothy turned back, he had one more reason to do so.

In fact, he was so angry after Dorothy left that morning that, instead of walking to Brown's Hill, he walked to a nearby farm to buy a jar of bootleg liquor, then took the liquor to a friend's house and started drinking and talking about his troubles. The more he drank, the angrier he got. Finally he told his friend that Dorothy was running around on him. "She is going with a white man as sure as you're born," he said.

Roger Malcom's friend wasn't surprised by this revelation. Earlier in the summer, he'd seen Dorothy curse at Weldon Hester on the road, and when Weldon Hester didn't retaliate—didn't beat her, didn't even threaten to beat her—he'd immediately suspected they were having sexual relations. Other black people in Hestertown believed Dorothy was having sex with Barnette Hester—not Weldon Hester. They claimed they had relations while she worked in the Hester house and Roger worked in the field. Dorothy herself had once told Roger's sister that Barnette Hester had given her liquor. Roger's sister assumed Dorothy had given him something in return. Even Mama Dora thought Dorothy was "fast."

But still others in Hestertown had heard that Dorothy had tried to fight off Barnette Hester, that he'd forced her to have sex with him. They'd heard she told him, "Quit bothering me, before the other hands know about this mess." They knew the tradition; they knew their mothers, sisters, and wives—or they themselves—had been forced to have sex on the mornings or afternoons when the white landlord sent the men in their family to the most distant field on the farm. Some even suspected Roger Malcom was going to be killed so one or both of the Hester brothers could have easier access to Dorothy.

No doubt Roger and his friend discussed these possibilities that Sunday before Roger left to visit his old friend Allene Brown, a black woman who lived on a nearby farm. In Allene Brown, Roger found a sympathetic ear; she'd harbored suspicions about Dorothy for a long while. "She always go with white folks," says Allene Brown. "I told her to leave them alone." But even though she agreed with Roger, she tried to convince him not to confront Dorothy. He kept saying he was going to get her from Barnette Hester, and that scared Allene Brown.

"Don't go," she told him.

"I'm going," Roger Malcom said, "if I have to die with my shoes on."

Allene Brown begged him not to start trouble. "I tried to shame him out of it," she says. "I said, 'Why don't you do right?' He didn't pay me no attention."

Roger left Allene Brown's house that Sunday just before 6 P.M. and came in sight of the Hester farm in time to see Dorothy stepping into a car with a group of black people. He ran up, pulled her

out of the car, and confronted her in the road. When she ran into
the Hesters' front yard, he followed her. Then Barnette Hester
stepped between them and confirmed Roger's suspicions.

Mama Dora was standing in the road when Roger plunged his
knife into Barnette Hester's side. As he pulled it out, she heard him
say, "I thought you were going with my wife, and now I know it."

When Mama Dora turned and began to run, she saw the white
men chase Roger into the cornfield. She ran to get Roger Jr., and
when she returned to the Hesters' yard, she saw the white men
binding Roger's ankles and wrists. She knew they were going to
lynch him. With two-year-old Roger Jr. in her arms, she fled into
the woods surrounding Hestertown.

By then, some of the black people who lived in tenant houses
on nearby farms had heard the commotion and begun walking
toward the Hester house. A white farmer stopped one black couple
on the road. "No use in you all going down there," he warned from
the driver's seat of his car. "We done got him and are going to make
away with him." A few minutes later, the same white farmer told
another black man that he'd never see "that black SOB Roger walk
this road again." If the sight of Roger Malcom bound in ropes, lying
in the dirt, didn't convince them, the white farmer's comments did.
The black people hurried away to tell others that Roger Malcom
was going to be lynched.

Then Barnette Hester's thirty-nine-year-old brother, Weldon,
drove into the Hesters' front yard. Stepping out of the car, he
pushed through the crowd, walked straight to Roger, and kicked
him in the face. Years before, Weldon Hester had lost an eye in a
hunting accident, and on this evening—as at any time when he was
nervous or angry—his glass eye stared blankly as his other eye cast
about. "I am going in and get my shotgun," he said to the men in
the crowd. "Let's kill him now."

But Weldon Hester's mother told him to go to the hospital to see about Barnette. She told him he couldn't kill Roger Malcom. "You would have to serve time," she said. "You let the others do it."

Weldon Hester obeyed his mother and drove off. When the deputy sheriffs arrived, Roger was still lying in the dirt, still alive.

Roger Malcom had never been arrested before, yet he was well acquainted with Deputy Sheriffs Lewis Howard and Doc Sorrells. The two men had held their positions for nearly a decade; everyone knew them. "They run the county," people said. "Anything happen in Walton County, they know about it." At six foot two and 250 pounds, Lewis Howard was legendary for his ability to withstand pain; after a bank robber shot him point-blank in the stomach with a double-barreled shotgun, he walked into the Walton County Hospital holding his intestines. But he was even more legendary for his quickness at the trigger, and, according to black people in Walton County, Lewis Howard was quickest when his targets were black men. As the stories went, he'd arrest them and use his gun to make them confess to crimes, whether they'd committed them or not. His partner, Deputy Sheriff E. J. "Doc" Sorrells, was also a big man, also known for his reputed tendency toward violence. On this evening, as at any time when he was patrolling the county, he had an unlit cigar clamped between his lips. The last member of the trinity, High Sheriff E. S. Gordon, had held his position since 1933. He was known as a white-haired Wyatt Earp, but at age sixty-seven, he was content to let his deputies handle most matters. So it was the deputies who transported Roger Malcom from Hestertown to the jail in Monroe that Sunday evening.

For Roger Malcom, as for most of the black field hands or sharecroppers who lived and worked on Walton County's farms, a trip to Monroe was usually a treat. It meant an escape from chopping, hoeing, and picking, and a chance to spend a little money—even though it was usually borrowed from the landlord and would have to be paid back after the cotton settle. For Roger Malcom, a trip to Monroe often meant a visit to Standpipe Street, out near the ice plant. There, black men sold jars of liquor out of their houses and let customers stick around to drink and dance to records. Roger had met Dorothy up on Standpipe nearly one year before.

But on this evening, Roger Malcom wasn't headed to Standpipe, because he'd stabbed his white landlord. He didn't know if Barnette Hester was still alive, but he knew he himself wouldn't live much longer. Tonight or the next night, he would be taken out of jail and lynched. The thick cement walls wouldn't protect him from a mob of white men.

CHAPTER THREE

By the time Mama Dora emerged from the woods with Roger Jr. the next morning, Barnette's father and brothers had returned to Hestertown after their long night at the hospital. They gave her the news that Barnette was seriously wounded, but alive. They told her that Roger had been taken to the county jail and was also alive. It was better news than Mama Dora had hoped for during the sleepless night in the woods, and she walked down to tell Dorothy. But the tenant house was empty.

Dorothy had set out from Hestertown just after dawn that morning. She'd walked north on one of the countless footpaths that led through the cotton fields of Blasingame district, then crossed two narrow creeks, both of which were low due to the summer's scant rainfall. Continuing on, she'd passed through the tiny village of Good Hope and cut a path east of the thick pine forest known as Jones Woods. On her left as she walked north were two of the three "mountains" that rose up from Walton County's rolling hills. Everywhere around her were rows of cotton stalks, their bolls still closed like fists.

As a young girl, Dorothy had earned a reputation as a fast runner. Though, at age twenty, she was better known as a fine dancer—she'd taught herself by holding on to a tree limb and twirling in the dirt—she was still lean and lithe and quick. By noon, she'd covered nearly fourteen miles and was crossing the Apalachee River on the narrow wooden bridge at Moore's Ford. When she crossed the river, she left Walton County and entered Oconee County.

Like Walton, Oconee was an agricultural county, with roughly 90 percent of its land in farms. But, at half the size and roughly one-quarter the population of Walton, Oconee was a more desolate place. Its county seat was nothing like Monroe; tiny, dusty Watkinsville had no textile mills, no libraries or swimming pools—not even a bank. Because many people in Oconee County traveled to Monroe to do their business, the border between the counties was more fluid than the borders between most of the state's 159 counties. The Walton–Oconee county line was less a political or cultural division than a geographical marker.

Climbing up the steep hill from the river, Dorothy traveled a mile and a half more before reaching a two-story white stone house with a large *H* set into the chimney. Walking around the back of the house, she stepped onto a path that led alongside a tiny spring into the woods, to the concrete-block house where she'd lived with her family before moving to Hestertown. One month before, she and Roger had visited this house on a Saturday night. There'd been a party, with music and dancing—and her uncle had supplied three and one-half pints of bootleg liquor for the crowd. But this was a Monday, and Dorothy was alone. She walked inside and told her mother and stepfather, Moena and Jim Williams, that Roger had gotten into some trouble with the landlord.

That day, Moena was dressed identically to Dorothy, her short hair wrapped in a brightly colored kerchief, her slight body sheathed in a thin cotton shift. Though Moena was forty-six years old, the skin on her face was smooth. She looked like Dorothy's sister, not her mother. Only her hands, which were lined and calloused from nearly four decades of fieldwork, and her left eye, which drooped slightly as a result of a farm accident, distinguished her from her daughter.

Dorothy and her two older brothers—twenty-eight-year-old George and twenty-five-year-old Columbus, who went by the

name Charlie Boy—were from Moena's marriage to a man named
Columbus Dorsey. When Columbus Dorsey left Georgia in 1930
to move to North Carolina, Moena married Jim Williams, and he
quickly became a stand-in father to her children, though they kept
the Dorsey name. Now sixty-four and nearly blind, Jim Williams
suffered from a bad hip. He remained in his rocking chair that
Monday when Moena and Dorothy left the house, retraced the dirt
path out of the woods, and followed it to the back door of the large
stone house, where the white landlord, Loy Harrison, lived.

Loy Harrison came out after he finished dinner, dressed, as
always, in the standard uniform of the cotton farmer: khaki shirt,
khaki pants, and a snap-brim straw hat. Six feet tall and weighing
275 pounds, he towered over Moena and Dorothy, neither of whom
was more than five feet tall. Every part of Loy Harrison was massive: his head, his neck, his forearms, his hands. At forty-three, he
was renowned for hoisting engines out of cars with one hand, lifting
cotton bales as if they were babies. Addressing him as Mr. Loy or
Cap'n, as did all tenants on the farm, Moena told him that Roger
Malcom had gotten into trouble with his landlord and been lodged
in the county jail. If he'd go there and post bond for Roger, she said,
Roger could work for him on the farm.

Farms in Oconee County, as in Walton, averaged roughly one
hundred acres. To work a plot that size, a landowner needed one
tenant or sharecropper family, plus a few hired hands at harvesttime.
Loy Harrison, in contrast, owned roughly one thousand acres,
which stretched across Oconee County and into Walton. In addition
to Moena's family, Loy Harrison had five other black families and
two white tenant families working for him. But, like many large
landowners in Georgia in 1946, he was perpetually in need of more
help than those tenants could provide. There were few prospects in
the immediate community; as in much of the rural South, the area

surrounding Loy Harrison's farm had shrunk massively in population in the past decade. Since 1930, 114 black people—or roughly 60 percent of the black population—and 376 white people—or roughly 55 percent of the white population—had moved away. Without a sufficient supply of "free" workers to fill his needs, Loy Harrison often did just what Moena and Dorothy were asking him to do: he'd pay off a prisoner's fine, or post his bond, and let him work off the debt on his farm.

Loy Harrison was far from unusual in that respect. Large landowners all over the rural South, faced with both war-induced and urban migration, used the local jail as a labor pool. And often the local sheriffs and city police made sure the pool was stocked. They'd lock black people up on a Saturday night on minor—or trumped-up—charges, such as gambling, possession of liquor, or public drunkenness. When a landowner came to the jail on Monday morning to pay a prisoner's fine, the police claimed part of it for making the arrest, the jailer claimed part of it for "turning the key," and the landlord took home a cheap, reliable worker who was bound to him until his debt was paid. "They'd get old Hector for walking in the side of the road, wobbling in the ditch," recalls one white Walton County farmer of a black farmhand. "They'd get him every weekend and I'd get him every Monday. I'd pay the fine and he'd work it off on my farm." As one black man described it, "You could walk down the street and stagger a little, and they'd arrest you." The practice of landowners buying prisoners—particularly black prisoners—out of jail was so common in Walton and Oconee counties that it had its own slogan. "If you keep yourself out of the grave," landlords told their black tenants, "I'll keep you off the chain gang."

Moena Williams had lived on Loy Harrison's place for nearly four years. She knew the rhythm of the farmwork, and she knew that, since it was lay-by time, Loy Harrison would soon be starting up his sawmill. Given that he'd need workers for that, and for the cotton harvest that followed, she and Dorothy expected Loy Harrison to grant their request.

But that day Loy Harrison surprised Moena and Dorothy. He said he wouldn't bond out Roger Malcom. He said he didn't think Roger would be a good worker, and that he'd probably have trouble with him if he brought him to the farm.

Walking back to her mother's house, Dorothy was disappointed and frightened. She knew that every night Roger Malcom remained in the county jail was another night a lynch mob could get him. But if Loy Harrison posted Roger's bond and brought him back to the farm, he'd be safe. No one—not even the Walton County sheriffs— came onto Loy Harrison's farm without permission. And no lynch mob would dare insult Loy Harrison's authority by harming one of his workers—not without his permission.

Moena promised Dorothy she'd ask Loy Harrison to bond out Roger Malcom again the next day, but Dorothy couldn't wait. Later that afternoon, she walked down the hill to the Apalachee River, crossed back over the Moore's Ford Bridge, and reentered Walton County. Following the road up from the river, she came to a fork. To the right, the road led out to the Atlanta–Athens highway; to the left, it led back the way she'd come that morning, through Good Hope to Hestertown, to the dirt yard where Roger Malcom had stabbed Barnette Hester. Set twenty feet back from the fork in the road was the Fanny Wright place, a faded two-story house named after the original owner's wife, who'd fallen down the stairs, broken her neck, and died in a heap. Loy Harrison owned the house and the surrounding 145-acre farm, and Dorothy's oldest brother, George, was sharecropping there with his common-law wife, Mae Murray.

At twenty-eight, George Dorsey was slight like his sister and mother, though five years in the army had filled him out. He'd been drafted in 1941, and during an overseas tour that lasted from January 1942 to December 1944, he'd island-hopped throughout the South Pacific, toting, cleaning, hauling, and helping to maintain the infrastructure needed for the Northern Solomons campaign. His military occupational specialty was Duty Soldier III, which meant, in army terms, that he possessed no useful skills beyond those of a laborer; his enlistment records indicate he'd had no schooling at all. In spite of the manual labor, George Dorsey liked the army and might have wished to reenlist after the war's end. But, with his lack of education and limited skills, he didn't have the option. In September 1945—one month after President Harry S. Truman announced Japan's surrender—George Dorsey was released from the army at Fort McPherson, Georgia, and given $3.40 for bus fare home to Walton County. He stepped off the bus at Aycock's store on the Atlanta–Athens highway wearing his soldier's cap and his khaki uniform decorated with three medals: the Asiatic Defense Medal, the Asiatic Pacific Medal, and the Good Conduct Medal. In his pocket, he carried the first $100 of his $300 mustering-out pay.

Dorothy walked up from the road, past the pen where George's mule—bought with a portion of that $300—stood stamping its feet. Near the front door was a row of flowers planted by twenty-three-year-old Mae Murray, who'd moved out from Monroe to live with George that spring. Mae was known as one of the loveliest black women in Walton County. Both men and women talked enviously of her pale yellow skin and long, straight hair; many, in fact, were surprised when she took up with George Dorsey, whose skin, like the rest of his family's, was dark black. They were even more surprised when she began calling herself George Dorsey's wife, given that she'd always been a free spirit, a woman who didn't have just one lover. "She really must have liked him to settle down," one man said. Indeed, those who saw the couple dancing together in the houses on Standpipe Street were convinced they were deeply in love. Like Dorothy and Roger, George and Mae planned to leave Walton County after the cotton harvest. Maybe they'd go to Chicago, maybe to New York City.

Inside the Fanny Wright house, Dorothy told George and Mae about the fight between Roger and Barnette Hester, and soon afterward, the three walked the mile out to Aycock's store on the highway and caught the bus to Monroe. When they stepped off, they walked past the courthouse square, where groups of white men continued to rally votes for the impending election. They crossed Broad Street with its row of storefronts and continued on Washington Street as the pavement ended and the road became dirt. They passed the side door to the Troy Theatre, its neon sign reading COL-ORED ENTRANCE, and walking on, they reached the intersection of Washington and Jackson Streets, known as the Corner. Huddled around that intersection were a black-owned café, barbershop, pool hall, and taxicab stand. There were black-owned cafés, and another black-owned funeral home, in other sections of town, but the Corner was the only all-black business district in Monroe. As such, it was the heart of black public life. So much happened there daily that one man who washed dishes in a restaurant across town hoofed it back to the Corner on his break, just to see what he'd missed. Beyond the Corner was Tabernacle Baptist Church—one of several black churches in Monroe—and a grove of trees, including one known as the "hanging tree" ever since a black man was lynched from it in 1911.

Crossing the wide dirt street, Dorothy, George, and Mae climbed two steps and pulled open the screen door to the tin-roofed cement building that housed Young Funeral Home. Inside, Dan Young, a slender, bespectacled forty-year-old, was busy. But since

Mae Murray was kin to him—a second cousin—he stopped what he was doing to talk with the three. In the dim light of the funeral home, Dorothy, Mae, and George asked Dan Young the same question Moena and Dorothy had asked Loy Harrison: Would he bond Roger Malcom out of jail?

Dan Young was one of the wealthiest black men in Walton County. In addition to running one funeral home in Monroe and another in a town farther south, he owned much of the real estate on the Corner; according to the 1940 census, he was the only black man who owned commercial property in Walton County. Unlike most blacks in Walton County, who earned their living farming, cleaning, or toting, Dan Young was a professional. That meant he wore a suit every day, not just on Sundays. And it also meant that, unlike most blacks in the county, Dan Young enjoyed some degree of financial independence. Rather than relying on white people for his livelihood, he was paid by black people, black life insurance companies, or the mutual aid societies and lodges run by black churches. He'd grown up in the southern part of Walton County, then left to study at Morehouse College in Atlanta. After that, he'd lived briefly in New York City and attended mortuary school. Through these experiences, he'd forged ties with other powerful black men both within Georgia and without. He was a member of several black undertakers' associations, as well as the black Masons organization, the Prince Hall Masons. His brother-in-law, C. A. Scott, was editor of the nation's first black daily newspaper, the *Atlanta Daily World*.

Both Dan Young's wealth and his independence made it customary for blacks in need of a loan, a property owner to sign for bond, or assistance with nearly any matter to visit his funeral home at the Corner and ask for his help. When, for example, a black man in a nearby town was picked up by a group of armed white men and charged with peeping into a white woman's room, Dan Young "went his bond"—pledging $500 of his property as collateral to ensure the man's appearance in court—and arranged for a black lawyer from Atlanta to represent him. "Dan Young was a fixture," says a reporter for the *Atlanta Daily World*. "He was strong and fearless." A man like Dan Young, who could go between the white establishment and the black citizenry, was a vital member of every Southern town.

It wasn't unusual, then, that Dorothy, George, and Mae sought out Dan Young after their first avenue for aid—their white landlord—had failed. But that afternoon Dan Young also turned them down. He was too busy preparing for the primary election on July 17, which was now just two days away. It would be the first primary election in fifty years in which black Georgians would be able to vote.

Blacks had been denied the right to vote in the state's Democratic primaries starting in 1891, when the Georgia General Assembly ruled that the Democratic Party was allowed to set the rules for the state's primary elections. Atlanta pioneered the whites-only primary, and from there the practice spread to Augusta, Macon, and Savannah, until, by 1900, it was standard statewide. Barred from voting in Democratic primaries—the only elections that mattered in the one-party politics of the state—black people in Georgia were effectively disenfranchised.

But, in April 1944, the U.S. Supreme Court had handed down a decision that historians would later argue was as crucial to the modern civil rights movement as *Brown v. Board of Education of Topeka*. The court ruled in the Texas case *Smith v. Allwright* that the right to vote in a primary election was guaranteed by the Constitution and couldn't be denied to black people. Three months after the ruling, on July 4, 1944, a black preacher named Primus King arrived at the courthouse in Columbus, Georgia, to test the court's decision. When he was denied the right to vote on the grounds that he wasn't a member of the state Democratic Party—which was open only to whites—he filed suit in federal court. More than one year later, in October 1945, federal judge T. Hoyt Davis of Macon decided in Primus King's favor, ruling that *Smith v. Allwright* applied to Georgia. While the leaders of the state Democratic Party readied their appeal in the wake of that decision, black leaders in Georgia focused their attention on a special election to fill a vacant seat in Atlanta's fifth congressional district, which would be held in February 1946. They launched the most massive black voter registration drive in Atlanta's history.

Black businessmen and black clergy spearheaded the drive, but nearly a thousand black veterans in Atlanta were its foot soldiers. They'd returned from service abroad demanding better living conditions, fairer policing, increased access to public services—and above all, the right to full citizenship. In their front windows, they posted the "double V," which called for victory for democracy at home and abroad. And, dressed in their service uniforms, they went door to door signing up black voters, enlisting them in a homeland "war for democracy." Their efforts paid off. When registration closed, the names of seven thousand black people appeared on the voter rolls, more than ever before in Atlanta's history. On the night before election day, the city's black leaders—John Wesley Dobbs, A. T. Walden, E. M. Martin, and the Reverends J. H. Borders and Martin King Sr., among others—waited until after the last radio broadcast aired to hold a mass meeting at Wheat Street Baptist Church near Auburn Avenue. There they gave a message to be sent through the grapevine: *vote for the woman*. The next morning, nearly seven thousand black people in Atlanta voted for "a cussin', whiskey-drinking, cigarette-smoking lawyer" named Helen Mankin—and she won, becoming Georgia's first female member of Congress. By waiting until the last minute, black leaders had given their support to Mankin—the only candidate who'd campaigned for their votes—without causing a backlash from her white supporters. Black voters had voted in a bloc, and for the first time since the end of Reconstruction, they'd played a role in a congressional election in Georgia. As the news of Mankin's win traveled through the state, it energized black leaders and terrified many white leaders. Both reached the same conclusion: if enough black people voted throughout Georgia on July 17, what had happened in Atlanta in February could happen statewide.

That prospect became ever more real on April 4, 1946, when the U.S. Supreme Court refused to hear an appeal of Judge Davis's decision in the Primus King case. It was now definite: the whites-only primary in Georgia, which had reigned for more than fifty years, was history. Black Georgians would have the right to vote in the gubernatorial primary on July 17, 1946, and in all primaries thereafter. *Atlanta Daily World* editor C. A. Scott called the Supreme Court's ruling "the Negro's second emancipation," saying that, "politically speaking, to have been a black man in Georgia before April 4, 1946, was to have been nothing."

Building on the momentum of both the Mankin victory and the abolition of the white primary, that spring Atlanta's black leaders enlarged their efforts beyond city boundaries, launching the largest statewide drive to register black voters anywhere in the South. Late in April, when a group of black men gathered at a church in Monroe, they joined the statewide movement by creating the Walton County Civic League. That day, the roughly ten members of the newly formed Civic League elected Dan Young president. Then each member selected a section of the county and pledged to register every eligible black man and woman in that section in time to vote in the July 17 primary. Boyzie Daniels, a tall, light-skinned, twenty-two-year-old black man with blue eyes, was assigned to Blasingame district, where he himself lived. He accepted the assignment, though he knew it wouldn't be easy. In asking black people in Blasingame to vote, he'd butt right up against the sharecropping system, which had formed the bedrock of rural life in the South since the end of the Civil War.

Sharecropping was essentially a feudal system in which a relatively small number of landowners owned the bulk of the land, and a majority of people worked for those landowners as tenants. In Walton County, where most of the land was in the hands of seven hundred white men, the tenancy rate was 72 percent—meaning that nearly three-quarters of the county's farms were worked by people who didn't own them. These people belonged to various categories of the tenancy hierarchy. At the top were those who paid a fixed rent for their house and fields and provided their own mules, plows, seed, and fertilizer. Below them was the greatest number of tenants, sharecroppers, some of whom farmed on "thirds" (meaning they supplied their own equipment and paid the landlord one-third of their crop as rent for the house and acreage), and some of whom farmed on "halves" (meaning the landlord supplied equipment as well as the house and fields and took one-half of the crop in return). At the very bottom were laborers paid by the day.

While there was fluidity within the hierarchy—a family could farm on halves one year, and on thirds the next—there was very little chance of leaving tenancy behind permanently, particularly for black people. Boyzie Daniels, who'd been able to purchase a small farm in Blasingame with the help of his parents and in-laws, was one of only forty-seven black landowners in Walton County. His black neighbors in Blasingame were mostly sharecroppers, like George Dorsey, or day laborers, like Roger Malcom. They were people whose livelihoods—and very lives—were totally dependent on their white landlords. They were people who, like the majority of black people in the rural South, toiled in virtual serfdom, even as late as 1946.

No law governed the relationship between landlord and tenant, and even if one had, a black tenant's word would have held little weight against his white landlord's in court. That left black tenants vulnerable to a range of abuses. When one black man and his wife tried to move off their white landlord's farm in Hestertown, he found them, brought them back to the farm, and beat them. They weren't allowed to leave the farm, he said, because they owed him $48. Another black man in Hestertown had seen at least five white farmers whip their black tenants for attempting similar escapes. One black man in Hestertown said simply, "Negroes would not be permitted to move away." Just as Roger Malcom had once been forcibly "returned" to the Malcom farm by Weldon Hester, many other black tenants in Hestertown lived, year after year, as virtual prisoners.

And because the tenants were essentially powerless against their landlords, there was also no way to escape "enslavement by the pencil." It was customary for tenants to borrow money from their landlords throughout the growing season to buy medicine, clothing, meat, or liquor. But when they went to repay these loans, or the "furnish," after the harvest, they often discovered they owed the landlord as much as they'd earned. A well-known joke told of the landlord who added up his black tenant's debts for the year after the cotton was sold in December. "Let's see," he said, "I bought you a mule—that's seventy dollars. I furnished you one hundred and twenty dollars, and rent is four bales of cotton." After pausing to do the math, he said to his tenant, "You sold two hundred fifty dollars worth of cotton and you owe me two hundred forty dollars. So you get ten dollars back."

"Does that mean that one bale of cotton I hid is mine to keep?" the black tenant asked.

"Dammit, nigger," the landlord said, "now I got to refigure the whole thing."

The joke got to the heart of the sharecropping system: even when black tenants knew their landlords were cheating them, there was rarely anything they could do to stop it.

Thus, when Boyzie Daniels went from farm to farm that spring, asking black people to register to vote, he was asking them to go against their landlords, many of whom had made it clear they thought voting was for whites only. He was asking them to buck the social system, jeopardize their financial livelihood, and risk their lives. Again and again, blacks in Blasingame district—like most blacks throughout Georgia's rural areas—refused. "They was free, but they were bound to the landlords," says Boyzie Daniels. "They didn't want to cut off their meat and bread with their tongues."

For a while he tried to convince people, but he soon got frustrated and, even worse, disgusted. "They believed in God, and they believed in their white landlords, and believed they'd get justice in the fall of the year, after the harvest," he says. "Right back then you couldn't get much help out of them. The older ones were just plumb lost. They was deep in love with their misters and their masters."

But it wasn't only fear that kept many black people in Blasingame and elsewhere in the rural South from registering that spring; it was also doubt about the importance of voting. After all, their lives weren't governed by the laws of the state; they were governed by their landlords.

Out of 389 black people in Blasingame district, Boyzie Daniels found only 12 willing to register to vote in the primary election on July 17, 1946.

But in Monroe, where black people didn't contend with the share-cropping system—though most worked for whites, either as domestics or laborers—the members of the Walton County Civic League had more success. By the time voter registration closed, they'd convinced roughly eight hundred black people to register to vote, more than had ever before registered in Walton County. This increase was mirrored in towns and cities throughout Georgia. By the close of registration on July 5, the number of blacks registered statewide had jumped from 30,000 in January 1946 to a staggering 135,000, giving Georgia far more registered black voters than any other state in the nation. Louisiana had 7,000 and Mississippi had 5,000; even by 1947, Arkansas and South Carolina would have only 40,000 and 50,000 respectively. As the election drew near, anticipation built on the part of Georgia's black leaders, who wondered if the power of black voting could be demonstrated statewide as clearly as it had been demonstrated in Atlanta in February.

Undertaker Dan Young was one of those leaders. All spring, as the Civic League ferried black people to the registration office to fill out their registration cards (yellow cards for black voters, white cards for white voters), he'd observed no overt resistance. The absence had allowed him to hope for a peaceful election day. But, on the afternoon of July 15, when Dan Young learned that Roger Malcom had stabbed his white landlord, some of that hope drained away. The stabbing was a bad thing in itself, but that it had happened three days before the first primary election in fifty years in which black people in Georgia could vote was worse. That's why he had to refuse when Dorothy, George, and Mae walked into his funeral home and asked him to post Roger Malcom's bond. To help Roger Malcom would be to risk too much.

CHAPTER FOUR

That Monday afternoon, as Dorothy, George, and Mae left Young Funeral Home and caught the bus back to Loy Harrison's farm, Barnette Hester's family continued their vigil at the hospital. After returning home early that morning, Bob Hester had eaten a meal, slept for a few hours, and then driven back to the hospital. Barnette's wife, Margaret, and their five-year-old son, Nelson, accompanied him, but Barnette and Margaret's daughter, Linda, who would have her first birthday in just eight days, stayed home with her grandmother. At the hospital, the risk of infection was too great for Margaret to take Nelson into Barnette's room, so she stood in the doorway and held him up to the glass. She knew Barnette was barely conscious, but she hoped the sight of his son would somehow get through to him.

Throughout the day, a steady stream of neighbors and friends came to pay their respects and talk about the tragedy in hushed tones. Barnette had only been trying to prevent Roger Malcom from hurting his wife, one man said. If Barnette hadn't intervened, said another, Roger Malcom would have stabbed Dorothy that evening—maybe killed her. The friends and relatives talked as a way to take in the stabbing of a young man—a good son and father, a decent farmer—who had done nothing wrong, and incorporate it into what they knew of the world. And they talked to calm their greatest fear, which was that Barnette would survive the stabbing only to die from an infection.

Naomi Studdard, a close friend of Barnette's who lived near his farm in Hestertown, remembers her shock and disbelief. "Roger didn't have no reason to stab Barnette," she says. "The only thing that Barnette did was say he didn't want no trouble."

Two weeks earlier, gubernatorial candidate Eugene Talmadge had stood on Monroe's courthouse square and warned that blacks in Georgia were dangerously out of control. The white people of Hestertown had always been strong Talmadge supporters. When they saw Barnette Hester lying in the hospital—or heard about the attack against him—Eugene Talmadge's warning must have seemed all the more accurate.

Eugene Talmadge had made his political debut in 1926 as Georgia's agricultural commissioner, and since then, he'd run in every statewide Democratic primary save one. In 1932, 1934, and 1940, he'd campaigned for governor, giving stump speeches that quickly became legendary. While the faithful availed themselves of free food and drink—barbecued pork or fried fish, potato chips, and iced tea—Fiddlin' John Carson and Moonshine Kate provided entertainment. A roster of lesser speakers would warm up the audience, paving the way for Ole Gene, as he was known. Then, when the crowd was on the brink of frenzy, he'd step onto a raised platform, snap his trademark red suspenders, raise his fist, and point his finger heavenward. His eyes would roll and a forelock of his hair would quiver, and above the din, he'd shout to the people the words they already knew. Even Talmadge's most fervent detractors acknowledged his brilliant rhetorical skills, as time and again he framed his campaigns as a defense of true Georgians—the farmers and blue-collar workers known as the woolhat boys—against urbanites and carpetbaggers—the Northern-based businessmen who forever threatened to colonize the state. With his emphasis on farm-to-market roads and agricultural reform, and his own history as a south Georgia plowboy, Eugene Talmadge made it clear that he was for farmers—white farmers, that is. His strategy worked again and again, despite the fact that, once in office, his policies generally benefited the big businesses he'd railed against, rather than the poor whites he'd championed.

Then, in 1942, in the first election to award a four-year term for governor, rather than a two-year term, Eugene Talmadge's strategy failed. Ellis Arnall, the former attorney general of Georgia, campaigned against Talmadge with the pithy slogan "Eliminate the dictator"—and won. When he took office in 1943, he proceeded to abolish the poll tax, lower the voting age, revoke the Ku Klux Klan's corporate charter in Georgia, and support the prosecution of thirty-eight Atlanta police officers for their Klan membership. Governor Arnall didn't believe in social equality for black people. But he was, as black lawyer and leader A. T. Walden put it, "as liberal as it is possible for a white man to be and hold office in the South." As Arnall ushered in the most striking period of reform the state had ever seen, many people predicted the end of the reign of Eugene Talmadge.

But they spoke too soon. On April 16, 1946, twelve days after the Supreme Court declined to hear the Primus King case on appeal—thereby securing black Georgians' right to vote in state primaries—sixty-one-year-old Eugene Talmadge announced his candidacy for a fourth term as governor. Advisers pleaded with him to step aside and let his grown son, Herman, a lawyer and World War II veteran, run instead. "Naw," said the elder Talmadge in his country-boy drawl. "I'm the only goddamn son of a bitch that can win."

In his previous campaigns, Talmadge had always painted himself as a proud white supremacist. He'd bragged of beating and flogging the black people who worked on his farm in south Georgia, and told of chasing a black chauffeur with an ax handle because the man walked next to a white woman on a street in his hometown. He publicly proclaimed his sympathy for the Ku Klux Klan (he never joined outright, but helped out with "a little whipping" when he could) and his hatred for the Rosenwald Fund ("Jew money for niggers"), as well as anything that reeked of the federal government or civil rights. But in the wake of the Primus King decision, Talmadge focused his racism as never before. His message was simple: he was the lone candidate against "nigger voting." His platform was direct: he'd defend white supremacy in Georgia.

Just as *Atlanta Daily World* editor C. A. Scott called the Primus King decision a "second emancipation," Eugene Talmadge called it a "second Reconstruction." "Look beneath the smoke," he said in one speech, "and you will see a raging holocaust burning away at the very foundation of our Southern traditions and segregation laws." But though the Primus King decision gave Talmadge the ammunition to cultivate and exploit white Georgians' fear, he didn't have to create the fear from scratch. It was already there, a brew of postwar anxieties about the increasing mechanization of farming, the severe job and housing shortages, and the return of nearly a half million black soldiers to the South. During World War II, when more than one hundred thousand black soldiers had been stationed in Georgia, there had been "race riots" at Camp Gordon, near Augusta, and at Fort Benning, in Columbus. In June 1943, black troops at Camp Stewart, near Savannah, had mutinied in rage over segregated and substandard facilities. Such uprisings were unprecedented in Georgia, and they'd struck fear into the hearts of white Georgians. By the time Talmadge launched his campaign in April 1946, there had already been several clashes between returning black soldiers and white policemen, bus drivers, and military officers. That such clashes had occurred was, for many white Georgians, evidence that black veterans had returned from the war more aggressive and more dangerous—more "uppity," at the very least.

And yet, at the same time many white Southerners feared the return of black veterans to the South, they also worried about the record numbers of black people leaving. Both phenomena, after all, signified a loss of white control. As a result of the exodus, white landowners confronted labor shortages and resulting higher wages, both potentially disastrous. And industrialists had their own fears; in the spring of 1946, the Congress of Industrial Organizations (CIO) launched Operation Dixie, a recruiting effort aimed at bringing one million Southern laborers, black and white, into the union's fold. Black soldiers, black union members, black voters—taken together, they made the spring and summer of 1946 a threatening time for white people in the South. Nowhere was this more true than in Georgia, where whites contended with the largest black population of any state in the country. In Atlanta, the Ku Klux Klan, which had been largely dormant since the 1920s, responded by signaling its rebirth with a mass cross-lighting atop Stone Mountain on May 9, 1946. At the same time, a Nazi-style white supremacist group known as the Columbians was goose-stepping through Atlanta's streets, preaching Anglo-Saxon purity and warning blacks against moving into white neighborhoods.

When Eugene Talmadge hit the campaign trail in 1946, he was mindful of the gravity of the situation. For the first time, there was no food or drink, no fiddling or festivity, at his campaign stops. Instead, there were warnings. "If the Negro vote succeeds in defeating me . . . you will have to go around and politic with the Negroes," he said in a speech in Augusta, "go to their homes and knock on their doors with hat in hand, shake hands with all of them, and kiss the babies if you want to be elected." If black Georgians were given the right to vote, he said in a speech in Statesboro, they'd "become arrogant and drunk with their own power." They'd repeal the laws requiring segregation in schools, hotels, and trains—and even the laws that prohibited intermarriage. Always a clever campaigner, Talmadge paid a man who looked like his main rival for the governor's seat, James Carmichael, to tour the state accompanied by two well-dressed black men. These black men, in turn, were paid to puff big cigars and smile wide when they stopped at roadside filling stations—offering a glimpse of Georgia's apocalyptic future, if Talmadge weren't elected. And at one of James Carmichael's campaign rallies, Talmadge supporters paid black people $10 to sit on the main floor with the white people, rather than in the Negro section in the balcony. The message was clear: a vote against Eugene Talmadge was a vote to end life as white Georgians had always known it.

On June 28, when Talmadge and his entourage stopped in Monroe, he'd spoken to the crowd from atop a wooden platform on the courthouse square. After praising Mississippi senator Theodore Bilbo for warning black people against voting in the Mississippi primary, he'd launched into his classic rhetoric: "My opponents say it is the law—that you have to let the Negroes vote. They say I've stirred up the issue. But I ask you, who brought forth that Supreme Court decision making it possible for Negroes to ride by the side of white people on buses?"

On June 3, the U.S. Supreme Court had ruled that states could no longer segregate black and white passengers who crossed state lines in public transportation. Just as he'd spent all spring pledging to reinstate the whites-only primary, Talmadge claimed that day that, if elected governor, he'd "put inspectors at the state line to look into every sleeping car and see that there's no mixing of the races in Georgia." Once again, Talmadge took a "liberal" move by the federal government and molded it to fit his message that Georgia was on the brink of racial chaos, if not complete upheaval. The recent Supreme Court decisions, he said, were "gnawing like termites at the foundations of Southern traditions." He was the only man who could stop the destruction.

Of the six hundred people in the crowd on Monroe's square that day, most were farmers, dressed in their khaki shirts and pants, wearing straw hats. It was sweltering—the ice plant was having trouble meeting the demand for ice and cold water. But even in the heat, the crowd cheered and hollered, issuing rebel yells as if on cue. They had voted for Talmadge for governor three times before, and they would do so again on July 17.

Eugene Talmadge closed his speech that day with a plea: "I'm facing the guns this time. If Negroes agree with me, I urge them to stay at home and not attempt to vote."

Then he offered one last warning for his supporters' benefit. "You're going to see something new on July 17," he said, "and if it's a hot day, you'll smell it, too."

Afterward, Talmadge remained on the courthouse square for a long time, shaking hands and collecting donations. Bob Hester and many of the farmers from Hestertown talked with him. Loy Harrison likely did too. He was a longtime supporter. He'd named his first son after himself, but he'd named his second son for Talmadge.

One week after Talmadge's visit, a record crowd had turned out in Monroe to listen to James Carmichael, the thirty-year-old Atlanta-area businessman and lawyer running as the progressive alternative to Eugene Talmadge. Carmichael, who managed the Bell aircraft plant in Marietta, Georgia—the largest bomber and modification plant in the country—billed himself as a liberal. But he was a staunch segregationist, a fact he'd struggled to make clear throughout the campaign as Talmadge painted him as a "nigger lover" and spoke gleefully of his "colored friends." Carmichael's only real defense was to appeal to moderate whites with his own warning. "If we permit the present forces stirring up race hatred in Georgia to continue," he said in one radio broadcast, "we will have . . . four years of chaos, turmoil, and bloodshed in Georgia."

The two candidates for governor couldn't have been more different in style or substance. Whereas Talmadge dressed in red galluses and delivered his speech from a stand on the courthouse square, Carmichael dressed in a suit and addressed his crowd from a podium inside one of the courtrooms in Monroe's stately courthouse. After pledging aid to teachers, veterans, and farmers, he devoted his speech to articulating the flaws in Talmadge's vow to reinstate Georgia's whites-only primary. The issue, he said, wasn't about race, but about the rule of law. Reinstating the whites-only primary wouldn't be possible without abolishing all of the state's primary laws, he said, and without those laws there'd be no laws governing the election at all. "The successful candidate for governor, unhampered by law, would control the entire election machinery of the state," he said. "He would fix the qualifications for voters, could prescribe a poll tax, could bar anyone he wished from primaries; in short, he could do anything he wished."

James Carmichael's "good government" message resonated with the townspeople of Monroe, who, like townspeople all over the South, had realized that law and order, or at least the appearance of it, was crucial for business success. Though they didn't welcome black voters any more than most white Georgians, they weren't willing to risk the national reputation of the town, county, and state by defying the Supreme Court's ruling. Since the start of the campaign, the people of Monroe had thrown their support behind Carmichael, and when he concluded his address on July 8, many agreed it was the strongest they'd ever heard. A few days later, the *Walton Tribune*, which heartily endorsed Carmichael, reported that several statewide polls—including one that had correctly predicted the last four elections—indicated he'd win the governor's race. James Carmichael's supporters were confident of victory. As they saw it, Eugene Talmadge was obsolete, provincial, merely "a ghost's voice hell-bent on halting the future."

Three days later, when the last serious contender for governor gave a speech in Monroe, it was hardly noted. By then, the race was clearly between Eugene Talmadge and James Carmichael, the south-Georgia farmer and the Atlanta-area businessman who symbolized the crossroads at which Georgia was poised in 1946. For the primary wasn't simply the most bitterly contested governor's race in state history—it was a referendum on life in Georgia: Would the citizens elect Eugene Talmadge, moving back toward the traditions of the state's past, traditions built on unquestioned white supremacy? Or would they go for James Carmichael, moving forward toward industrialization, urbanity, and a semblance of racial equality—in other words, toward the rest of the nation?

With full knowledge of what the governor's race meant, Dan Young, Boyzie Daniels, and the other members of the Walton County Civic League gathered on the evening of July 16 at Carver School, the only black school in the county that had electricity, to offer final instructions for voting in the next day's election. As the black people filed into a classroom, the members of the Civic League handed each a piece of paper printed with a list of names and a warning: "Read this ballot carefully and memorize the names thereon, and vote for those persons on the list, but do not take this ballot to the polls." This was a marked ballot; it had been distributed to black voter registration clubs throughout the state in an effort—an illegal effort—to produce exactly what Eugene Talmadge and many white Georgians feared: widespread black voting in a bloc. But even without the marked ballot, it went without saying that the black people in the room would vote for James

Carmichael. Eugene Talmadge had made it clear he didn't want their votes; at one campaign stop he'd bragged that if he got a black vote, it would be by accident.

When the meeting ended at 11 P.M., the attendees scattered from the school to travel back to the farms where they lived and worked. Two and one-half miles south of Monroe, four black men veered off the highway onto a road that cut through Towler's Woods and came upon a row of parked cars. The moon was shining brightly, and the men recognized the cars as belonging to white farmers in Hestertown. A pair of fog lights was on one, a crooked antenna on another. Fifteen or twenty white men stood in a group near the cars, talking and smoking, the lit ends of their cigarettes glowing in the darkness.

On any other night, the black men wouldn't have worried—so many people drank, played cards, and "parked" in Towler's Woods that a nearby farmer often shot off his gun to get some peace. But on this night they did worry. They feared what this group of white men intended for the black people who would vote in the next day's election. And they feared what the group intended for Roger Malcom, who was locked in a jail cell in Monroe.

Late that night, a group of white men did park their cars in Towler's Woods, leaving their headlights burning while they stood in a group to drink the free whiskey provided by Eugene Talmadge's campaign. Most of the men were Barnette Hester's friends or relatives; many had visited him at the hospital. Some were angry about an incident that had happened the same day Roger Malcom stabbed Barnette Hester. The daughters of several Blasingame farmers had been driving together to Monroe when a carload of black men tried to flirt with them. The black men were drunk, and the white girls got frightened. They stopped at a filling station along the Atlanta–Athens highway, told the white owner what had happened, and waited fifteen minutes before driving off again. Then, when they turned off the highway at Aycock's store, near the Moore's Ford Bridge, they saw the black men again. In the end, they made it home safely. But one of the girls was so distraught that she had to stay out of school the following day.

Thirty-five years earlier, on a June night in 1911, a group of white men had stopped a train traveling from Atlanta to Monroe and pulled off a black man named Tom Allen, who was returning to Walton County to stand trial for allegedly raping a white woman from Blasingame district. The white men had marched Tom Allen away from the train tracks and lynched him from a telegraph pole just a few miles south of Towler's Woods. Ten hours later, the mob—which numbered twelve hundred to fifteen hundred men by then—took a black man named Joe Watts from the jail in Monroe and lynched him from a tree at the edge of town, just a block beyond the Corner. The handiwork was the same in each lynching: the mob strung the black man up, a leader barked an order, and they shot him to death.

All of the men at Towler's Woods that Tuesday night knew of the double lynching in 1911. Some had relatives who'd taken part in it; some had no doubt taken part themselves. As they talked about Roger Malcom stabbing Barnette Hester, and the black men harassing the white girls on the road, it became clear to them what they had to do.

They had to pile into their cars, drive into Monroe, surround the jail, demand the key or break down the door, and take out Roger Malcom. Then they had to lynch him. That lynching would punish Roger Malcom and keep black voters away from the polls. And it would scare black people in Walton County, and the surrounding counties, back into place for a long, long while.

But no leader stepped forward to activate the plan, and as time passed, the men drank away their outrage. Soon they were getting into their cars to drive home to their farms, dark and silent at this late hour.

Early the next morning, which was election day, Boyzie Daniels gathered several black people from the farms in Blasingame, and they climbed onto a wagon furnished by a white farmer to make the trip to the courthouse in Monroe. The farmer didn't put any condition on the use of the wagon, yet Boyzie Daniels knew what he expected. In the last few days, the landlords in Hestertown had paid visits to their black tenants. "You vote for Talmadge, here's five dollars," they'd said. Then they'd turned to another, saying, "You vote for Talmadge, here's five dollars." Watching black people take the money—"Thank you, sir," they said, "thank you, sir"—Boyzie Daniels had begun to reconsider whether he'd vote at all. Yet, that morning, he got on the wagon.

At the courthouse, Deputy Sheriffs Lewis Howard and Doc Sorrells came out to escort Boyzie Daniels and the others inside. The sight of the two deputies walking down the courthouse steps—their metal badges and guns the only things distinguishing them from other white men—was something Boyzie Daniels couldn't understand. He assumed the escort was a pretense, designed to make it seem as if black people's votes would be taken seriously. Or, he thought, it was a show of power. By taking the black voters inside safely, the sheriffs displayed their authority over whites as well as blacks. Either way, Boyzie Daniels made a seemingly contradictory conclusion: "We weren't welcome, but we were protected."

Inside the courthouse, Boyzie Daniels looked for other members of the Walton County Civic League, those who'd sat near him at meetings and pledged they'd be there to vote. "All those who owned land had spoke up and talked about voting for Carmichael. But then when voting day came, I didn't see them there," he says. "I learned that day that talk is cheap."

When he walked to the voting table, he heard the two white women sitting there say, "Looks like there's some black clouds rising."

He'd heard Eugene Talmadge on the radio, broadcasting from Atlanta every Monday and Saturday afternoon since May. He'd listened to what Dan Young and the other men had said at the Civic League meetings: that a vote for Talmadge was a vote for white supremacy, that a victory for Talmadge would erase all the progress black people had made, that Talmadge was in thick with the Ku Kluxers. Boyzie Daniels himself had spent months urging other blacks to register to vote for James Carmichael. And yet, when he took the voting paper and pencil that day, he circled Eugene Talmadge's name. Then he gave his paper to one of the white women, gathered up the people who'd come into town with him, left the courthouse, and went back home and into the field.

Later he'd say he voted for Eugene Talmadge because it didn't matter. "Our votes went into the garbage," he'd say. "They didn't count them."

Then he'd say: "I didn't have enough friends out there, so I went along with the whites. I just went along with the system. I said, 'I'll go up with the crowd and vote for Gene Talmadge,' and that's what I did. I voted against my own will, my own desires."

He'd say Talmadge wasn't as bad as he seemed. He just told the voters what they wanted to hear, like any politician.

Then a final reason: "I voted for the white man's buddy. I voted for peace and brotherhood. I thought maybe if Talmadge won, they'd be happy and treat us better."

He feared that if Talmadge lost, the whites in Walton County would take it out on the blacks. They might lynch Roger Malcom, maybe lynch some others. So Boyzie Daniels voted for Eugene Talmadge, for safety and security.

Election day had dawned sunny and clear throughout much of Georgia, prompting long lines of black and white voters to form in Augusta, Albany, Savannah, and Atlanta and its suburbs. In Columbus, black voters let the Reverend Primus King step to the front of the line, and he became the first black person in the city to cast a vote in the 1946 Democratic primary. By noon, some Atlanta precincts had already received twice as many votes as they had four years before. Workers used coat hangers to jam the ballots into the ballot box at one voting place. At another, voters were locked inside to await an extra delivery of ballots.

When the polls closed that afternoon in Monroe, the town leaders declared they'd never seen "a better planned or more orderly election." Though one man in Walton County had heard that three black people were killed in Monroe after a white man trying to vote was "brushed aside" by a black man, he heard wrong. The voting in Monroe had gone peacefully, as it had in most of Georgia's larger towns and cities. There'd been no physical attempt to bar black people from the polls, a fact that prompted the *Chicago Defender* to label Georgia's primary election as "the greatest black vote ever recorded in the South." The lack of violence reinforced many Georgians' belief that James Carmichael would win.

But the results proved otherwise. At 10 P.M. on July 18, Eugene Talmadge declared that he'd been "overwhelmingly elected," setting off a celebration that rocked Atlanta's staid Henry Grady Hotel. There was drinking and fighting, but mostly the crowd was in good humor, because Ole Gene had won. "This is our answer to those who brought the Negro into our primary," one supporter shouted from atop a chair in the hotel lobby. In his first address as governor-elect, Talmadge claimed he was "prouder of this victory than of any race I ever won," and once again issued his campaign pledge: "No Negro will vote in Georgia for the next five years." In his hometown the next day, the crowd cheered as Talmadge made his official victory speech. He greeted their cheers not with his customary firebrand rhetoric, but with exhaustion. He said the campaign had taken fifteen years off his life. "I'm just about spoke out," he said. "I'm real tired."

At the news of Eugene Talmadge's victory, those who'd been sure his rhetoric was too extreme to gain a following reeled in shock. Yet they hadn't been wrong; a majority of Georgians had voted for James Carmichael. In fact, Carmichael had won the popular vote by sixteen thousand, polling more popular votes than any other successful candidate for governor in Georgia's history. But he'd won only 146 of the state's 410 county unit votes, while Eugene Talmadge had won 242. And since the county unit votes were the ones that mattered, Talmadge would be Georgia's next governor.

Georgia's county unit system, which had been adopted at the beginning of the twentieth century as a way to subvert the tyranny of city political machines, functioned like a statewide electoral college. Each of the state's 159 counties was assigned either two, four, or six unit votes, according to its population. For example, Fulton County, which contains Atlanta, had six electoral votes, while Walton County had two. So, despite the fact that on July 17, 1946, Fulton County's popular vote (83,057) was more than *sixteen* times as large as Walton County's (4,976), it only had *three* times as many county unit votes. Therefore, one vote in Walton County, and in any of the state's many small rural counties, carried the strength of several votes in the state's few large urban counties—meaning that Georgia's rural areas overpowered its urban areas on the state political scene. As one Georgia politician said, "What was important in Georgia is not how people voted, but how the votes were counted." In the days following the election, a coalition of liberal and veterans groups would ask the courts to declare Talmadge's victory—and the county unit system itself—unconstitutional, but they'd lose their bid. The county unit system would continue to dominate Georgia politics until 1962.

But the county unit system was far from the only factor that contributed to Talmadge's victory, a fact that became clear as a picture of the election emerged in the ensuing days and weeks that was in stark contrast to the one initially painted. It was soon revealed that, at the close of voter registration on July 5, the Talmadge camp had mounted a full-scale exploitation of a little-known provision in the Georgia legal code that allowed citizens to challenge any registrant's right to vote. Talmadge headquarters in Atlanta had mailed boxes of blank challenge forms to its local campaign offices, where supporters simply filled in the names of black registrants—the color-coded registration cards made it easy. As a result, black people all over Georgia had received forms in the mail stating: "You are hereby notified to appear at the Court in _____ County, Georgia, on _____ day of _____, 1946, at __ o'clock to show cause why your name should not be stricken from the list of registered voters. Your right to register and vote has been challenged; and at the above time specified, we will hear evidence as to your qualifications as a voter and as to your right to register and vote." At the hearings themselves, the questions ranged from the obtuse to the blatantly racist— "What is an ex post facto law?" "What is a bill of attainder?" "What white person asked you to register?" "Was you ever in the stockade?"—but they were always intended to disqualify black voters.

After black leaders in Atlanta contacted the Civil Rights Section of the U.S. Department of Justice, agents from the Atlanta office of the Federal Bureau of Investigation opened an inquiry into the voter purges. Though FBI agents began investigating on July 9, eight days prior to the election, their efforts were aimed largely at documentation, rather than prevention. They did little to halt wholesale voter purges. And so, as the FBI's report would later reveal, there were attempts to prevent black voting in 90 of Georgia's 159 counties. In Crawford County, all 340 black people who registered were challenged, and 274 were disqualified. In Calhoun County, 456 black people registered, and 390 were disqualified. In Hart County, 489 black people registered, and 284 were disqualified. In Houston County, all 808 registered blacks were challenged, and 735 were disqualified. In Taylor County, 200 black people registered, and 178 were disqualified. All told, between July 5 and July 17, the names of an estimated 16,000 black voters were purged from voting lists throughout Georgia.

The FBI's report indicates there was no formal attempt to purge black voters in Walton County, though a group of Talmadge supporters met in Sheriff E. S. Gordon's office to discuss the possibility. But, out of the 810 registered black voters in Walton County, only 493 ballots were counted on election day. As the *Walton Tribune* later revealed, the elections registrar had quietly disqualified "a large number" of black people's ballots in Monroe because they were "improperly marked." That meant 317 blacks either registered and had their names purged; registered but were too frightened to vote; or voted and had their ballots destroyed.

And purges were hardly the extent of it. As the news trickled out from Georgia's small towns, villages, and rural areas in the weeks following the election, it became clear that many black voters had suffered the same threats and violence that characterized the last election in which large numbers of black Georgians had voted, in 1870. During that election, Georgia's only black congressman was forced to hide in a belfry after the Ku Klux Klan killed seven of his supporters. One newly elected black representative was murdered, and others received notes from the Klan indicating they'd meet a similar fate unless they resigned. Now, more than seventy years later, similar things had happened. On July 16, the night before election day, a cross was burned in a black section of the small town of Greenville. That same night in Cairo, Georgia, a crowd of masked white men shot off rifles and shotguns outside the homes of prominent black men, warning them not to vote. In Augusta, circulars reading "Keep Away from Polls . . . Or Death" were placed at the front doors of potential black voters. Other black people opened their morning newspapers to find threatening notes folded inside.

On election day itself, white men armed with sticks and rocks prevented about fifty black people from voting in the village of Manchester. And in the worst of the violence, a white man from Taylor County shot a black man named Macio Snipes. Though a coroner's jury would later rule that the white man had committed the killing in self-defense after an argument over a $10 debt, it was also true that Macio Snipes had been the only black man to vote in his district.

And despite the peaceful voting in Monroe, there had been trouble in rural Walton County. Late on the night before election day in the village of Gratis, which lay about six miles northeast of Monroe, six white men had gone to the home of a black man named Albert Hunter, taken him to a nearby creek, and whipped him with a hose, a pistol, and sticks. The men later claimed the whipping was punishment for an argument that had occurred several weeks earlier between Albert Hunter and a white storeowner. But, just as the men gathered in Towler's Woods knew that lynching Roger Malcom on the night before the election would serve several purposes, the men in Gratis knew that the beating would serve as both a specific punishment for Albert Hunter and a general warning for black people in Walton County.

The warning worked. No black people voted in Gratis, where polling was held at the store of the white man with whom Albert Hunter had supposedly argued. "I know that no Negroes voted in my store on that day," the white storeowner later admitted, "and the only ones who came into my store that day for any purpose was before the polls opened." Then he added, "I think this election was as fair as any election I have known about."

The two black men who did attempt to vote at the store were prevented by a pair of white farmers, who told them "not to put their damn foots across that road."

Not a single black person voted in Blasingame district—and only sixty black people voted in Walton County outside of Monroe. Though it's impossible to know how many were warned, directly or indirectly, not to vote, it's certain that few black people felt secure voting at the county polling places at the local country stores. These stores guaranteed neither the right to vote without intimidation nor the opportunity to vote anonymously. And it's also certain that this lack of security benefited Talmadge, who narrowly won the county unit votes in Walton County—despite losing Monroe by 600 votes—because he swept the rural areas. In Blasingame district, Talmadge got 119 votes, while Carmichael got only 14; in Gratis, Talmadge got 84 votes, while Carmichael got 3; and in Mountain district, the district closest to Loy Harrison's farm, he received 115 votes, while Carmichael got 39. The rural residents of Walton County, like other rural residents throughout Georgia, had given Eugene Talmadge his fourth term as governor.

On July 5 there had been 135,000 black people registered to vote in Georgia. But only 85,000 black votes were counted on election day. Whether through purges or bureaucratic mishandling, intimidation or outright violence, roughly 50,000 potential black ballots had gone uncounted in Georgia. Given that 98 percent of black people whose ballots were counted voted for James Carmichael, these missing votes could have altered the election's outcome. Certainly that was the case in Walton County, where Talmadge had won by the slimmest of margins: 78 votes. Those 317 missing black votes would easily have tipped the county in Carmichael's favor.

As the real picture of the election emerged, black leaders who'd once viewed the primary election with optimism were disheartened both by Talmadge's victory and the lengths to which he'd gone to secure it. "Most of the people here in Atlanta, both whites and Negroes, were disappointed and disgusted at the outcome of the election," commented one black man. "We overestimated the amount of democracy here in the state of Georgia." As if to underscore the disappointment of July 17, Helen Mankin, the congressional candidate whose victory in February's special election had epitomized the power and potential of black voting in Atlanta, lost the regular election to a candidate who, like Talmadge, had campaigned on a white supremacist platform.

In the aftermath of Talmadge's victory, the editor of the *Walton Tribune* penned an open letter, asking him to publicly assure black people they wouldn't be "embarrassed and persecuted" under his administration. "This section has many excellent colored citizens— hard working, industrious, and law-abiding," he wrote, "and should they decide to leave we would suffer an almost irreparable loss." This was the essence of the liberal position in Georgia in 1946: black people didn't deserve equal rights, but they did deserve a safe environment in which to work for white people. More than a month later, the editor would reissue his public plea to Governor-elect Talmadge, noting "a feeling of unrest among the colored people of Walton County, some of whom . . . plan to move away."

"This will be a great mistake," he wrote, "as the better element of the white people are the friends of the colored people, and the negro is happier here than he would be anywhere he might go."

Eugene Talmadge won the district surrounding Loy Harrison's farm by more than 400 votes, but the election results meant little to Moena, Dorothy, George, and Mae. They hadn't numbered among Oconee County's 320 registered black voters; even if they'd wanted to register, their illiteracy would have prevented them. Besides, they were worried about Roger Malcom's safety. Each day since July 15, they'd asked Loy Harrison to post Roger's bond and bring him back to the farm. And each day Loy Harrison had said no.

Fifteen miles away, in Hestertown, Barnette Hester's family and friends greeted Eugene Talmadge's victory with satisfaction. But it didn't ease their concerns—because the infection they'd feared had come to pass. On election day, the skin around Barnette's wound had become swollen and inflamed, and then burst.

A black man who worked as an orderly at the hospital remembers mopping up the fluid that spilled from Barnette's wound. "He had something in his side and it busted. Sticky stuff splattered all over the room. It smelled like sickness," he says. "I thought he was going to die."

So did the doctors, and so did the Hester family and friends. Barnette was too weak even to sit up.

When news of Barnette Hester's infection reached the county jail on the evening after the election, Deputy Sheriff Lewis Howard visited Roger Malcom in the group cell. "If that fellow dies that you stuck," several inmates heard him say, "you better be praying if you want to go to heaven, because your time won't be long."

As Lewis Howard walked away, Roger Malcom turned to another inmate and said, "I'll never be a free man anymore."

A few days later, when Roger Malcom's father brought him a change of clothes and a one-dollar bill from Mama Dora, Roger told him the same. And when Mattie Louise, his first wife, brought him her wristwatch to use in jail, Roger told her as well. "I won't get out of here alive," he said.

When Barnette Hester died, he would die too.

And then, early on the morning of Thursday, July 25, after eleven days spent hovering on the edge of death, Barnette Hester sat up in his bed at the Walton County Hospital. His father, Bob, who'd stayed by his side throughout the night, was there to witness his son's crucial step and hear the doctors' conclusion. The infection had run its course, they said. Barnette would live.

For the past eleven days, Bob Hester had been so concerned about Barnette's welfare that he hadn't discussed the stabbing with the sheriffs. But that morning, on the way back to Hestertown to tell relatives and friends of Barnette's recovery, he stopped at the county jail and told Deputy Sheriff Lewis Howard he wanted to file charges against Roger Malcom for assaulting his son. When Lewis Howard told him he'd already executed a warrant, Bob Hester asked if Roger Malcom would be allowed to post bond. Yes, Lewis Howard said—now that the charge was attempted murder, not murder. If Roger Malcom could post a $600 bond, the deputy said, he could go free.

Moena, Dorothy, George, and Mae had no knowledge of Barnette's infection, or his recovery. All they knew was that that Thursday at noon, after refusing for ten days, Loy Harrison finally agreed to go to the jail in Monroe and see about bonding out Roger Malcom. On top of that, he said he'd take Moena, Dorothy, George, and Mae with him when he drove into town.

Later that afternoon, the four walked up to Loy Harrison's house, with George and Mae's little dog Spot in tow. When they'd all gotten into Loy Harrison's Pontiac, Moena saw the car would be too crowded once Roger Malcom joined them. At the last minute, she climbed out, saying she'd stay home and finish her ironing for Loy Harrison's wife.

With George in the front seat, and Dorothy, Mae, and Spot in back, Loy Harrison drove off at 2:30 P.M. His farm lay between two roads that led out to the highway, giving him the choice of heading northeast along Moore's Ford Road to Bethelbara Road, or turning southwest, driving across the Moore's Ford Bridge, taking the right fork at the Fanny Wright house, and following the Mountain Lodge Road to the highway. That day, he opted for the northeastern route, a route lined on both sides by his fields, his tenant houses, his pine forests. At Bethelbara Road, Loy Harrison turned left, reached the Atlanta–Athens highway, and took that all the way into downtown Monroe. It was a twelve-mile trip, and it took roughly twenty minutes.

After he'd parked at the courthouse, Loy Harrison told Dorothy, George, and Mae to wait while he went alone to the sheriff's office in the basement. When he informed Deputy Sheriff Lewis Howard that he wanted to talk with Roger Malcom, Lewis Howard told him to drive to the jail. There, George, Dorothy, and Mae again waited in the car while Loy Harrison and Lewis Howard walked to a narrow window cut into the side wall of the jail.

"You gonna work for me if I get you out?" Loy Harrison called to Roger Malcom through the window.

From inside came the sound of Roger Malcom's voice. He said he would.

"You gonna leave that whiskey alone?" asked Deputy Sheriff Lewis Howard.

Again, Roger Malcom's muffled reply: he would.

Loy Harrison returned to his car and drove back to the courthouse, where he signed the bond papers—guaranteeing Roger

Malcom's appearance in court with $600 of his property—and told Lewis Howard he'd pick up Roger Malcom in about two hours, on his way home.

Back outside, Loy Harrison told Dorothy, George, and Mae to meet him at the water fountain on the courthouse lawn at 5 P.M. Then he drove off, and they headed down to the Corner. As they were leaving the courthouse square, they passed Major Jones, the black trusty at the jail, who was on his way to a nearby café. Two years before, Major Jones had been convicted of killing a black man and sentenced to fifteen to twenty years in the county prison camp. Through the arrangements of Lewis Howard, he'd been transferred to the jail, where he cleaned and ran errands.

"Thought you were going to get that boy out of jail," Major Jones called to them.

"We are going to get him," Mae Murray called back. "We're going to get him at five o'clock."

At Briggery's Café on the Corner, Dorothy and Mae each bought ten cents' worth of penny candy, then all three walked the several blocks to Standpipe Street, Spot in the lead. A young black woman who'd often watched George and Mae, and Roger and Dorothy, dance in the houses on Standpipe noticed they were in high spirits that afternoon. Boyzie Daniels, who'd driven into town from Blasingame to buy canning supplies for his wife, saw them on their way back downtown. They were walking arm in arm, almost marching. They called out hello and he called hello back.

By then it was nearly five o'clock, so Dorothy, George, and Mae hurried to the drinking fountain. When Loy Harrison drove up, they asked him for $3. With the money in hand, they went into the basement of the grocery store and bought a scrap of meat left over from another customer's purchase. The man behind the counter wrapped the meat in brown paper, and George Dorsey put it in his back pocket. Since a little money still remained from Loy Harrison's loan, Dorothy, George, and Mae went to the black-owned café near the bus station and shared two pieces of custard pie. Loy Harrison met them there with his car.

A few minutes later at the county jail, Lewis Howard unlocked the cell and Roger Malcom marked an *X* on the signature line at the bottom of the bond paper. For eleven days he'd feared that a mob would come to the jail, take him out, and lynch him. Now he'd been proven wrong; he was getting out of jail alive. After telling another inmate that he was happy to be going home with "his wife's people," he walked outside. He climbed into the backseat of Loy Harrison's car with Dorothy, Mae, and Spot, and George Dorsey got into the passenger seat. It was nearly 5:30 P.M. when Loy Harrison drove out of Monroe.

Instead of retracing the same route he'd taken earlier that afternoon, Loy Harrison turned off the highway just after Aycock's store, onto Mountain Lodge Road. The dirt road wound past one empty cotton field after another. At any other time, the empty fields would have been unusual. But the cotton and corn had been laid by, and what little fieldwork there was could be done in the mornings, leaving the afternoons free. A half mile off the highway, Loy Harrison drove past the tenant house where a family of black sharecroppers lived. A third of a mile later, they passed the turn-off to Mt. Enon Church, where the dirt was worn down to the rock by the wagon wheels and footsteps of black people on their way to and from services. Farther on was the tiny white house that sat at the edge of the Fanny Wright place. One of Loy Harrison's tenants had been found hanging there six months before. The dead man's family immediately moved out of the house, and Loy Harrison moved another family in, but they said the place was haunted and left after two nights. The house had been empty since.

Later that night, Loy Harrison would tell what happened after he reached the fork in the road in front of the Fanny Wright house. He'd say he slowed the car and asked George Dorsey if he should let him and Mae out. He'd say George told him to go on across the river, because Moena was waiting for them. So Loy Harrison took the left fork and drove toward his farm.

He had just passed the last house before the Moore's Ford Bridge when he glanced in his rearview mirror and saw the car behind him. As he continued on toward the river, he saw three cars parked on the far side of the bridge. Four or five men with guns stepped out from the cars and began crossing the bridge. Then the car behind Loy Harrison's pulled close and touched his bumper, and more men suddenly appeared from the trees on either side of the road. Within minutes, Loy Harrison's car was surrounded by a mob of roughly twenty armed men.

At first, Loy Harrison thought the men were federal revenue agents. But when they pointed their shotguns at him through his open car window, he realized his mistake. "Stick 'em up," they said.

Just then, two more men emerged from a car on the other side of the river and walked across the bridge. One of the men was roughly sixty-five years old. He stood more than six feet tall and weighed more than two hundred pounds—and, despite the late-afternoon heat, he wore a brown double-breasted dress suit and a large-brimmed black hat. His face was tanned a deep brown, as though he'd just returned from a Florida vacation. Immediately, Loy Harrison identified him as the leader of the group. Flanking him was a slight man in his early twenties who had dark hair, a dark complexion, and gray eyes. He wore a khaki army uniform.

When the two men reached the car, the leader ordered his young companion to train his shotgun on Loy Harrison. Then he motioned the rest of the men to gather at the passenger side of the car.

"This," he said, pointing inside to Roger Malcom, "is the SOB that we want."

At that, several men forced open the car door and pulled Roger Malcom from the backseat. They held him down while others bound his wrists and tied a long rope around his neck. The rope work was "expertlike, prettylike," Loy Harrison would later say.

When the men finished with Roger Malcom, the leader turned to George Dorsey and said, "We'll just as well take you along too, Charlie."

From the driver's side of the car, Loy Harrison tried to intervene. "This ain't Charlie," he said, "this is George."

"Keep your damn mouth shut," said the young man guarding Loy Harrison. "This is our party."

The men pulled George Dorsey out of the car and bound his hands with the other end of the rope they'd used to bind Roger Malcom's wrists. Then they pushed both men down the small hill that sloped off the road.

Still inside the car, Dorothy yelled out, cursing the name of a man in the mob. After her words rang out, the leader called, "Hold it," and pointed to three or four men. "Get those bitches too," he said. Like well-drilled soldiers, the men pivoted and ran back up onto the road.

Dorothy held tightly to the car seat and then to the car door. The men had to use the butts of their guns to pry her hands loose. Then they dragged her and Mae down to their husbands, who stood fifty yards off the road, in a clearing on the old wagon trail that ran alongside the Apalachee River.

Up on the road, the young man with the shotgun gave Loy Harrison orders, and he stepped out of the car with his hands raised. As instructed, he stood on the left side of the car, facing the man, looking across the bridge, toward Oconee County and his vast plantation. Out of the corner of his right eye, Loy Harrison could see his black farmhands lined up abreast. Mae Murray stood closest to the river. Next to her was Dorothy, then Roger, then George. Loy Harrison heard the leader count to three, and then he heard a volley of shots. Then came the leader's voice: "One, two, three." Then another volley. Later Loy Harrison would say he'd never felt as powerless as he did standing on the bridge with the shotgun pointed at him. "I didn't have anything but a pocketknife," he'd say. "What could I do?"

Then the counting came again, then one more round of shooting. After a few minutes, the men walked back onto the road.

"Now that we are here, let's take care of all of them," said the young man guarding Loy Harrison. At that moment, Loy Harrison believed he'd be the mob's fifth target. This mob, he knew, wouldn't leave witnesses.

The leader walked past Loy Harrison once, turned around, and walked past him again. "Do you recognize anyone?" he asked.

"No," said Loy Harrison.

The leader didn't register his answer.

"No," Loy Harrison said again, he didn't recognize any of the men.

After a silence, the leader said, "You know what to do with him." When he and the other men had walked across the bridge to the cars, the man pointing the shotgun at Loy Harrison put it down and said, "Leave when you're ready." Then he got into one of the cars and drove away. Soon Loy Harrison was alone on the Moore's Ford Bridge. It was quiet, except for a rustling in the clearing by the river, where Spot was nosing around in George Dorsey's back pocket for the piece of meat he'd bought in town.

Loy Harrison got into his car, turned around, drove back up the hill, took the right fork, and sped out to Aycock's store on the highway. "Mrs. Aycock, call the sheriff for me quick," he said. "They took all my Negroes from me and I suppose they shot them."

"All of them?" Mrs. Aycock asked as she telephoned the jail.

"I suppose so." Then Loy Harrison took the phone.

"A group of white men took my Negroes from me at Moore's Ford," he told Deputy Sheriff Lewis Howard. "What should I do?"

Lewis Howard told Loy Harrison to drive home. Since he didn't want to use the Moore's Ford Bridge—the bodies of the four young black people were still lying in a heap there—he retraced the route he'd taken to Monroe that day. At a narrow spot on the highway, he was forced to slow down to pass four parked cars. When he did, a man stepped out from one of the cars and peered into Loy Harrison's backseat. The man didn't say a word, but Loy Harrison knew he was looking for his black tenants. The mob had covered its bases, he concluded. They'd stationed men along both of the routes between Monroe and his farm.

It was nearly 6:30 P.M. when Loy Harrison's car appeared on the path to Moena and Jim Williams's tenant house. Moena had finished her ironing hours before and was eager for Dorothy and Roger, and George and Mae, to return from town. But when the car stopped, Loy Harrison stepped out and said something had happened to the two couples. He told Moena and Jim to get in the car with him and ride to his house. They could wait in his yard for news from the sheriff.

After an hour passed without any word, Loy Harrison got into his car and drove back to Aycock's store. There he met Deputies Lewis Howard and Doc Sorrells and, at their request, accompanied them to the Moore's Ford Bridge. Coroner W. J. "Tom" Brown was standing by the bridge, holding a flashlight in his only arm. He'd pulled his car as far off the road as he could without its sliding down the bank and shone his headlights into the clearing. Soon the doctor arrived, and Coroner Brown called his jury—five men selected from the county's most recent grand jury—out of the car, so they could conduct a legal inquiry into the cause of death of the four black people. Nearly a dozen other white people stood on the periphery. A white sharecropper named Riden Farmer, who lived with his family in the house closest to the bridge, had walked down with his twelve-year-old son, Emerson. A white man named James Verner had driven to the bridge with his girlfriend. She stayed in the car while he joined the others.

It was 8 P.M. There were still shreds of daylight on the road and in the nearby fields, but the trees blocked the light in the clearing by the river. The sheriffs huddled close with their flashlights. Coroner Brown and the doctor knelt and began examining the body nearest to the road.

George Dorsey lay on his side, facing away from the river. One bullet had entered the right side of his jaw; one had entered just above his right ear; and a third bullet had entered the left side of his abdomen. There were shotgun wounds on his left hip and left forearm. When the men turned him over, they also found shotgun wounds on his back.

Roger Malcom lay on his back, facing upward, with a gunshot wound on the left side of his forehead. A bullet had entered the left side of his chest and exited the right side of his back. Another bullet had entered his right hip. A rope nearly twelve feet long was tied in a noose around his neck. His hands were tied with one end of a plow line that also bound George Dorsey's wrists.

Dorothy Malcom lay on her left side, facing Roger Malcom. There was a shotgun wound on her right jaw and a bullet wound behind her left ear. Both bones in her left forearm were fractured.

After the first three bodies had been inventoried, Riden Farmer backed away from the group and vomited into the bushes. Once he and his son had left the area, the coroner resumed the examination. Mae Murray Dorsey lay crouched on the ground, facing the river, a large-caliber bullet wound through the top of her head, and both a bullet wound and a shotgun wound in her left shoulder.

The inquest that followed the medical examination was brief and routine. Coroner Brown administered the jurors' oath, then questioned the lone witness, Loy Harrison. He took notes from Loy Harrison's testimony: "Left Monroe 5:30 P.M., drove straight there, car blocked him at bridge, man stuck shot gun thru window and told him to stick his hands up. Then said to negro, 'Charlie, I want you.' About 20 or some men, 3 Fords and one Chevrolet car."

Since Loy Harrison was the only witness, and since he couldn't identify any of the men in the mob, the jury promptly issued the verdict that was standard in the wake of a lynching. "Death at the hands of persons unknown," the coroner wrote on four separate pages in his notebook that night. When the death certificates were issued, the cause of death would be more specific: assassination, with contributing causes listed as "gun shots (many times)." Coroner Brown estimated that roughly sixty shots had been fired in all. And though he didn't note it on his report that night, the nature and location of the wounds led him to make several other conclusions. He knew, for instance, that the victims hadn't tried to run or even turn away. They'd faced the shooters, or stood with their profile toward them. He also knew that the victims had been shot repeatedly after they'd fallen to the ground. Before leaving the bridge that night, Coroner Brown, who'd served Walton County in that capacity for thirty years, took a bullet from one of the bodies. It was a .22 rifle bullet, sticking halfway out of the flesh on an arm: the first souvenir.

After the inquest, Loy Harrison drove back to his farm, where

Moena and Jim Williams had been waiting for nearly four hours in his yard to learn what happened to their children. Loy Harrison told them a mob had shot all four of the young people, and they were dead. Then he told them he'd already made burial arrangements, and he went inside. Moena stayed in the yard, weeping, for a long time before walking back to her tenant house. By then Coroner Brown, according to Loy Harrison's instructions, had driven to Aycock's store and placed a call to Almand's Funeral Home, the only white-owned funeral home in Monroe. Unlike most undertaking establishments in the South in 1946, Almand's—which was owned by E. L. Almand Jr., the mayor of Monroe, and ranked among the leading funeral homes in north Georgia—embalmed and buried both white and black people. But given the existence of two black-owned funeral homes in Monroe, they didn't do a huge black business. "The ones we buried chose us," remembers Ed Almand III, the son of E. L. Almand Jr. "They were friends."

That Thursday night after receiving the telephone call from Coroner Brown, E. L. Almand Jr. dispatched his hearse to the Moore's Ford Bridge and summoned his longtime black employee, Isaac Brooks, to ready the funeral home. Nearly an hour later, Isaac Brooks was waiting when the hearse returned and two white funeral home employees opened its back doors and pulled out four large baskets. Isaac Brooks helped with the baskets, and he saw the dead people's clothes. They were speckled with blood, he later told his family. They looked like the ground after you wring a chicken's neck.

Inside, the men pulled the clothes from the bodies, sprayed off the blood and dirt with a hose, and then embalmed them. After that, they wrapped the bodies in sheets, put them back into the baskets, scrubbed their hands and hung up their aprons, and left. Later that night, Isaac Brooks returned to his house on Standpipe Street, walked into the kitchen, took out a half-pint of liquor, and sank into a chair. He'd lifted money and jewelry off the bodies in the funeral home many times before. They wouldn't need it where they were going, he'd always say, and his wife was inclined to agree. But that night when Isaac Brooks laid a wristwatch and a scrap of meat on the kitchen table, Isaac Brooks's wife shook her head. She picked up the things, walked out of the house, threw them into the yard, and hurried back inside.

If Isaac Brooks's wife had lingered outside, she'd have noticed that Standpipe Street, always lively on a summer night, was deserted. In fact, all of Monroe's black neighborhoods were quiet by then. Under orders of the city police chief, officers had gone through town clearing black people off the streets. One policeman told the black woman who ran the beauty shop on the Corner to close up for the night. Another entered the Troy Theatre and ordered the manager to cut off the movie. Isaac Brooks's step-daughter, Mary Alice Avery, was sitting in the Colored section, transfixed by *Do You Love Me?* when the screen went blank. "Some-one started talking loud and telling us some kind of tragedy had happened and we had to go home," she says. "Me and my sister locked hands and come up those streets and come straight home."

Still later, the night police chief had driven by the Troy Theatre's Colored entrance and warned black people lining up for the late movie to return home. "We were told to get off the street and go home and don't turn on no light and don't be sitting on porches or whatnot," says a black man who was waiting there that night. "Because something had happened, and something else could happen."

More than a few black people remember policemen driving slowly through their neighborhoods, telling them to go inside, cut off their lights, and be still. Though the police chief would later say he imposed the curfew in the interest of protection, most blacks interpreted it as a threat. White men driving through a black neighborhood at night were too much like night riders, too much like the Ku Klux Klan, to be anything helpful. And yet, whether threat or protection, black people left their porches and stoops, went inside, locked their doors, and shut their windows. It was the hottest night of the month; the mercury didn't drop below seventy-four degrees. And besides the heat, there was the torture of not knowing what had happened.

On the outskirts of town, in his room at the Walton County Hospital, Barnette Hester was hazy from the medicine he'd been taking for eleven days. He was weak and disoriented, dreamy. When a black hospital aide brought him his tray, he spoke to her.

"I told them not to do anything to Roger," he said.

The aide was startled. She didn't understand what he meant. But it didn't matter. She was black, and Barnette Hester, in his dream state, wanted forgiveness.

CHAPTER SEVEN

Early the next morning, white people all over Walton and Oconee counties hurried through their breakfasts and their chores, cranked up their cars, and drove off from their farms. Some stopped to ask for directions at Aycock's store, because they'd never heard of the Moore's Ford Bridge before they heard the news. Then, one after another, they turned off the Atlanta–Athens highway onto Mountain Lodge Road, retraced Loy Harrison's route to the bridge, and walked in the mob's footsteps along the trail that led to the killing place.

More than one hundred years before the white people gathered at Moore's Ford that morning, the first white settlers in the area had waded across the Apalachee River there, holding tightly to their children and their horses. After a heavy downpour, the river swelled, and the ford became dangerous, and so, in the 1840s, the settlers built a simple wooden bridge. By 1946, that bridge had changed little. Set low on the river, it flooded after two days of steady rain, the steep dirt road leading to it rendered slick and impassable. Since 1939, when the highway between Atlanta and Athens was put through, most people crossed the Apalachee on the wide cement highway bridge roughly one mile upriver. Whole days now passed without a single driver braving the bridge at Moore's Ford. When one did, the wooden floorboards, which were warped and loose, knocked loudly as the car passed over.

But the people who lived nearby still went to Moore's Ford, because to them it wasn't just a river crossing or a path between Walton and Oconee counties; it was a place in and of itself. In the afternoons when they were set free from the field or the classroom, local children would pedal their bikes to Moore's Ford, take hold of a rope tied to an overhanging branch, swing out, and drop into the river. Sometimes black men would be tending lines in the shoals there. In earlier days, they could just slide their hands into the crannies between rocks and pull out catfish by the fistfuls. But recently, several local white men had adopted a more modern method of fishing that was depleting the Apalachee's abundance. They'd squat on a flat rock, crank a telephone, and drag its wires in the river, sending electric shocks into the water below. Within seconds, ten or twenty or fifty catfish would rise to the surface. The men would skim them off and drop them into a pail, their tiny silvery antennae still quivering. Then they'd crank the telephone again.

Along the riverbanks near Moore's Ford, wild mountain laurel and wild rhododendron bloomed, and river cane grew up in thick groves called canebrakes. When farmers lit fires to clear the land for planting, the heat caused the hollow cane stalks to explode. On those days the river carried the sound of the explosions—a sound like gunshots—for miles. From the riverbank, countless footpaths led into a forest of privet, pine, and hardwoods draped with wisteria. Men and boys hunted quail, doves, fox, and rabbit in that forest, and girls and women searched for the best straw for their brush brooms. Even at midday, it was shadowy in there. You could nap in the shade of a tree, escape the visibility of the fields, retreat. You could drink moonshine or meet a lover. Moore's Ford was a small patch of wildness in a landscape tamed and cultivated into rows of cotton and corn. It was a rare place that wasn't associated with work, a place of small sounds and small secrets: the rustling of birds, the lapping of the river, the footsteps of a person getting away.

But the crowd gathered in the clearing that morning wasn't interested in Moore's Ford except as a killing place, for they'd come to participate in the long tradition of collecting lynching souvenirs. Walton County's first recorded lynching had occurred in 1890, when a black man named Jim Harmon, who was accused of touching a white woman's face while she slept, was shot to death, his body sunk to the bottom of a pond; it had produced no souvenirs. But some of the county's citizens were likely among the huge crowds that witnessed the lynching of a black man named Sam Hose near Atlanta nine years later. After Sam Hose was hung and burned to death, men rushed at him with knives. They cut off his fingers, ears, and penis, then scavenged for limbs from the lynching tree, ashes from the fire—anything that bore the mark of the lynching. This urge to collect and preserve provided young W. E. B. DuBois a glimpse of Sam Hose's knucklebones on display at an Atlanta grocery store a few days later.

No doubt there were also some citizens of Walton County among those who flocked to nearby Watkinsville, the Oconee County seat, on June 30, 1905, to collect "cartridge shells and other things as momentoes [*sic*]" from the bodies of eight men who'd been taken out from the county jail the night before and lynched. The mob that lynched Tom Allen near Towler's Woods in Walton County six years later discouraged such souvenir-collecting by pinning notes to his body that instructed people to leave it hanging as long as possible. The mob members reasoned that the longer Tom Allen's body hung, the longer it could serve as a warning to black men inclined to commit similar "crimes." Those who wanted souvenirs made do with photographs of Tom Allen's body, which sold briskly in Monroe. Some were mounted and framed for display. With the addition of a postage stamp, others became postcards, carrying family news and gossip—as well as a record of the lynching—from Monroe to places all over the country.

On this Friday morning in 1946, there was no possibility of

retrieving body parts or photographs of the lynch victims, since the four bodies had been transported to Monroe late the evening before. So the souvenir collectors made do once again. A white student who'd detoured to Moore's Ford on his way to class at the University of Georgia in Athens found a length of rope with a few cords clipped off by a bullet. As he was leaving the clearing with his souvenir in hand, another man snatched it. After hunting again, the student found a tooth, which he later gave to a friend for her charm bracelet. "Four-leaf clovers, wishbones, good-luck charms on bracelets. You know, Indian-head pennies," he says. "She felt like that tooth would be something."

As the morning wore on, more and more white people appeared at Moore's Ford: a carload of women, a farmer and his young son, a group of men from Hestertown, and a preacher, among others. They listened to white sharecropper Riden Farmer, who stood by the bridge and told the crowd that the shooting the night before had sounded like a fire in a canebrake. They walked the path that led from the road to the clearing and peered at the four sheets of newspaper that covered the bloodstains on the ground where the bodies had fallen. One woman had her photograph taken as she pointed to a bloodstain. Others pointed to leaves, branches, and tree trunks perforated with bullet holes. The white people looked and talked and scavenged with confidence, sure that the lynching marked the end of something, not the beginning. The double lynching of Tom Allen and Joe Watts in 1911 had drawn a few days of outsiders' scrutiny—nothing more. In articles headlined "Walton Runs Red with Blood; Lynchings at Dawn and Noon," newsmen reported that "the people of Monroe and of the entire county have always been known as the state's best, most conservative and law-abiding citizens. They do not relish the notoriety given them . . . knowing as they do that the lynchings were largely the work of men from adjacent counties . . ." The people of Walton County, newspapers in Atlanta and Athens reported, were determined to mount a full investigation, identify the lynchers, and clear the county's good name. But no arrests were ever made, despite the fact that the unmasked mob members had freely called each other's names before, during, and after the lynching; and despite the fact that a crowd of spectators had watched the mob commit the lynching. Two years later, when a "quiet, but desperate and determined mob" in Walton County lynched a black man named General Boyd, who was accused of entering a white woman's bedroom while she was sleeping, county citizens were able to contain the news within the county's borders for four days. Even after it leaked out, there was no investigation, and no arrests were made. The white people at Moore's Ford that morning had no reason to think this most recent incident would be any different.

What they didn't consider, however, was that the men who'd killed Roger and Dorothy Malcom, and George and Mae Murray Dorsey, had committed a murder so extreme that it would become an icon of postwar violence, a symbol of the chasm between the promise of democracy and the reality of life for black people in America in 1946. What they couldn't predict was that the men who fired the shots at Moore's Ford had made history; the nation would never again see as many victims lynched on a single day after July 25, 1946.

What the men and women gathered at Moore's Ford also didn't know was that early that morning, as they rushed through their breakfasts and hurried to the bridge, Walter White, executive secretary of the National Association for the Advancement of Colored People (NAACP), had received a long-distance telephone call from Georgia.

*　　　*　　　*

When the phone rang at NAACP headquarters in New York City on Friday, July 26, delivering the news that four black people had been shot to death by the side of a country road in Georgia, Walter White was undoubtedly horrified, but it's unlikely he was shocked. He was born in Atlanta in 1893, and his childhood coincided with a decade that saw more lynchings than any before or since: more than one hundred blacks were lynched each year between 1890 and 1900. Though the earliest lynchings in America had occurred in the Northeast as well as the frontier west, and had claimed mostly white victims, by the end of the Civil War nearly all of the nation's lynchings occurred in the South, and most of the victims were black. Lynching, originally a tool to levy outlaw justice, had, by the time Walter White was born, become a terrorist tactic used largely to punish blacks accused of transgressing the rules of white supremacy. Of the 1,545 people lynched between 1890 and 1900, just 438 were white—meaning 1,107 (or 72 percent) of the victims were black. Even these figures, as high as they are, are surely under-estimates, because the incidence of lynching was impossible to doc-ument accurately. One key challenge was overcoming the fear and secrecy that kept many lynchings local, underground, or far from the public eye. But another challenge was the difficulty of distin-guishing lynching from the more general crime of murder. Some scholars and activists argued that community sanction was the dis-tinguishing factor; others claimed it was the presence of a mob. Either way, the conditions that surrounded lynchings, in addition to the inexactness of its definition, prevented—and continues to prevent—the compilation of accurate statistics. It is safe to say, however, that the incidence of lynching declined after its peak in 1892, though it continued to claim roughly twenty-five black vic-tims a year through the 1920s, and roughly ten black victims a year through the 1930s. And it is also safe to say that, by the time Walter

White received the news that July morning in 1946, more than three thousand black people had been lynched in America.

At fifty-three, White had more than two decades of professional experience with lynching and racial violence. He'd joined the NAACP's national staff in 1918 and quickly become their most daring on-the-spot investigator. Arriving in town after a lynching, he'd mingle with police, judges, and the lynchers themselves; his light skin, blue eyes, and blond hair afforded him a natural disguise as a white man. On one occasion, he was deputized, handed a badge and a gun, and authorized to "go out and kill niggers." On another occasion, he himself only narrowly escaped being lynched. From this risky investigative role, White had moved easily into all aspects of the NAACP's antilynching struggle. He'd written exposés, drafted federal anti-lynching bills and lobbied Congress, negotiated for action at the highest levels of the executive branch, and authored two novels about lynching. By 1946, he was the foremost antilynching activist in the nation.

Like many white Southerners, White and the NAACP were alarmed by the clashes between black veterans and white bus drivers and policemen that had been occurring frequently since the war's end. But, while many white Southerners interpreted such clashes as evidence that black veterans had gotten "uppity" and aggressive, the NAACP viewed them as evidence of white people's increased aggression, the sort that had plagued the nation during the Red Summer following World War I. By July 1946, White and the NAACP had already mounted massive responses to two of the year's most brutal incidents of racial violence. The first had occurred on February 13, when the local police chief in Batesburg, South Carolina, bludgeoned a black veteran named Isaac Woodard in the face, permanently blinding him. At the time of his beating, Isaac Woodard was still in uniform; he'd been discharged from an army base in Georgia only hours before and was then arrested after fighting with a bus driver. The second incident occurred twelve days later, after a black veteran in Columbia, Tennessee, fought with a white storeowner over the repair of a broken radio. When black people in Columbia mobilized to protect the black veteran from a white mob that had gathered on the town square vowing to lynch him, a "race riot" ensued. Two black men were shot dead by police, hundreds of other black men were arrested, and the town's entire black business district was destroyed. Immediately after learning of each incident, Walter White had started a nationwide publicity campaign. Then he sent a NAACP investigator to the scene to gather information, as he'd once done himself.

That July morning when he got the news of the Moore's Ford lynching—a lynching that, in claiming four victims, instantly shattered the historical trend toward fewer lynchings—Walter White followed the same protocol. He sent a press bulletin about the lynching to the nation's major newspapers and radio networks, as well as to every black newspaper. Then he fired off two telegrams, one to U.S. attorney general Tom Clark, and one to President Harry Truman. In the telegram to Attorney General Clark, White reported the lynching as the "direct result of [a] conspiratorial campaign to violate federal constitution by Eugene Talmadge and Ku Klux Klan." In the telegram to President Truman, White cited the lynching as the latest incident in an "outbreak of lawlessness which threatens not only minorities but democracy itself." Walter White knew few specifics about the lynching victims—in fact, his press release contained inaccuracies about the way they'd been lynched, as well as an incorrect surname for George Dorsey—but specifics didn't matter because the victims were now symbols of injustice: a NAACP cause.

After seeing to the initial publicity, White next contacted the director of the NAACP's Atlanta office—a branch he'd helped form in 1916, and the one closest to Walton County—and asked him to hire a white investigator to travel to Monroe immediately. This investigator, White instructed, was to "get as much specific evidence against individual members of the mob and information as to any connection which the Ku Klux Klan may have had with the lynching." The investigator should also probe into "possible complicity by local police and the sheriff's office"—and rush the information to NAACP headquarters as quickly as possible.

About the time Walter White received his long-distance call that morning in New York City, Walton County sheriff E. S. Gordon placed a telephone call to the headquarters of the Georgia Bureau of Investigation (GBI) in Atlanta. Over the wire, Sheriff Gordon—who'd roused himself that morning despite being too ill the evening before to attend the coroner's inquest at the Moore's Ford Bridge—reported the four murders. He repeated the familiar lynching verdict, "death at the hands of persons unknown," and stated that since the lone eyewitness, Loy Harrison, had provided no leads, the investigation was at a standstill.

The phone call was protocol, and Sheriff Gordon almost certainly thought the matter would end when the line went dead. While Walter White's impulse was to maximize what he viewed as a national lynching, Sheriff Gordon's goal was to downplay what he termed a local murder. But he failed. The GBI's director, Major William Spence, immediately notified Governor Ellis Arnall of the lynching. In turn, Arnall, who'd become a lame-duck governor at Eugene Talmadge's victory eight days before, ordered Major Spence and four other GBI agents to drive to Monroe and launch a murder investigation.

By the time the GBI agents escorted Loy Harrison to Moore's Ford later that afternoon, the stream of souvenir collectors had tapered off, a consequence of both the heat of the day and the diminishing supply of souvenirs. Dressed in his khakis, his face flushed in the afternoon sun, Loy Harrison looked even more the farmer next to Major Spence, who appeared less like a lawman than a teacher in his suit, tie, and metal-rimmed glasses. Standing in the road at the spot where the mob had ambushed his car, Loy Harrison explained to Major Spence and his agents that he hadn't decided for certain to post Roger Malcom's bond until roughly 3 P.M. the day before, when he'd signed the papers in the sheriff's office. Then, after telling his black tenants to meet him at the drinking fountain on the courthouse square at 5 P.M., he'd driven to a filling station, visited several stores, and spent time talking to both the day and night manager at the Monroe ice plant. Since he'd told no one about his decision to bond out Roger Malcom that afternoon, he assumed the mob had learned of his plans from his black tenants, who "got drunk and talked all over the place," he said. Although the men in the mob were unmasked, Loy Harrison said he hadn't seen them clearly and wouldn't be able to recognize them again. He was positive, however, that he'd never seen any of them before. He ended his statement by saying, "I had no intention of getting anybody in trouble. I just needed a farmhand." At the conclusion of the interview, Major Spence posted a guard at Loy Harrison's large stone house, to offer protection in case the mob members should try to take revenge against him for his testimony.

Later that afternoon, two assistant U.S. attorneys drove into Monroe to visit the Walton County sheriffs in their office in the courthouse basement. It was a brief visit; the federal lawyers had only one question to ask before returning to their headquarters in Macon. Was there any indication of trouble during the eleven days Roger Malcom was in jail before the lynching occurred?

Sheriff Gordon answered the question immediately. No, he said, there hadn't been a hint of trouble. When he turned to his deputies, both Lewis Howard and Doc Sorrells confirmed his answer. No, they said, not a bit.

As the attorneys were leaving Monroe, reporters and photographers from the Associated Press, the United Press Syndicate, and *Life*, as well as representatives from newspapers in New York, Chicago, and Atlanta—and the NAACP's hired investigator, a white lawyer from Macon—were making their way into town. By that evening, the boys hawking newspapers on the streets of Atlanta were yelling, "Mob violence breaks out in Monroe. Four Negroes lynched!" The next day's *Chicago Tribune* featured the words MASS LYNCHING IN GEORGIA spelled out above the nameplate in huge block letters usually reserved for news of war or peace. The *Atlanta Daily World*'s headline read "Nation's Worst Lynching," and the headline of its rival, the *Pittsburgh Courier*, read "Monroe Massacre Shocks Nation."

Friday evening on NBC's national nightly radio news, the lead story reported that the U.S. military had detonated the world's fifth atomic bomb underwater near the Pacific island of Bikini at 8:35 A.M. on July 25. The second story reported that, in Nuremberg, Germany, American Supreme Court justice Robert Jackson was calling for the death penalty for twenty-two top Nazi officials for their crimes against humanity. And finally, there was an item from Monroe, Georgia. "One hundred forty million Americans were disgraced late yesterday, humiliated in their own eyes and in the eyes of the world by one of the most vicious lynchings to stain our national record in a long time," the announcer said. ". . . A gang of armed and degenerate poor whites waylaid a Negro man and another man and their wives on a country road forty miles from

Atlanta. The brief and sadistic orgy ended in the bodies being rid-dled by sixty bullets."

By then, the bodies of the four lynching victims had been trans-ported from Almand Funeral Home in downtown Monroe to Young Funeral Home on the Corner. This move occurred because, contrary to Loy Harrison's instructions the night before, the vic-tims' families preferred that Dan Young, not E. L. Almand Jr., arrange the funerals. And E. L. Almand no doubt preferred the move as well. Though he embalmed and buried black people, it was difficult for him to allow their families to hold viewings or visita-tions at his funeral home; to do so would have meant risking the patronage of his white customers. And too, there was the issue of money. Neither Roger Malcom nor Mae Murray had burial insur-ance, and George Dorsey and Dorothy Malcom had policies worth only $25 each. That meant the funeral director would likely be stuck with the cost of the caskets, the funeral, and the burial plots. By turning the bodies over to Dan Young on Friday, E. L. Almand relieved himself of any worries about getting paid; he charged the city $140 for the embalming and was finished with the matter.

In mortuary school, Dan Young had been trained to make the dead look like the living. But on that Friday night nothing in his "undertaker's art" could make Dorothy and Roger Malcom, and George and Mae Murray Dorsey, look as they'd looked two days before. As one reporter commented, "Shotgun shells fired at point-blank don't leave much face." Whether Dan Young was most affected by his inability to conceal the young people's injuries, or by his own refusal to help them nearly two weeks before, it's impossi-ble to know. But he told his friends that preparing the bodies for the viewing knocked him off his feet.

Dan Young and his assistants were still working late that night when a crowd of young black people pounded on the basement door of the funeral home. They'd heard through the grapevine that he "had the bodies," and they wanted a peek. After Dan Young refused to open up, they scattered, and one black man decided to play a joke on his girlfriend as they walked home along the dark streets of Monroe. "There they are!" he cried out suddenly. He laughed as his girlfriend screamed, and then waited for her to run to him for protection. But he underestimated her fear of "they," of the lynchers. His girlfriend ran home, and though he chased her, he couldn't catch her in time for a good-night kiss.

That night, the sky above Walton County, like the sky above the entire South, shone with the aurora borealis, the northern lights. The aura was so bright that a man in Atlanta was able to read his newspaper outside at midnight. But few black people in the rural areas of Walton County enjoyed the light show that Friday night. Some barred their doors with a chest of drawers and hung quilts over their windows, as their ancestors had done when the night riders came. Others loaded shotguns and placed them by their beds. They were fearful, and they were ready. "If they kill four," one black woman said, "they'll kill more."

CHAPTER EIGHT

The next morning in Monroe, a crowd of black people formed into a loose line that stretched the length of three city blocks, from the corner of Broad and Spring Streets to the entrance of Young Funeral Home, on the Corner. By noon, several hundred people had gathered, enough to draw murmurs from those who'd come to town to do their weekly errands. Those who hadn't yet heard about the lynching learned of it that Saturday morning, because the crowd was impossible to miss. "There was so many black people down there," says one black man, "they looked like ants."

A few women were waiting in line that morning, dressed in light summer dresses and sandals, but most of the people leaning against the buildings were young men, some wearing suits, ties, and felt hats, some wearing overalls and straw hats, and some still wearing their army uniforms. When Dan Young opened his doors, those at the front surged inside, past a plaque with four names lettered on it: Mr. Roger Malcom, Mrs. Dorothy Malcom, Mr. Geo. Dorsey, Mrs. May M. Dorsey. Next to the plaque hung a poster left over from the July 17 primary election. Its message proclaimed: "U.S. is ready to protect 'Negro Balloting.'"

After the double lynching in Walton County in 1911, white crowds had flocked to a certain telegraph pole south of Monroe, and a certain tree near the Corner. But, as one newspaper reported, "not a negro in Monroe could be induced to go near" either place. Thirty-five years later, Moena Williams didn't walk to the clearing by the Moore's Ford Bridge on the morning after her children were killed—nor would she ever. She said she didn't want to see the place. Similarly, those blacks who'd once fished and necked and drunk liquor at Moore's Ford wouldn't do so for a long while, and never without the knowledge of what had happened there. In the days after the lynching, even the rope swing hung by children from an outlying branch looked ominous to the black people who hurried past it on their way to and from the fields.

Had the bodies of the four lynch victims remained at Moore's Ford until being buried, most black people in Walton County wouldn't have seen them. Instead, they would've relied on white people, on rumors, or on their nightmares, for information about the lynching. But the bodies had been transferred from the lynching scene to a black-owned funeral home located in a black business district. And so, that Saturday, black people in Monroe had the rare chance to personally witness the victims of a lynching, to examine the injuries and inventory the harms in a safe place. Many of those who passed through Dan Young's funeral home that day were there to mourn. But just as many were there to confront the truth of the lynching, to look upon what one black reporter called the "mute evidence in human form." Nine years later, after Emmett Till was lynched in Mississippi, his mother would allow his mutilated body to be exhibited so the world could see what had been done to her child. That day in Monroe, many would see what had been done to four black citizens, and more than a half century later, black people all over Walton County would remember.

Mary Alice Avery, the stepdaughter of Isaac Brooks, the black man who'd helped clean the bodies at Almand Funeral Home, went to the viewing on a date with her fiancé. They passed through the entrance and entered the main room of the funeral home, where the four bodies lay on a row of stretchers. Even at midday, it was dark in there, the windows shrouded by heavy curtains, the room's bare wooden floors and stained walls illuminated by a few dim bulbs.

While some passed by the bodies quickly, looking and not looking, Mary Alice Avery and her fiancé studied them. At the far end of the row lay Roger Malcom, his face pocked with the plaster of paris Dan Young had used to conceal the damage to his face. But nothing could hide the hole in Roger Malcom's cheek. It was larger than a quarter, the result of a shotgun fired at close range.

Dorothy's body lay next to Roger's, a bandage covering her face where the right side of her jaw had been blown away. It was evidently her tooth that the white student had found on the ground near Moore's Ford the morning before and given to his friend for her charm bracelet.

Next to Dorothy lay her brother George. His right eye was covered with a bandage—it had been shot out—and his right ear, which had been partially shot off, was attached to his head by tape.

And last in the row was Mae Murray Dorsey, whose eyes, nose, and ears were unmarred, and whose long, straight hair—the envy of local black men and women alike—framed her pale face in death as it had in life. Mae Murray looked as if she were sleeping; her face, unlike the others, wasn't a record of her death.

That day, Mary Alice Avery looked closely and tried to remember everything as she walked past the row of bodies: Dorothy with her swollen jaw, George with a bump like a thimble on the top of his head, Mae with a neat, round bullet hole in the back of her head. When Mary Alice Avery and her fiancé returned to stand in front of Roger Malcom, they peeled back the funeral blanket and looked at his body.

"They kind of lacerated Roger. They had stuck him or cut him. He was tortured for sure," she says. "The others just had bullet wounds, but he had been attacked."

They'd heard he'd been castrated, so they pulled the blanket all the way down.

"He *was* castrated," she says, "like the privates halfway cut off, something kind of hanging."

After they'd finished viewing the bodies, people walked outside, blinking in the sunlight. Some, like Mary Alice Avery, reported that one or both of the men had been castrated. Some said Roger Malcom's genitals had been stuffed into his mouth. Some said the women's genitals had been carved out and tossed up into the trees by the Apalachee River. And others said that one or both of the women had been pregnant, and that their babies had been ripped from their wombs and murdered too. There was no proof of these things—neither the newsmen who reported on the viewing, nor Dan Young, in his comments to others, said anything about castration or pregnancy. Yet those who told the stories and those who listened to them didn't need proof. The history of lynching made the stories believable, even if they weren't true.

Other people walked out of Young Funeral Home that day with unanswered questions. When did Roger and Dorothy, and George and Mae, sense they were in danger—was it when Loy Harrison turned off the highway, or not until they neared the Moore's Ford Bridge? Did Roger and George try to fight off the lynchers? Were they able to hurt any of them? Did they try to break free and escape—or did they think the white men were only going to beat them? Did they scream when they realized all was lost—or did they go silent? Did they die instantly, or at least quickly? Did they die with the knowledge of why they were lynched?

Still others walked out of the funeral home laughing bitterly. "There were so many holes you could see daylight through the bodies," they said. "Their faces were like screens. You could sift flour through them." This gallows humor served to take in shock, to mask surprise and fear and anger. As one black reporter noted, some people on the Corner that day "were as loud-mouthed and hilarious as if the stark tragedy . . . had never occurred." Indeed, life went on, in a fashion. Briggery's Café—where Dorothy Malcom and Mae Murray had purchased their penny candy two days before—was doing a brisk business on soda pop, pork chops, and fish sandwiches. The beauty parlor and barbershop were full. Along the road that led from the Corner up to the paved main street, groups of black veterans, still wearing khaki shirts and army fatigue caps, played checkers. Though the reporter described them as "loud-mouthed and hilarious" from a distance, they quickly turned somber when he approached with questions about their experiences since returning from the army.

"They're exterminating us," said one black veteran. "They're killing Negro vets and we don't have nothing to fight back with but our bare hands. In Italy and Germany we knew which way they were coming, but here . . ." When the reporter asked the man why he didn't leave the South, he replied that if he did, the white people in Monroe and Walton County would take it out on his mother and sister. "They need us to work their farms," he said, "and they need us over at the saw mills and the cotton mills"—even though the only jobs there for black men were on the janitorial crews.

Another black veteran told the reporter that the white people he'd worked for before the war had begun harassing him to work for them as soon as he returned from the army. After he put them off, they checked on his account at the local bank, which made it appear that he'd stolen from them. The police would arrest him for being "drunk" any day now, he said. Then the white people would pay his fine and he'd be forced to work for them once again.

The men playing checkers viewed their experiences as evidence of the particular hardships faced by black veterans. And, even though only one of the lynching victims was an army veteran, they saw the lynching through the prism of their veteran status as well. But the truth was that the hardships faced by black veterans in 1946 weren't so different from the hardships faced by black people everywhere in the rural South. Many veterans just responded more assertively.

Even so, the black men playing checkers that Saturday didn't speak of avenging the deaths of the four people lying in Dan Young's funeral home, or uniting in any kind of reprisal for the lynching—it was still too soon for that. They simply vowed to defend themselves and their families against white people. "My mother tells me to be careful and good, and she tells me to pray. But she don't understand. The days of [Uncle] Tom are over," said one black veteran. "I know they're going to get me sooner or later, but I've got a pistol and three cartridges. That'll make four of us in hell together."

Later that day, after the crowds had disappeared from the Corner, Dan Young smuggled a reporter and a photographer from the *Pittsburgh Courier*'s Atlanta bureau into his funeral home. As the relatives of the victims lingered over the bodies, the photographer documented the grim tableau. In one of the photographs later featured in a special section of the *Pittsburgh Courier* titled "Victims of Georgia Hate Campaign," Moena Williams stands over Mae Murray Dorsey's body, her head bowed, her fist clenching a handkerchief. Wearing a red dress with a white pinafore, she looks far too young to be the mother of two of the lynching victims. Near her is Jim Williams, his body bent over, evidence of his bad hip. Farther down the row of mourners stands an elegantly dressed black woman, the sister of Mae Murray. She gazes toward her dead sister, whose head rests on a cloth pillow. A week-old newspaper, headlined "Voters Pour into Polls," serves as the only pillow for the other three.

Next to the photograph, under a headline reading, "Look Closely Mr. Talmadge," close-ups of the victims' battered bodies ran large, so black people all over the nation could see, as had those who'd visited Young Funeral Home, what a mob of white men had done.

That Saturday evening, after one full day of investigation in Walton County, Major Spence and his GBI agents made their first arrest. They took into custody a bouncer from the County Line Beer Garden who they believed was the leader of the mob at Moore's Ford.

Both at the coroner's inquest and in his first interview with the GBI, Loy Harrison had offered the same description of the mob's leader: a sixty-five-year-old man with a tanned face, brown eyes, and brown curly hair streaked with gray. According to Loy Harrison, the man wore a double-breasted suit, pointed shoes, and black hat, and he had a young man's gait and an intelligent voice. That Major Spence and his agents had located a man who fit such a specific description boded well. When they brought the beer hall bouncer— a local man named Lester Little—to the county jail that evening, they were hopeful for a quick break. If they could prove Lester Little was the leader, they could pressure him into revealing the members of the mob.

But when Loy Harrison arrived at the county jail and saw Lester Little, he shook his head. "No," he said. "He isn't the one. He's twenty pounds heavier."

Without a positive identification from Loy Harrison, Major Spence was forced to release his suspect. And in the wake of the release, his hopes for a quick solution to the lynching evaporated.

On the brink of frustration after only one full day on the case, Major Spence revealed to reporters two key conclusions he'd already made. The first pertained to the lynching itself: "It looks like it was a rehearsed affair. It looks like it might have been planned since the Negro was first confined to jail." The second addressed the "wall of silence" in Walton County: "The best people in town won't talk about this. They have an idea who it is." Like the phrase "death at the hands of persons unknown," the phrase "the best people" resonated. While newspapers often reported that the "lower classes" of white people seemed to delight in lynchings, they claimed "the best people" deplored such acts.

At a press conference that morning in Atlanta, Governor Arnall had said, "This mass murder is one of the worst incidents ever to take place in our state." After declaring that "civilization is incensed over this atrocity," he'd announced a $10,000 reward for information on the lynching, the maximum allowed by state law. Given the long history of inaction against lynching by authorities in the South, this was an unusually decisive and progressive move. Certainly it contrasted sharply with the reaction of Governor-elect Talmadge, who deemed the lynching "regrettable" and went on to claim that there had been no lynchings during his three previous terms as governor of Georgia—when, in fact, there had been fourteen. But that Saturday night in Monroe, Major Spence went one startling step further than even his liberal boss: he voiced his support for federal antilynching legislation. "We need federal backing," he said. "With conditions that now exist in Georgia we can't cope with them."

When Major Spence's comments appeared in newspapers the following day, Walter White and the NAACP's 450,000 members nationwide were heartened. But most white Walton countians, like most white Georgians, were outraged. In characterizing the lynching as a "rehearsed affair," Major Spence implied there'd been community knowledge of—if not participation in—the lynching. And in stating that the "best people" in town were keeping silent, Major Spence intimated local leaders were withholding information that could identify the guilty parties. The editor of the *Walton Tribune* was so "burned up" by Major Spence's comments that he confronted him several days later. Major Spence softened his statements then, but it was too late. His comments had caused the white citizens of Walton County to close ranks even tighter against the outsiders who'd already arrived in town, and against those who were still to come.

The streets of Monroe were deserted by the time two agents from the Atlanta office of the Federal Bureau of Investigation descended into the basement of Dan Young's funeral home late that Saturday night. They'd received a telephone call from FBI headquarters that afternoon and had immediately driven to Monroe to secure an autopsy order from a Walton County judge; time was of the essence since three of the four victims would be buried the next day. The two agents were told they'd be in Monroe for a few days or a week at most, presiding over the autopsy, investigating the crime scene, and aiding the GBI.

That night, the two agents stood among the cases of embalming fluid and plaster of paris while Dan Young's employees walked down the long stairway with the first body. When they reached the bottom, they laid the body on a cement slab, took up metal sticks, and began digging out the bullets. As they did, one of the agents, Louis Hutchinson, stood by the table with his notebook and diagrammed the location of each bullet's entry and exit. He noted the slugs were clustered around the chest and the face, with almost none in the body's lower region. That confirmed what the coroner had concluded the night before: the victims had sunk to the ground after the first volley of shots. After extracting the visible bullets, one of Dan Young's workers took a scalpel, made a long incision in the center of the chest, and folded back the skin. Then he took a saw and cut through the rib cage. After that was done, the men dug out the shotgun pellets and the bullet slugs embedded there.

When they finished with the first body, the workers brought the next one down. They laid it on the cement slab and again took up metal sticks and extracted the bullets and slugs. Then the scalpel and the saw.

It was early Sunday morning by the time the FBI agents let themselves out of the funeral home, leaving Dan Young's assistants to sew up the bodies. The two agents carried with them the fruits of the night's labor: three .38-caliber Smith & Wesson bullets, one each taken from the bodies of Roger Malcom, George Dorsey, and Mae Murray Dorsey; two .32-caliber Smith & Wesson long bullets taken from Roger Malcom's body; and seventeen number-six chilled shotgun-shell pellets extracted from the bodies of George Dorsey and Mae Murray Dorsey. The next day, agents would find several more bullets and a few lengths of rope at the scene of the lynching, the few items overlooked by souvenir collectors. These would comprise the only physical evidence in the case.

Louis Hutchinson was a rookie agent, a young man of thirty-three who'd been an accountant before joining the FBI and was thus known among his colleagues as a "stool sitter." He'd begun in the FBI's Newark, New Jersey, office investigating wartime espionage, and in his one year in Atlanta, he'd worked bank fraud and war-materials fraud. He'd never investigated a murder before. That night after returning to his room at the Monroe Hotel, Louis Hutchinson slept little. In his mind, he kept seeing a body coming down the stairs at Young Funeral Home—first the feet, then the middle, then the head.

Others in Walton County also lay awake that Saturday night. Many black people continued to live with fear now that, as one newspaper reported, "lynching is on the loose." And too, the white men who'd fired the shots that Thursday evening contended with a degree of surprise: how quickly the nation had learned they'd shot four black farmhands. And how many people outside Walton County seemed to care.

CHAPTER NINE

Just after midday on Sunday, people began arriving at Mount Perry Baptist Church to attend the joint funeral for George Dorsey and Dorothy Malcom, the first of the lynching victims to be buried. The church had been full earlier that morning, and now cars and trucks and wagons streamed in from the road once again. The mourners stepped out and stood in groups in the dirt churchyard, which had been swept smooth for the occasion. White reporters threaded through the groups, asking questions and getting a "blank wall." White photographers perched on ladders, fixing their lenses on the scene below. The reporters' questions and the clicks and flashes of the cameras reminded these mourners, in case they'd forgotten, that this was no ordinary home-going.

That morning, as people all over the nation opened their newspapers to find the Moore's Ford lynching in the headlines for the third day in a row—"Georgia Mob of 20 Men Massacres 2 Negroes, Wives," "Lynch Law Back in Georgia," "White Supremacy in Georgia," "Fight Until Lynch Evil Dies"—Dan Young had driven through the countryside, searching for a preacher willing to preside over the afternoon funeral. Again and again, the clergymen refused him. They were unwilling to take such a risk for two people they didn't know; they didn't want to put themselves or their families in danger. When Dan Young did finally find a preacher, he drove him immediately to the tiny clapboard church, so as to minimize the opportunity for the man to change his mind. Luckily, Dan Young didn't have to scramble to find a place to hold the funeral. As a member of Mount Perry Baptist Church, which sat in Morgan County,

just across the line from Oconee County, Moena Williams was enti-
tled to have her children buried in its cemetery. Just the same,
church leaders no doubt feared the liability. With the lynching victims interred in its cemetery, Mount Perry faced great danger of
vandalism, or even destruction—and the church had already burned
twice in recent history.

The funeral was to begin at 2 P.M. and most of the crowd had
moved inside by then, the men hanging their hats from nails on the
wall before taking seats in the slatted pews. Nearly fifty people filled
the church, and the deacons' section, populated each Sunday with
elderly men dressed in dark suits, was half-full. Though the group
was noticeably smaller than the one that had flocked to Dan
Young's funeral home the day before, it was a good crowd, considering. But when it came time to start the funeral, the first pew
was conspicuously empty. Moena and Jim Williams, along with
Moena's surviving son, Charlie Boy Dorsey, hadn't yet arrived. In
fact, the only relative of Dorothy and George's seated in Mount
Perry was a distant cousin.

Dan Young instructed the preacher to delay the funeral and went
out with another man in a car to look for Moena Williams and her
family. The reporters and photographers covering the funeral soon
joined him in the search, but after more than an hour, all returned
to the church. They'd driven to Moore's Ford, where GBI and FBI
agents were sifting the dirt at the crime scene to recover stray bullets and wading the river to search for abandoned murder weapons.
They'd driven to the cement-block house on Loy Harrison's farm
and found it empty. "They ain't nowhere," one black man concluded. When, at 4 P.M., Moena Williams's aged uncle opened the
door of the church, he told Dan Young that Moena had disappeared. He himself had held off coming to the funeral until he knew
it was safe.

By then, Dan Young had waited two hours, and he couldn't wait any longer. He gave the signal and the Reverend Joseph Ingram positioned himself behind the two white coffins and began the funeral service. There were no wreaths or bouquets. The only decorations inside the church that day were two small vases of dahlias, and an American flag draped over one of the coffins.

Rev. Ingram likely began the service with a prayer, then followed by reading the names of the medals George Dorsey had earned during his four and one-half years in the army. Perhaps he talked about George Dorsey's love for music, his smile, his skill as a farmer. Perhaps then he turned to Dorothy Dorsey Malcom, talking about her spirit, her friendliness, her youth. As he stood fanning himself in the afternoon heat, it's likely he didn't discuss the lynching directly. His role was to read from the Bible that lay open on the lectern, and to use biblical words to assure those in church that Dorothy and George were no longer suffering, that they were with God in heaven, and that justice would be done there. These words might have offered some comfort to Moena and Jim Williams, but they weren't there to hear them.

When the service was over, the mourners fell into line behind Rev. Ingram and Dan Young and followed a dirt path to the far side of the cemetery, where Dan Young's employees had dug a wide pit. In the pit were two wooden boxes placed side by side. The men lowered George Dorsey's coffin into one, then lowered his sister's down next to it. They piled the dirt in two mounds on top as the preacher offered one last prayer. Afterward, Dan Young turned his hearse toward Monroe, where Mae Murray's funeral would be held later that afternoon. The reporters and photographers followed him there, and the rest of the mourners returned home, wondering why Moena Williams and her family had missed the funeral. What trouble had happened now?

*   *   *

The trouble was finding a ride to the funeral.

Early that morning, Charlie Boy Dorsey, Moena's surviving son, had asked one of his black neighbors to borrow his car to travel to the funeral. The black man said his car was broken; in truth, he'd anticipated Charlie Boy's request and "broken" the car himself. Like the clergymen who refused Dan Young, the man either feared the risk of helping the family of the lynching victims or simply didn't want to get involved. Either way, he sent Charlie Boy down the road to ask another black man, Rufus Foster, for a ride.

Rufus Foster, who'd worked on a farm near Loy Harrison's for years, agreed to carry the family to the funeral that afternoon. But when Moena, Jim, and Charlie Boy arrived at his house at 1:30 P.M., they found him too drunk to drive. "Rufus got drunk," one black man speculated, "to make sure he couldn't go."

At that point, Charlie Boy walked the quarter mile back to the first man's house, to ask if his car was still broken. It was. So Charlie Boy walked back to Rufus Foster's house and asked if he could drive his car. Rufus Foster refused, but said he would allow Ed Jackson, a black man who lived nearby, to drive it. Luckily, Ed Jackson wasn't afraid to take the family to the funeral. "I guess I was crazy," he says. "I had just got out of the army. I didn't know why everyone was so scared." After hours of delay, Charlie Boy, Moena, and Jim Williams climbed into the backseat of Rufus Foster's car, Ed Jackson cranked it up, and they finally headed toward the church. At nearly 5 P.M., they crested the last hill before Mount Perry, and Ed Jackson spotted Dan Young's hearse coming toward them.

"Oh my God," he said, "we missed the funeral."

He drove on into the empty churchyard. Moena Williams stepped out of the car and walked to the back of the cemetery, to the freshly dug double grave. She stood there for a long time. Then she returned to the car and Ed Jackson drove her, Jim Williams, and Charlie Boy back to their house on Loy Harrison's farm.

Later that day—a day one newspaper deemed "Black Sunday"—Mae Murray's funeral was held at Tabernacle Baptist Church, just a block from Young Funeral Home and the Corner. A larger crowd gathered there than at the earlier funeral, perhaps because it was more convenient, perhaps because Mae Murray was better known in Monroe. Her family had lived on a plantation at the edge of town since the Civil War. She was a beautiful young girl, with her long, straight hair, and pale yellow skin. She'd finished high school. These were the only details about Mae Murray available to the reporters that day, and they'd be the only details available a half century later. Whether Mae Murray was "friendly" or "fast"; whether she went with white men, or only black men, would never be clear. When asked why Mae Murray was killed, her grandfather and great-uncle were "clammouthed" and "tight-lipped." They did, however, intimate that she was the most innocent of the four victims, that she'd been lynched by association. And, by burying her separately from George Dorsey, Mae Murray's relatives indicated that, in their eyes, she wasn't married to him. Mae was laid next to her parents in Zion Hill Cemetery, which sat on land donated by the white family for whom the Murrays had worked for generations.

When Dan Young held the last funeral the next day at Chestnut Grove Baptist, a tiny country church a few miles from Hestertown, only a handful of people attended: Roger Malcom's grandmother, Mama Dora; his sister, who'd made the trip from Chicago; his first wife, Mattie Louise; and a few cousins. One of Roger Malcom's aunts, Rosa Bell Ingram, had attended the viewing at Young Funeral Home, but was too frightened to appear at the funeral.

Mama Dora was frightened too. When reporters asked to interview her at the funeral, she refused, but, weeks later, after leaving Hestertown for the safety of her granddaughter's Chicago apartment, she'd talk to a reporter from the *Chicago Defender.* She'd speak of Roger's plans to move to Chicago after the cotton settle. She'd recall his love for black molasses and for the color blue. She'd say he was a "real scholar" who would've been a preacher had he lived. "He was jovial and always gave good advice, and everyone listened to him," she'd say. "I can't explain the way I felt when I was notified of his death. But something in me died too. They took my boy away from me like a dog. He was always gentle, sweet and kind, trying to please me and everyone else."

On the day of the funeral, Mattie Louise, who was still legally married to Roger Malcom though she'd left him the summer before, was more conflicted in her feelings than Mama Dora. Mattie Louise believed Roger had changed after their son, Roger Jr., was born. He'd started hanging out with a "bad crowd," she says, playing cards and gambling away money he'd borrowed from her. He started returning home late from the fields and making excuses to skip church. One day he walked into their house with another woman's lipstick staining the collar of his good white shirt. When Mattie Louise confronted him, he hit her. She hit him back. He ran outside, and she ran after him. They yelled and tussled, but the fight didn't leave their yard. Mattie Louise didn't seek protection from their landlord or from any white man—not during that fight with Roger, nor any of the many others. She defended herself alone, and when it was over, she walked up to Mama Dora's house to get a poultice for her black eye. Mama Dora would tell her that Roger was mean because his mother had died when he was so young, and since Mattie Louise had been abandoned by her mother as a baby, she understood that meanness. For a long time she stayed with Roger, in spite of his drinking and gambling and cheating, and in spite of the fights. "I loved him," she says, "and I thought that love could go a long way."

But on a Saturday in the summer of 1945, Mattie Louise had walked into the store in Hestertown to find Roger giving the money she'd lent him, money she'd worked for, to another woman. Worse, that other woman was Dorothy Dorsey. Mattie Louise had been friends with her when she was a child, but when she discovered that Dorothy was, as she says, "a little teenaged whore," she broke off the friendship.

Roger and Mattie Louise went home that day and fought, and in that fight Mattie Louise sensed a new danger. "Roger would have killed me sooner or later," she says, "because he wanted to have that other woman and I wouldn't stand for it."

So she began taking walks, looking for a path through the thick woods that led from the Malcom farm out to the nearest main road. One evening, she asked Roger to walk two miles to borrow a straightening comb and some hair grease for her. It was a trick; she had her own hot comb and grease. When he was gone, she packed a bag, delivered Roger Jr. to Mama Dora—who took him on as she'd taken on his father twenty-odd years before—and walked through the woods to the road. Then she caught the bus and rode to Atlanta.

"I knew Roger was the devil," she says, "and I got out of there."

After leaving Hestertown in August 1945, Mattie Louise had returned several times to visit her son, and to give money to Mama Dora for caring for him. During one of those visits, Roger Malcom saw her in his grandmother's house and barely recognized her; she had a new big-city hairdo, and a new gold star on her front tooth. As soon as he did recognize her, he slapped her. Then she chased him with a knife, slashing the air as she ran. She returned to Atlanta and didn't come back to Walton County until the spring of 1946, when her father asked for her help with his cotton crop. Mattie

Louise was living on her father's place when she heard Roger had stabbed Barnette Hester. Despite their troubles, she'd visited him in jail. She'd lent him her wristwatch and never got it back.

Now that Roger was dead, Mattie Louise remembered their years together as a series of snapshots. There were the nights they were courting, when they'd sit on the porch swing and make a wish on the moon. Those nights, Roger always talked about leaving Walton County, about moving to a city, or up North, to live. She never talked like that. "I felt like I know I was making a living where I was," she says. "All he know was farmwork. All I know was farmwork and cleaning house. Why take a risk?" And there was the day they moved out of Mama Dora's house into a little house set out in the middle of a field on the Malcom place. That little house was the first place Mattie Louise ever called her own—though it belonged to the Malcoms—and she loved it. But she also remembered when Weldon Hester, the overseer of the Malcom farm, came there two days after she'd given birth to Roger Jr., calling for Roger to come out and work. When Roger got outside, Weldon Hester accused him of getting drunk and ruining the farm wagon, and then he charged at him. Weldon Hester would've beaten Roger, but his wife arrived and restrained him.

"One day you're gonna get yourself killed, nigger," Weldon Hester said as he walked away. And Roger Malcom cursed him back.

"There was hate amongst those two people," says Mattie Louise. "I saw the hate in both of them."

She'd thought of that hate when she saw Roger's body in Dan Young's funeral home. "I seen folks kill hogs. Four or five hogs, hang 'em up, and let the blood drain. I'm a strong woman," she says. "I looked at that, and I fainted. They shot Roger worse than they shot the others. Maybe that was Weldon shooting him. He had all that hate in him from way back."

And yet Weldon Hester was not the only one Mattie Louise blamed for Roger's death. She blamed Dorothy Dorsey—she refused to call her Mrs. Dorothy Malcom, as the newspapers did—for voodooing Roger into taking up with her. And she blamed Dorothy for running around with white men. If she hadn't been doing that, she says, Roger wouldn't have stabbed Barnette Hester, and he wouldn't have been lynched. "One whore," says Mattie Louise, "nothing else."

But then she also blamed Roger.

"It was his fault. He brought it on himself. He used to just want to fight," she says. "He acted like the world owed him something. I told him he would die with his shoes on. He died like he lived."

On the Monday of Roger Malcom's funeral, Mattie Louise was sure she'd loved him—she still loved him. But she didn't think he'd ever loved her.

"I don't think Roger loved anyone," she says. "I don't think I ever saw him smile."

By sundown that day, the four victims of the Moore's Ford lynching lay in their unmarked graves—two at Mount Perry in Morgan County, one at Zion Hill in Monroe, one at Chestnut Grove near Hestertown. They'd been buried in sleek white coffins with brass handles, and thanks to a $773 check provided by a black civic committee in Atlanta, Dan Young wouldn't be stuck with the cost.

The four's few possessions were divided. Mattie Louise got one suit of Roger Malcom's clothes, two beds, and all of his furniture, because Mama Dora couldn't take much with her to Chicago. Charlie Boy Dorsey paid the remainder on a gun George had been buying from Loy Harrison and kept it for himself. A female relative in Shelby, North Carolina—where George and Dorothy's father, Columbus Dorsey, lived—got Dorothy's wool sweater. She hated it

because it was scratchy, and because of what had happened. Barnette Hester got Dorothy and Roger's cotton crop because they
died owing him $300. And the owner of Aycock's store near Loy
Harrison's farm got stuck with a debt, because George Dorsey died
owing $17.

That Monday, the first reward posters appeared in Walton and
five surrounding counties, offering $12,500 for "information lead-
ing to the arrest and conviction of persons involved in the killing of
4 Negroes . . . on July 25, 1946." And that day, the first letters
arrived at the office of Attorney General Tom Clark in Washington,
D.C. "I am a Negro woman living way down here at the tail end of
the South," one letter began. "Mr. Clark, what are you and your
people going to do about my poor people. . . . I am speaking about
those four youth that was killed in cold cold bloody murder in
Georgia. . . . Try and do something In the name of God try and do
something."

"Dear Pres. Truman," another letter began, "I am a little girl
about 12 year old and I think that someone up there in Wash DC
ought to put a stop to these murder and slavery because it is getting
terrible to walk down the street any moore."

Other writers were more hardened in their anger, as they pointed
to the clash between the ideals the nation had waged a war to
defend, and the reality of racial violence. "He the colored man . . .
go marching breast to breast back to back for Democracy," wrote
one citizen of New Jersey, "unregarding the hate and discrimination and disfranchise, murdering of his people which he left behind
which gets no protection in the South by the unjust laws but he die,
die, die and when he get back from the war the same thing is waiting for him."

A man who called himself "one of fourteen million disgusted
Negroes" wondered why those convicted of war crimes at Nurem-

berg were being "sentenced to pay the supreme price when these same atrocities are committed here in our own United States." Another writer asked, "How can we propose standards of democracy for other countries when in our own millions of colored citizens are at the mercy of lynch law?"

One after another, the letters that flooded into the attorney general's office—and the telegrams that arrived at the White House at the rate of one every two minutes—implored the federal government to take action. "I urge that you immediately intervene in Georgia to punish the murders and restore law and order for all its citizens," wrote one man. "The corrective measure lies in your hand, Mr. Clark," wrote another. "Use it." Like many Americans, these letter writers looked to the federal government, the guarantor of inalienable rights, for justice.

But it wasn't that simple. The federal government couldn't prosecute lynchers for murder because murder was a state crime, prosecutable only in state courts. For many years, the federal government had claimed that jurisdictional limitation prevented it from taking any action against lynching. Then, in 1939, in response to the continued failure of local authorities to prosecute—since 1880, less than 1 percent of lynchers nationwide had been convicted—President Franklin Roosevelt created the Civil Rights Section (CRS) of the U.S. Justice Department. And three years later, in 1942, he issued a formal directive ordering the CRS to investigate all Negro deaths where the possibility of lynching existed.

But neither the establishment of the CRS, nor the directive from President Roosevelt, enabled the federal government to prosecute for the crime of murder. The only option was to prosecute lynchers for violations of the federal civil rights statutes. And since nearly all of the civil rights statutes passed after the Civil War in an effort to enforce the newly created Thirteenth, Fourteenth, and Fifteenth amendments had been ruled unconstitutional in 1883 by the Supreme Court, only two statutes remained that could be used in lynching cases.

The first, Section 51 of Title 18 of the United States Code, gave the federal government jurisdiction in a lynching only if the victim was lynched while in the process of, or because of, his or her "free exercise or enjoyment" of a federal right. Those convicted under Section 51 would face a fine of no more than $5,000, and a prison term of no more than ten years. The problem with Section 51, at least in terms of its use in lynching cases, was the wording of the Fourteenth Amendment, which established the federal right of a person accused of unlawful conduct not to be deprived of life or liberty by state action, except by a fair trial. The key words were *state action;* the Fourteenth Amendment protected a person's right to life and liberty only against infringement by the state—not by a private individual.

The second civil rights statute, Section 52, gave the federal government jurisdiction in a lynching case if it could be shown that a public officer had subjected a person to "different punishments, pains, or penalties" than prescribed by the Constitution or federal laws "on account of such inhabitant being an alien, or by reason of his color, or race." Section 52 applied to cases in which a sheriff or a police chief gave mob members the key to the jail, or to cases in which they refused to send officers to protect a victim from a lynch mob—thereby subjecting a prisoner to death and the deprivation of his federal rights. Those convicted under Section 52, which was known as the "color of law" statute, would receive a fine of no more than $1,000, or imprisonment of less than a year, or both. Since the punishment was so light for conviction under Section 52, CRS lawyers planned to use it in conjunction with Section 88 of Title 18, a conspiracy statute.

Four years before the Moore's Ford lynching, lawyers from the Justice Department's newly created Civil Rights Section had made their first attempt to prosecute lynchers under Sections 51 and 52, after a mob in Sikeston, Missouri, broke into a state jail, seized a black prisoner named Cleo Wright, tied his feet to the back of a car, dragged him through the city streets, and finally burned him to death. The CRS ordered an investigation by the FBI, then turned over the findings to Missouri state prosecutors so they could pursue the lynchers on murder charges. When a state grand jury failed to indict, the CRS presented the FBI's findings to a federal grand jury in an effort to indict under Sections 51 and 52. But the federal grand jury also failed to indict, this time on the grounds that no violation of federal rights had occurred during the lynching.

In 1943, CRS lawyers made a second attempt, after a black man named Howard Wash was taken from a jail in Laurel, Mississippi, and lynched. This time a federal grand jury returned indictments against five people, including the local jailer, based on Sections 51 and 52. But after the defendants' attorney raised the issue of states' rights during trial, the trial jury found all five not guilty of civil rights violations—even though one had signed a confession stating he'd participated in the lynching. A state grand jury also failed to indict anyone for murder.

Later in 1943, the CRS tried again, after local authorities refused to prosecute three lawmen in Baker County, Georgia, who'd arrested a black man named Robert Hall, taken him to the county courthouse, and beaten him to death with a blackjack. After CRS lawyers presented the case to a federal grand jury, they obtained indictments against Sheriff Claude Screws and his two fellow lawmen based on both Section 52, the color of law statute, and Section 88, the corresponding conspiracy statute. At trial in a federal court in Georgia, all three defendants were found guilty on both counts, fined $1,000, and sentenced to three years in prison. The punishment, which was obscenely light given the crime, was less important than the fact that three white law officers had been convicted in the South for lynching a black man. When the Fifth Circuit Court of Appeals affirmed the conviction, the CRS claimed what it hoped would be the first of many victories in using the federal civil rights statutes to prosecute lynchings.

But after hearing the *Screws* case on appeal, the U.S. Supreme Court overturned the lower courts' verdicts. In a four-way split decision whose opinions totaled more than twenty-five thousand words, the justices held that to convict under Section 52, the federal government had to prove that Screws and his men had beaten Robert Hall in order to *willfully* deny his civil rights—not just out of general vengeance or personal hatred or racism. Since the issue of willfulness hadn't been a factor in the original case, the Supreme Court ordered a new trial.

In 1945, CRS lawyers took the *Screws* case to court once again. Not only had it gotten cold, but the burden to prove willfulness had built up "very high hills to climb," as CRS chief Turner Smith said. "The jury tended to believe that the personal side of the quarrel between Screws and Hall was extremely important," Smith concluded, "thus making it more difficult for the government to convince them that Screws had willfully used his authority as sheriff to deprive Hall of his constitutional rights." The jury found the lawmen "not guilty," leaving them free to return to their posts. As one civil rights expert later commented, "It would have been little short of a miracle had the federal government persuaded two Southern juries, deciding the same case, to vote to convict white men for a crime committed against a Negro." At its conclusion, the *Screws* case became a perfect demonstration of the two massive challenges the CRS faced in prosecuting lynching cases: jurisdictional problems and jury problems.

The two assistant U.S. attorneys who'd visited Monroe on the day after the Moore's Ford lynching had had the jurisdictional constraints in mind when they asked the Walton County sheriffs whether there was any indication of trouble during the period Roger Malcom was in jail. After the sheriffs said no, the federal lawyers told a reporter "they didn't think there had been a violation of any federal law. They didn't think the civil rights statutes would apply." The reporter, in turn, penned a rhetorical question that underscored the federal government's powerlessness in lynching cases. He asked, "I wonder if it would comfort what is left of those four young Negroes, lying naked on slabs in the basement of Dan Young's funeral parlor, to know that their civil rights had not been violated . . . ?"

Given the severe limitations of the two federal civil rights statutes, the NAACP had, since its creation in 1909, lobbied for a new law that would specifically make lynching a federal crime. The federal government would then be able to prosecute lynchers for lynching—not just civil rights violations. But to make lynching a federal crime would require an amendment to the Constitution, an impossible feat given the absolute opposition from the powerful contingent of Southern legislators in the Senate. And so, for nearly four decades, the NAACP and its allies had been seeking to do the next best thing: lobby for a bill that would strengthen Sections 51 and 52 and make them more widely applicable in lynching cases. Between 1900 and 1946, 178 such bills had been introduced into Congress, one at nearly every legislative session. Again and again, they'd died at the hands of Southern Democrats in the Senate. These senators not only claimed that a federal lynching law would infringe on a state's right to prosecute crime within its borders, but they also argued that the decline in the incidence of lynching proved there was no need for such a law. Lynching, they claimed, was becoming obsolete naturally.

The Moore's Ford lynching denied the obsolescence of lynching in a spectacular fashion and, in doing so, made Walter White "horribly hopeful" for change. As he explained in his regular column for the *Chicago Defender*, the fact that two women were among the lynching's four victims had greatly increased the public's outrage about the lynching and thus greatly increased its power as a mobilizing event. "If the mob . . . had been content to kill Malcom only, who had cut a white man for fooling around with his wife," White wrote, "or even if they killed Dorsey too there might have been . . . little comment." But in lynching Dorothy Malcom and Mae Murray Dorsey—adding two more names to the list of roughly one hundred black women lynched in the entire history of the nation— the mob "may have blasted America into doing something about lynching." In the days immediately following the lynching, White intensified his lobbying efforts for HR 1689, the federal antilynching bill that had been introduced in January 1945, but hadn't yet been put to a vote. The window of opportunity was narrow. The 79th Congress would close in just one week, and if the nation's lawmakers didn't pass an antilynching bill in the wake of the Moore's Ford lynching, Walter White feared they never would.

Then, on July 30, came the news of another lynching. This time it was in Lexington, Mississippi; this time a thirty-five-year-old black man named Leon McTatie had been flogged to death by six white men for allegedly stealing a saddle. The fact that two other men confessed to stealing the saddle several days after Leon McTatie's body was found made the lynching appear all the more senseless and

ratcheted up nationwide outrage even further. As newspaper headlines reported "Mania Grips Dixie," fifty members of the National
Association of Colored Women picketed in front of the White
House with signs reading, "Speak! Speak, Mr. President!" and
"Where is Democracy?" Five thousand people attended a rally at
New York's Madison Square Park while, in Harlem, attendees at the
largest mass meeting held in a decade cheered as their state representatives called for federal intervention in Georgia. Thousands
marched in Buffalo, Pittsburgh, Tampa, Boston, and Detroit, and
organizations as varied as the Screen Writers' Guild, the Congre-
gational Conference of South Dakota, and the National Lawyers
Guild drafted formal declarations demanding federal action. The
Chicago chapter of the American Youth for Democracy sent Attorney General Clark a stack of petitions containing the signatures of
fifteen hundred people who demanded "the machinery of the armed
forces be put to use in bringing to justice those responsible for
these horrible crimes." Liberal and labor groups all over the
nation—which, like the NAACP, were at the peak of their power in
1946—applied the full weight of their political pressure.

Finally, after six days of silence, President Truman took action.
Speaking through Attorney General Clark, he expressed his "horror
at the crime and his sympathy for the families of the victims." Then
he publicly ordered the U.S. Justice Department to investigate the
Moore's Ford lynching "to ascertain if any federal statute can be
applied to the apprehension and prosecution of the criminals."

Most citizens interpreted the president's order as a firm commitment to solve the murder. But those familiar with the narrow basis
for federal jurisdiction read more deeply into it. They concluded
that, despite the assistant U.S. attorneys' public statement that the
lynching looked like a "state case," there had to be some possibility
of a federal civil rights case. And they were right. The Justice

Department decided to enter the case because "the circumstances under which one of the victims was released by State authorities to meet a pre-arranged mob" made it a distinct possibility "that some State officer had tipped off the mob." The possible involvement of a state lawman in the Moore's Ford lynching meant that Section 52, the color of law statute, could apply.

On the evening of July 31, FBI agents stationed all over the South received phone calls directing them to get to Walton County as quickly as possible. Within two days, the Monroe Hotel was full—out-of-town visitors and traveling salesmen had to bunk in elsewhere—and the FBI's makeshift office in a suite of rooms on the second floor was as fully staffed as a field office in one of the nation's midsized cities.

"See you've got a new industry," visitors to Monroe were soon remarking to the locals. "The FBI."

CHAPTER TEN

Within days of the lynching, Barnette Hester had grown strong enough to leave the hospital and return to Hestertown, though a tube remained in his side to drain the fluid from his lungs. When Mama Dora visited Barnette at the Hester house before leaving Walton County for Chicago, he told her he hadn't wanted anything bad to happen to Roger. He said he could have settled things with him in his own way, and that he was sorry about the way the situation had turned out. Mama Dora thought highly of Barnette Hester, and when he said he was sorry Roger had been lynched, she believed him. Indeed, Barnette's conversation with Mama Dora echoed his sentiments in the hospital on the night of the lynching, when he'd blurted out to the aide, "I told them not to do anything to Roger." Beyond communicating feelings of regret and shame, and possibly a sense of powerlessness, both statements indicated that Barnette Hester had known there was the threat of a lynching before it occurred, and knew at least some of the men who'd participated in it.

And yet, when FBI agents interviewed Barnette soon after they arrived in Walton County, he told them he had no idea who committed the lynching. No one, he said, had made any comments to him "relative to seeking revenge or reprisal against Roger Malcom." The openness and honesty Barnette Hester had exhibited in the hospital and with Mama Dora vanished, replaced by "careful ignorance." Agents quickly learned Barnette's father, Bob Hester, had adopted a similar pose. No, he said, he had absolutely no knowledge of who was in the lynch mob. When agents asked about his conversation with Deputy Sheriff Lewis Howard regarding Roger Malcom's bond, Bob Hester denied the conversation had taken place, though three other people had witnessed it. Both father and son were polite—unlike their wives, who accused agents of running the lynching "into the ground," and refused to be interviewed—but their intentions were clear. They would put as much distance as possible between themselves and the mob; they would deny any connection between Barnette's stabbing and the lynching.

And yet, agents had already come to a conclusion shared by most in Walton County: "The obvious motive for the lynching was Roger Malcom's stabbing of Barnette Hester on July 14." In fact, the cause-and-effect relationship between the two events was so obvious as to be nearly instinctual for both blacks and whites in the area. Though they disagreed on the motive for the stabbing, as well as the seriousness of the wound inflicted, they agreed that Roger Malcom had not only broken the law by stabbing Barnette Hester, but he'd also transgressed the rules of white supremacy—and most expected he'd be punished by a mob long before he'd have the chance to stand trial. As one reporter later commented, "There isn't a man in this town, white or black, who didn't know something was going to happen to the Malcom boy." Roger himself had predicted as much. "I'll never be a free man anymore," he'd told other prisoners in jail. "I won't get out of here alive," he'd told Mattie Louise.

Details from Loy Harrison's account of the lynching further reinforced its connection with the stabbing. Pulling Roger Malcom from the car that evening, the mob said he was the "SOB" they wanted. He was also the only victim found with a noose tied around his neck. Evidently mob members had planned to use the same methodology at Moore's Ford as was used in Walton County's 1911 double lynching: hang the victim, then shoot him. But after deciding to lynch the three others, perhaps the prospect of hanging the victims seemed too arduous. In the end, the long noose around Roger Malcom's neck served only to mark him as the mob's main target.

But if revenge for the stabbing was the motive, why did the lynchers wait eleven days to get it? That question could easily be answered by pointing to the one thing that distinguished Thursday, July 25, from every other day since the stabbing: it was the morning Barnette Hester sat up in bed for the first time since he'd been stabbed, signaling to doctors and loved ones that he was going to live. Once the news that Barnette was out of danger traveled to the jail, the charge against Roger Malcom, which had been murder, was amended to attempted murder, making Thursday, July 25, the first day that Roger Malcom could be released on bond. When the mob learned that he would, indeed, be freed that afternoon, they must have seen the chance to enact their revenge. By the time they set upon Loy Harrison's car at the Moore's Ford Bridge, they were so angry that they dragged George Dorsey from the car too. And when Dorothy Malcom called one of their names, they had to kill the women as well. Roger Malcom was the one they wanted; the others simply had the misfortune of accompanying him. In pleading with Loy Harrison to post Roger Malcom's bond, the three had unknowingly facilitated his murder, then perished with him.

This was the story the force of twenty-five FBI agents assigned to investigate the Moore's Ford lynching understood at the outset. And though the prosecutorial role of the federal government was constrained by the limits of federal jurisdiction in lynching cases, the FBI agents themselves didn't labor within such limits. In their minds, they'd been sent to Walton County to solve a murder, to find out who "pulled the job" and to gather evidence against them. It was no surprise, then, that they immediately organized their

investigation into three main areas of inquiry: the stabbing of Barnette Hester, the meeting at Towler's Woods, and the lynching
itself. And it was also no surprise that their earliest list of possible
suspects looked very much like the Hesters' extended family tree.
Agents began their interviews at the home of Weldon Hester, Barnette's brother and the overseer of the farm where Roger Malcom
had lived nearly his entire life.

At first, Weldon Hester refused to answer any questions, but
after agents applied pressure he agreed to be interviewed, though
he remained hostile throughout. When agents asked if he'd threatened Roger Malcom's life on the evening of the stabbing, he said, "I
don't know what I said about Roger, I was so damn mad I don't
know what I said." Then he added, "I did not say anything about
killing him, not that I know of." When agents asked if he'd attended
the meeting in Towler's Woods two nights after the stabbing, Weldon Hester claimed he didn't know where Towler's Woods was—
though it sat just a few miles from Hestertown. Finally, he offered
his alibi for July 25, 1946.

Both he and his wife had worked at the Monroe Manufacturing
Company from 8 A.M. to 5 P.M. that day, he said. After work, his
wife rode home in a neighbor's car, while he drove home in his own
car. When agents asked why he drove alone that day, given that he
usually rode in the neighbor's car along with his wife, Weldon Hester said he couldn't explain it. Continuing, he said he arrived home
about 5:15 P.M., ate supper, changed his clothes, and walked across
the field to attend the revival at Union Chapel Methodist Church,
which began at 7:30 P.M. His cousin Alvin Adcock accompanied
him, he said, and both learned of the lynching at roughly 9 P.M.,
when the revival ended.

Mapping the route between the Monroe Manufacturing Company and Moore's Ford, agents concluded that if Weldon Hester

had left work that day at 5:02 P.M., as the mill's records showed, he could've made the fifteen-minute drive to Moore's Ford in plenty of time for the lynching. After all, Loy Harrison hadn't left Monroe until roughly 5:30 P.M., meaning that 5:45 P.M. was the earliest possible time at which the lynching could have occurred. Loy Harrison told agents the entire affair took approximately fifteen minutes, and the ride from Moore's Ford to Hestertown took roughly twenty-five minutes. That meant Weldon Hester could have left work, driven to Moore's Ford, participated in the lynching, and made it home by roughly 6:30 P.M.—in plenty of time to eat dinner, change into his church clothes, and walk to the revival.

The issue of time became critical after several black people told the FBI they'd seen Weldon Hester and Alvin Adcock drive through Hestertown at roughly 6:30 P.M. on the evening of the lynching. By far the strongest testimony came from a young black woman named Elizabeth Toler, who was climbing a fence to leave the pasture where she'd been playing baseball when she fell and cut her arm on a piece of barbed wire. She was holding her bleeding arm as Weldon Hester drove by. He laughed out his car window at her, she said. She was certain it was him; she couldn't forget that laugh.

A few days after agents arrived in Walton County, an agent from the FBI's Chicago office convinced Mama Dora to allow him to interview her in her granddaughter's apartment. Once the summary of that interview was sent to Monroe, agents learned of Weldon Hester's longstanding enmity for Roger Malcom, as well as the fact that he'd often served as the ringleader in the beatings of black people in Hestertown. Then they learned something locally that further intensified their suspicions: several black people living in Hestertown reported they'd heard their white landlords say that the two black women had been lynched at Moore's Ford because one had called out Weldon Hester's name. Though he asserted his innocence again and again, Weldon Hester quickly became what agents termed "a strong suspect"; he had the motive, the ability, and the opportunity to have participated in the lynching.

Weldon Hester's cousin, forty-one-year-old Alvin Adcock, was also hostile when agents approached him, but he was extremely nervous as well—his hands trembled and he licked his lips continuously. When agents asked him how he'd learned about the lynching, he said he'd heard the news on a radio broadcast very early on July 26. This claim not only conflicted with Weldon Hester's alibi, it also conflicted with the fact that news of the lynching wasn't broadcast on Atlanta-area radio stations until 11 A.M. that Friday morning.

When agents asked Alvin Adcock for his alibi for July 25, he told them he couldn't recall his activities. But Jimmy Brown, a black tenant on Alvin Adcock's farm, told agents he saw Alvin Adcock remove a double-barreled shotgun from his car at dusk that day. He also said he later heard Alvin Adcock tell his wife that they'd "shot Roger Malcom and the others." A few days afterward, when Alvin Adcock gave Jimmy Brown a pair of his own pants in return for doing some work, Jimmy Brown gave the pants to agents, and they sent them to the state-of-the-art crime lab at FBI Headquarters in Washington, D.C. There, technicians determined the pants were stained with blood, but couldn't prove conclusively that it was human blood. Nonetheless, Alvin Adcock, like Weldon Hester, became a "strong suspect."

Agents then moved on to Jack Malcom, a twenty-six-year-old Hestertown man who'd returned to Walton County from the army on the day before the lynching—making him a possible candidate for the mob leader's sidekick, the young man who Loy Harrison said had held a gun on him. When agents asked Jack Malcom for an account of his activities on the day of the lynching, he said he'd spent the entire day at home with Melvin Hester, his father-in-law, and that neither of them had left the house at any time. Two discrepancies with this claim appeared almost immediately. First, agents had already learned that Melvin Hester, also a suspect, had left home several times that day. And two, they'd learned from another suspect, Clarence Hester, that both Jack Malcom and Melvin Hester had accompanied him to Monroe on the afternoon of July 25.

When agents confronted Jack Malcom with these contradictions, he got "considerably agitated," recanting his earlier statement and saying he had no recollection of his activities on July 25. Agents then pressed him about rumors that he'd brought home a souvenir weapon from the army. He denied it, and when agents read him the names of his close army friends who claimed to have seen him with a gun, he said he didn't know the men. In a final effort to elicit a straight alibi, agents interviewed Jack Malcom with his parents present. At their prompting, he told agents that on July 25, he'd gone to Monroe at 2 P.M. with Melvin and Clarence Hester. In town, he said, he'd stopped at the county clerk's office to leave his army discharge papers for recording, then gotten a haircut. He said he couldn't remember what he'd done in town after that, a statement agents regarded as "highly unreasonable" given that it was his first visit to Monroe since returning from the army. Jack Malcom said he returned home to Melvin Hester's house at roughly 5:30 P.M., then received a visit from his friend Hughlon Peters at roughly 7:30 P.M.

That led agents to Hughlon Peters, a twenty-five-year-old cousin of Barnette Hester's who'd visited him in the hospital three times, the last on the morning of the lynching. After returning from the hospital that day about 1 P.M., he said, he'd remained home until 5 P.M., at which time he drove to Melvin Hester's house to visit Jack Malcom. This would've put him at Melvin Hester's house at roughly 5:30 P.M., a claim that conflicted with Jack Malcom's claim that Hughlon Peters didn't visit until 7:30 P.M. That discrepancy, coupled with Hughlon Peters's insistence that he didn't learn of the lynching until hearing about it on the radio at seven or eight the next morning—a contention that, again, conflicted with the fact that no radio station that served Walton County had broadcast news of the lynching that early—made Hughlon Peters a suspect. Clearly he and Jack Malcom had conspired to arrange their stories. When inconsistencies surfaced despite their arrangements, agents concluded these men not only shared the same motive as Weldon Hester—revenge—but also had a window of opportunity in which to have participated in the lynching.

As agents fanned out to interview the rest of the Hester clan—brothers-in-law, cousins by marriage, and distant relations—they began to hear the same phrases again and again, like a chorus: "I have never been to Moore's Ford, don't even know where it is." "I was not around Monroe that day." "I have no idea who killed the Negroes." Certainly, lying was a defense mechanism and an evasion strategy, but it quickly became sport as well. Just as bootleggers had long been revered for outsmarting federal "revenuers," locals soon earned respect for ridiculing or lying to the FBI. More than one white man duped agents into believing he was working for them as a confidential informant, when he was really aiding suspects by alerting them of agents' plans. Although the FBI and GBI agents were Southern white men with accents to match, they were outsiders—most people in Walton County had never seen an FBI agent before, except in the movies. And against the outside threat, the locals constructed a "wall of silence," or an "iron curtain," as

FBI director J. Edgar Hoover would later say. This wall was built from both solidarity and fear of reprisal—as one white man in Hestertown said, "If I had anything to do with the lynching, and my brother reported it, I'd kill him." Within a week of the lynching, agents concluded in their report that the people of Hestertown, almost without exception, had "indicated in some way that they resented . . . the entire investigation. Many have admitted that they do not wish to see anyone punished for the crime. Others have stated that they are opposed to the mass killings, but have said they would not furnish information that might lead to a solution of the crime, if they had such information in their possession." Indeed, resistance to agents' efforts was so clearly the norm in Hestertown that when a white person did appear willing to aid the investigation, agents automatically became suspicious.

But the conclusions agents drew about the sentiments of the people of Hestertown could just as well have characterized many of Walton County's white citizens. In talking with the visiting newsmen, some made no effort to conceal their belief that the lynching was well-deserved punishment, not a crime. "I knew a fellow who knew a nigger who had lived in Africa and he'd boiled up his father's head and made soup out of it and ate it," said one retired Walton County farmer. "That's the kind of people niggers is. . . . They all lie and steal, and when they get drunk, all they want is a white woman."

Others declared the lynching was wrong only because it had claimed female victims. This was the opinion of Sheriff Gordon, who advised one reporter that the mob "hadn't ought to killed the two women," leaving the reporter to infer the unsaid: they "ought" to have killed the two men. Still others resented the attention being paid to the lynching when no comparable attention, they argued, was paid to crimes against whites. "The crime at Monroe, Ga. was no worse than many wholesale murders and rapes committed on whites in Ga., as well as elsewhere," one citizen wrote to Georgia senator Richard Russell. "For instance, three or four years ago near Savannah, Ga. a little family of five was slain. In their house. By a Negro. Down in South Ga. three or four years ago, a man and his wife and one or two little boys were shot cold blooded by a big negro. In broad daylight." Senator Russell, who'd been born in 1897 in a section of Walton County that had since become part of Barrow County, penned a collegial reply: "I deplore the murders, of course, but I feel as you do about the emphasis being placed upon this particular crime by propagandists from other sections of the country who take every opportunity to intensify sectional and racial hatred."

Using reasoning similar to Senator Russell's, a white Walton County man refused to cooperate with the FBI's investigation because, he said, it was being controlled by "Negro groups" from Alabama and New York; all the agents, he maintained, were from Northern states. (In fact, they were all Southerners.) And since the start of the investigation, 150 white men in the county had pledged to finance the defense of anyone arrested in the lynching. Clearly they'd view those arrested as victims of the Northern-based liberal conspiracy against the South: as political prisoners, not murderers.

And yet, despite these sentiments in the county, many white people in Monroe did condemn the lynching. Several white churches passed resolutions denouncing the murders and calling for justice; several of the town's leaders publicly expressed their horror. But these sentiments soon faded as Monroe's citizens began to focus less on the brutality of the lynching and more on what they viewed as their unfair treatment by both the national press and the FBI. As the white citizens of Monroe came to see it, the tragedy of the lynching wasn't only the deaths of four black people; it was the smudge on Monroe's reputation caused by those deaths. The *Walton Tribune* received a card from a white woman who was planning a car trip with her black maid and wanted to arrange "safe conduct" through Georgia, while E. L. Almand Jr. received a postcard addressed to "The Mayor, The Town Where Four Negroes Were Slain, Georgia." "We are today the target of a hostile press throughout the world," wrote the *Walton Tribune* editor. "Events of our soil are being construed and misconstrued to prove every belabored point of the racial discrimination theories so dear to so many who know so little about it."

Faced with the association of their town with a grisly crime, well-to-do citizens of Monroe made a choice. Rather than trying to clear their town's name by cooperating with the FBI's investigation and helping to bring the lynchers to justice, they resorted to the same rhetoric the "best people" had used throughout the South's long history of lynching. The Moore's Ford lynching was the action of "a wanton few," they said. It occurred seven miles away, nearly in the next county, and "no one from Monroe was involved." (Though the statement that "no one from Monroe was involved" contradicted people's testimony that they didn't know *who* was involved, most missed the contradiction.) It was the fault of Talmadge's supporters, they said, the rabble-rousers, the low-class folks. "I hold Eugene Talmadge guilty of murder," said one Monroe businessman who sometimes said *Negro* but more often said *nigger*. "You can't sow the seeds of racial hatred without bearing a crop."

But even if Monroe's "best people" didn't participate in the lynching, once they refused to cooperate with efforts to bring the lynchers to justice, they took on a portion of the guilt. For, in stonewalling the FBI, they strengthened the very system of white supremacy that had given rise to lynchings and perpetuated conditions in which lynchings could flourish. A white woman from south Georgia had written to Senator Russell asking, "Why is it that if a killing occurs here it is called a lynching, and if in another section just a killing?" The answer was that a *killing* described the act of an individual or individuals; a *lynching* described the act of individuals who killed, if not with the direct support of the community, at least not with its condemnation. Lynching, in short, was a form of collective violence.

By the first weeks of August, the townspeople of Monroe had aligned with the farmers of Walton County to make one thing clear: the FBI wasn't welcome.

At the same time agents were struggling against the hostility within Walton County, pressure on them from outside the county intensified. On August 6, a crowd of fifteen thousand people gathered at the Lincoln Memorial in Washington, D.C., to cheer as speakers from the National Negro Congress, the Southern Conference for Human Welfare, and the American Federation of Labor demanded federal action in the Moore's Ford lynching. That same day in New York City, Walter White—who'd watched the 79th Congress adjourn several days earlier after taking no action on HR 1689, the current federal antilynching bill—presided over an emergency meeting composed of representatives from sixty organizations, including the YMCA, the American Jewish Congress, the American Civil Liberties Union, and the Elks. The group, which called itself the National Emergency Committee Against Mob Violence, publicly condemned the lynching in Walton County and demanded the federal government throw its "full force" into bringing the lynchers to justice.

On August 11, the Kansas City Monarchs called a silent time-out during a Negro League baseball game to honor the lynching victims. In San Francisco that day, protesters wearing black armbands carried four coffins through the city streets, marching to a muffled drumbeat. On Broadway, the actors and producers of the play *Anna Lucasta* devoted a special performance to the lynching victims. In Boston, citizens formed the Committee for Action on the Georgia Lynching, later providing funds to relocate the family of Mae Murray's sister from Monroe to New York City. In Atlanta, a Citizens Defense League spearheaded by several black churches launched a drive to raise $100,000 to aid both the present and future victims of civil rights crimes.

As activism continued throughout the nation's cities, the reward for information about the lynching ballooned. Early on, the Civil Rights Congress, the Southern Regional Council, and the American Civil Liberties Union had bumped up Governor Arnall's reward from $10,000 to $12,500. From there, the reward grew as the Baptist Ministers' Conference of Chicago pledged $15,000, the NAACP pledged $10,000, the National Maritime Union added $5,000, and the *Chicago Defender* followed with another $2,000. By August 2, the reward totaled $30,000. By the anniversary of V-J Day, on August 14, it stood at $43,000; and by the end of August, the bounty would climb to $64,000. The mounting sum reflected rising outrage about the lynching, and rising expectations for justice.

And as those expectations went unfulfilled day after day, the liberal newspapers that had hailed the federal government's commitment in late July began to turn critical. "FBI Lagging in Monroe, Ga. Lynch Probe," the *Chicago Defender* reported, adding that "compared with many strange and mystifying cases affording only slender clues that have been cracked by the FBI, it seems the Georgia lynch case should not be so difficult." Another newspaper reported "few signs of a manhunt" in Walton County, and yet another concluded that the investigation presented "a rather sad picture, after the brave statements of Governor Arnall and President Truman about how the investigating resources of the state and nation were to be directed toward capture and punishment of the mobsters."

Within the vacuum of information, rumors flourished, and in the information they supplied—true or false—they made the FBI's efforts look even more inadequate. The Communist newspaper *Daily Worker* reported in an "exclusive" story that a meeting between Eugene Talmadge and Barnette Hester's family had taken place on July 16, two days after the stabbing. "There can be no doubt," the article stated, "that the conversation revolved around the subject of the Negro who had struck back at Hester's son." The article didn't attribute these facts to a specific source, nor did it quote any eyewitnesses to this meeting; nonetheless, several large newspapers ran the story. A few days later, the *Chicago Defender*, in an article headlined "Duluth Cleric Shows Up FBI," reported that a black minister "of no investigative experience" had located two witnesses to the Moore's Ford lynching—something FBI agents, who were the "world's best human bloodhounds," had failed to do. The minister's information came from the NAACP, which had taken an affidavit from the two "witnesses" and leaked its contents to the press, even though the account was clearly flawed, conflicting with such basic facts of the lynching as the location where it had occurred.

Since the first days after the lynching, White had funneled Attorney General Clark clues he'd learned through the NAACP's investigator in Monroe, or through other contacts in Walton County. At those times, it seemed the NAACP and the Justice Department were members of the same team, a team opposed to mob violence. At just as many other times, however, White broke ranks with Attorney General Clark and FBI director Hoover, criticizing them for an inaction resulting from racism. White had to play this protean role. He needed the Justice Department to help him achieve his goal, which was an end to lynching. But the federal government's history of passivity in the area of civil rights made it obvious White couldn't afford blind trust. In mid-August, he wrote a letter to Hoover, explaining that "so thorough a campaign of intimidation of Negroes was carried on in Walton County, that none of the local Negroes were willing to talk to any white person whatever credentials or connections he might have." Did the Bureau employ any Negro agents? he asked. If so, could they be sent to Walton County? At the time, the Bureau employed three black agents: Hoover's aging chauffeur, on whom he'd conferred agent status as a means of placating the NAACP; his office retainer; and a sixty-eight-year-old agent who was, for all intents and purposes, inactive. But even if the Bureau had employed other black agents, Hoover wouldn't have sent them into Walton County. "The particular type of Negro living in Monroe was a very ignorant type of Negro," he'd later say, "and for that reason they were scared, they wouldn't talk hardly to anybody, and I don't think they would talk to a Negro agent."

Hoover's racism—not to mention his grave misjudgment of the fear of black people in Walton and Oconee counties—inevitably filtered down to the agents, who thought little of disparaging the local black people in their written reports, labeling them "ignorant" or "below average Negro intelligence," and concluding they wouldn't make "good witnesses." Given that agents' ability to elicit valuable testimony depended almost entirely on their ability to gain witnesses' trust, it's not surprising they had little success with black people that summer and fall. As one black man in Walton County said, "The FBI said they were friends of the Negro people, and we were going to see justice. They said they were going to work it out, and we were going to hear results. I didn't believe a word of it."

Though the FBI required its agents, all of whom were lawyers or accountants, to undergo a special training course in civil rights, the very skills needed for those cases—approaching, relating to, respecting, and empathizing with black witnesses—weren't covered in the course's offerings. As Thurgood Marshall, special counsel for the NAACP, commented, "You don't investigate a lynching in the same way you investigate a hot automobile. . . . You have more local feeling to overcome. You have more unwillingness of people to talk." Agents must be specially trained, he said. Above all, they must "themselves believe in the enforcement of civil rights." As Walter White commented in a memo to an NAACP staffer, "The government will never get anywhere investigating lynchings and other crimes against Negroes in the South until it does some housecleaning and sees that assignments of FBI men to investigate these cases do not go in with prejudices against Negroes and on behalf of the criminals."

Mirroring the impatience and frustration of the NAACP, their liberal allies, and the national press, the citizen letters arriving in Attorney General Clark's office also changed in tone by mid-August. "Your lack of initiative in seeking out and uncovering the lynch mob that killed four Negroes in Monroe, Georgia is intolerable," wrote one man. "If you really were concerned with justice in this situation, you could find the guilty in no time at all." "I am sure that if 20 Negro people had killed four white people, the Justice Department would have found at least 200 Negro people who had done the horrible deed," another man wrote.

Then came the news of another lynching in the South. On August 8, two black men had been released from a Minden, Louisiana, jail, where they'd been held for allegedly attempting to enter a white woman's house, and delivered into the hands of a mob. The mob had taken them to a bayou, tortured them with a meat cleaver and a blowtorch, and left them for dead. One of the men survived; the other man, a twenty-eight-year-old World War II veteran named John C. Jones, did not.

The news of the sixth lynching within a two-week period added fuel to the nationwide hysteria. Thus, by mid-August, the twenty-five FBI agents in Walton County were positioned squarely between two opposing battle cries, one demanding they take no action in the lynching, and one demanding they take more. Since FBI policy prohibited agents from speaking to the press, they couldn't give updates on the investigation or explain their strategies. Instead, they soldiered on through the steamy August days, going door to door to interview suspects and witnesses, checking and rechecking alibis, and compiling a list of automobiles owned by white men in the area. These activities, more often than not, were exercises in frustration. When, for example, agents attempted to track down the cars that fit the descriptions of those seen near Moore's Ford on the day of the lynching, they found the descriptions were inexact, conflicting, or fabricated. One man told agents he'd seen several white men riding in a Ford station wagon near Moore's Ford that day. After weeks of searching for the station wagon, agents abandoned the lead, fairly certain their witness had lied.

Agents' search for the murder weapons was even more frustrating. According to the ballistics report produced by the FBI Crime Lab—which was based on the twelve bullets and casings, and seventeen shotgun-shell pellets, retrieved from the bodies and the crime scene—between six and twelve guns had been used in the lynching. Among the shotguns fired were a twelve-gauge and a twenty-gauge, and among the pistols were a .32 Smith & Wesson, a .38 Smith & Wesson, a .38 Special, and a 9mm revolver. Looking for the two shotguns was like looking for two needles in a haystack; nearly every grown man in Walton and the surrounding counties owned a shotgun for deer- or bird-hunting, or simply to shoot snakes on his farm. And given that a thriving trade in souvenir weapons had grown up since the end of World War II, locating the pistols presented nearly as challenging a prospect. In an effort to trace the origin and movement of various souvenir pistols, agents compiled a list of local white men who'd recently returned from overseas service and investigated anyone rumored to have bought weapons from them. These efforts proved futile, as again and again agents spent weeks tracing the trail of a pistol only to lose it. In the few cases in which they did locate the weapon, they discovered it didn't fire the same type of bullets taken from the crime scene or the bodies.

On one occasion, agents learned from two sources that a white suspect named Corrie Blasingame owned a .38 Smith & Wesson revolver, one of the gun types used in the lynching. Based on that information, agents confronted Corrie Blasingame. But when he denied owning the revolver, the lead went cold right there. Without a warrant, agents couldn't search his house, his barn, or his car. And in the case of Corrie Blasingame, as throughout the investigation, the FBI didn't have enough evidence to show probable cause that a federal crime had been committed, and therefore couldn't obtain a search warrant.

Without search warrants, agents could only investigate weapons on a voluntary basis. When a suspect handed over his shotgun, the agent took it, wrote the owner a receipt, and sent it off to the crime lab in D.C. When a suspect volunteered his pistol, the agent took it, stood over a burlap bag of cotton, and fired. Then he handed the pistol back to the owner, retrieved the bullet and shell casing from the cotton, and sent those to the lab for analysis. Despite the fact that it was highly unlikely a man who'd participated in the lynching would willingly hand over his murder weapon, agents asked again and again. They had to. As agent Louis Hutchinson said, "One good handgun ID would have broken the case."

And so, within weeks the investigation had taken on a familiar routine. In the morning, agents breakfasted in the dining room of the Monroe Hotel—the finest restaurant in town and the site of the Rotary Club's monthly meetings—before climbing to the office on the second floor to get their assignments for the day. Hot and weary, they'd return to the hotel in time for dinner. At night, while a staff of secretaries transcribed their notes from the day, they'd play Ping-Pong or listen to the teachers who boarded at the hotel play piano and sing in the lobby. When newspapers reported in early August that the FBI had earned nearly twelve thousand convictions in 1945—winning 97 percent of their cases that went to trial—the agents at the Monroe Hotel received a much needed morale boost. They'd gotten "their men" in all those investigations, and they'd get their men in Walton County. For them, it wasn't a political crusade or a civil rights issue; it was a murder investigation.

One August night a reporter cornered an agent in the hotel lobby and asked if the FBI would stay in the county until they cracked the case—regardless of civil liberties violations. Overcome by a need to defend the Bureau's record, the agent violated the FBI's policy on not talking with the press. "Hell, yes," he said.

On the day after the lynching, newsmen had flocked to Loy Harrison, the lone witness to the crime. They'd taken photographs of him sitting behind the wheel of the car from which the four lynching victims were dragged and posed him handling the rope used to bind Roger Malcom's and George Dorsey's hands. Nearly all of the reporters from the nation's mainstream newspapers based their articles on Loy Harrison's account of the lynching; in fact, a reporter from *The New Republic* was the only one to pen anything outwardly critical about him. "I of course do not accuse Harrison of complicity in this affair," the reporter wrote. "But to say the least, he was careless in seeking to employ a man against whom white sentiment was running so heavily. He was careless in allowing more than three hours to elapse between the time his intention became known and the time he left town. He was careless in not sticking to the main road." By early August, the newsmen had left. And since the FBI agents were focusing their efforts in Hestertown and Blasingame districts, Loy Harrison was left to dust his cotton with calcium arsenate, plant his winter crops, and begin operations at his portable sawmill, adding new mountains of sawdust to the ones that already dotted his plantation.

But though Loy Harrison went about his business as usual in the weeks following the lynching, he wasn't the same person, his family said. According to his wife, he'd grown sad. One day she found him in the basement of their house, holding a straight razor in one hand and a mirror in the other. "I believe he was going to kill himself," she told a black worker on the farm. He greatly reduced his cussing, and he suddenly devoted himself to religion, urging everyone in the family to attend church. Loy Harrison was, his family said, a changed man.

And to family members, the change made sense. In their eyes, Loy Harrison was a good provider and a generous landlord. "You could not find another caring, more sharing person," says Loy Harrison's niece Anne Harrison Manders, who lived a half mile from him. "He fed and clothed his farmhands. He took care of them just like they was family."

As his family saw it, Loy Harrison had almost been a victim of the same mob that lynched his farmhands; he'd been held at gunpoint and spared only because he didn't recognize anyone. And after his farmhands were lynched, he grieved for them. According to Loy Harrison's young daughter, he wept every time he drove over the Moore's Ford Bridge.

But, by the end of August, Loy Harrison could no longer work or grieve in peace. Because, after weeks of traveling the dirt roads of Hestertown, agents decided to return to the lone eyewitness to the crime and question him closely about several points in his account. The agents' first question had to do with Loy Harrison's failure to describe any members of the mob beside the leader and his side-kick, as well as his failure to describe the men who'd peered into the backseat of his car as he drove home on the highway. How were those failures possible given that none of the men wore a mask? And given that the mob members were most likely locals—those with a motive to avenge Barnette Hester's stabbing—how was it possible that Loy Harrison hadn't recognized a single one?

Agents also questioned Loy Harrison's inability to hear the name of the mob member that Dorothy had called out. After all, the mob's leader, who was standing at least fifty yards away, heard it clearly enough. And last, why had the mob allowed Loy Harrison to live? If they were indeed strangers, as he alleged, why would they trust him not to run immediately to the sheriff once they let him go? And if Loy Harrison had been as frightened of the mob as he claimed, why had he called the sheriff immediately, then provided such a detailed description of the mob's leader? Wasn't that risky?

Even without satisfying answers, the questions made it clear that Loy Harrison knew more about the lynching than he'd told; they made it clear that he likely knew at least some members of the mob. But each time agents confronted him, he held firm to the same account he'd given since the night of the lynching. He never appeared nervous, threatened, or even concerned. In fact, one agent found him so maddeningly blasé that he shot the head off a bird to show him he meant business. But that didn't shake Loy Harrison. Again and again he said, "If I knew anything, I'd sure tell it." And again and again, he returned to the financial bottom line, to the fact that, in lynching his farmhands on the eve of the cotton harvest, the mob had victimized him as well. "Why I'm as mad as anybody, the way they killed my niggers," he said. "I need all the nigger hands I can get."

After all, he was just a typical, respectable farmer, struggling to make a living.

But when agents began to investigate Loy Harrison's background, they learned he was far from a typical or respectable farmer. In fact, he had a history of assault and murder that stretched back more than two decades, to the day in January 1921 when he and several other young white men had shot a black man named Will Wheeler. Roughly five months after that, he and some of the same men had shot another man. On July 15, they'd shot yet another man, then attacked him with a wooden plank. All told, by mid-1921, seventeen-year-old Loy Harrison had been indicted in three separate attempted murders. One definitely involved a black man, and the other two may have as well—because the Oconee County prosecutor "wasn't able to make out a case" in any of the incidents and dropped all the charges in 1923.

By then Loy Harrison had left Georgia for South Carolina, adopted the alias John Barfield, and launched what would become a long and lucrative career in illegal liquor manufacturing. On the night of April 2, 1923, he was preparing to run six hundred gallons of mash through a still located in a secluded section of Darlington County, South Carolina, when he heard a rustling in the surrounding woods and went to investigate. Seconds later, two shots were fired, and a federal prohibition agent, who'd been waiting in the bushes for the right moment to raid the still, sank to the ground. "I am shot," he cried out to the other federal agents hiding nearby. "Come and get me."

As the federal agent lay dying, Loy Harrison fled into the forest. He stumbled in the dark, cut a deep gash into his arm on a barbed-wire fence, and fell on the ground, weak and delirious from blood loss. The next day he was found and taken to jail, where he learned that police had discovered his cap and coat lying next to the .45-caliber revolver that had fired the fatal shots. He was charged with the murder of a federal agent.

At the highly publicized trial that June, one officer after another testified that John Barfield (Loy Harrison's alias had stuck) had committed the murder. The local U.S. attorney testified that John Barfield had, in fact, confessed to the crime. "I am responsible for the whole thing," he'd said after the police had captured him. "Can't you give me life imprisonment instead of electrocution?"

When John Barfield took the stand, he claimed that another man working at the still had committed the murder. But the jury, unconvinced, found him guilty. After sentencing him to a life of hard labor in the South Carolina State Penitentiary, the judge concluded that twenty-year-old Loy Harrison had "the finest nerve of any young man I have ever seen. He has stood this trial as calmly as any man could, and . . . he did not tell the truth."

One year later, the South Carolina Supreme Court overturned the guilty verdict after ruling the judge had erred in handling both Loy Harrison's confession and the charge to the jury. Instead of waiting for his new trial, however, Loy Harrison sawed through the bars in the county jail and escaped. Then, after a few days, he returned to jail, gave himself up, and awaited trial once again. In February 1925, he was acquitted of murder, but sentenced to ten years for federal liquor violations. The sentence was reduced, and one year and one day later, Loy Harrison left South Carolina and returned to Georgia.

Before long, Loy Harrison had restarted his illegal liquor business in Oconee County. In 1938, he was convicted on two counts of violating federal liquor laws, and in 1939 and 1940 he was convicted again. By 1946, Loy Harrison had been arrested six times for liquor violations. Twice he'd paid several thousand dollars in fines, and four times he'd served prison sentences. But these convictions were minor setbacks compared to the gains. Four years after returning to Georgia a penniless ex-convict, Loy Harrison owned nearly two hundred acres in Oconee County. By 1946, he owned nearly one thousand acres, making him one of the largest landowners in the area.

When agents confronted Loy Harrison with a list of his liquor violations, he admitted to them, but swore he hadn't made or sold liquor since 1944. But that was a lie. Agents located a white man who admitted in a signed affidavit that he'd made liquor for Loy Harrison in 1945. And they learned that that same year local revenue officers had raided a still on Loy Harrison's farm. Moena

Williams's sister, Grace—who was interviewed at her Chattanooga, Tennessee, home by an agent from the FBI's Knoxville bureau— had seen smoke coming from the still for two days before the raid. Afterward, she'd walked down to see it. There were broken gallon jugs and rubber tubes on the ground, she said, and a pile of wet mash that gave off a strong odor of whiskey. That day, she learned from another worker on the farm that there were four stills on Loy Harrison's property that hadn't been discovered yet.

All over Walton and Oconee counties, people made home brew or bought liquor and resold it to friends and neighbors gallon by gallon, jar by jar. These were small-time, amateur operations; when the perpetrators were caught, they had their liquor confiscated (often by local lawmen who turned around and resold it), paid a fine, and then went free. Roughly one-third of all crimes recorded in Walton County's docket books between 1940 and 1946 related to making, transporting, selling, or having liquor, and the record in Oconee County was similar. But though liquor-making was illegal according to federal and state law, it wasn't viewed as criminal by the local community. There was a long and proud tradition of farmers selling their grain in liquid, rather than in solid, form.

Loy Harrison, however, was in a different league from most people in Walton and Oconee counties. He produced large quantities of whiskey from five stills hidden in the knolls and nooks and pine forests of his vast plantation, and this whiskey left his farm not jar by jar, but in trucks that carried it as far as Chicago. Loy Harrison was a liquor wholesaler. Aside from selling to his workers, to whom he readily extended liquor on credit, he didn't sell locally. He let his tenants handle that demand. Jim Williams, for instance, sold liquor out of the house he shared with Moena and the family. He kept a fraction of the sale of each gallon and handed the rest to Loy Harrison. "A little man go to Moena's house to get liquor," explains a black man who lived near Loy Harrison's farm. "A big man go to Mr. Loy."

Though making liquor was nowhere near as labor-intensive as growing cotton, Loy Harrison nonetheless needed workers to run the operation. Several of his tenants did no farming at all; their sole duty was to supervise the stills from sunup to sundown, and their payment was a barrel of mash. For each gallon of whiskey the mash produced, Loy Harrison gave them $10—good money compared to farming wages. If they got caught by the state or federal revenue agents, Loy Harrison would pay their fines and get them working his stills again.

The nature of an illegal liquor operation would seem to require that Loy Harrison trust his workers not to tip off the law, steal, or drink his product. But agents learned that instead of trust, Loy Harrison relied on violence and the threat of violence. A black woman named Lizzie Lou Vinson, whose father made liquor for Loy Harrison, remembers him charging into their house one evening, threatening to beat her father for drinking the profits. And once, when Loy Harrison noticed that some of his liquor was missing, he put poison in a few jars "to see who was stealing it," says a black woman who briefly worked for Loy Harrison. As recently as 1942, Loy Harrison had held a pistol on a black tenant while five of his other tenants (four of whom were black) beat him until he was unconscious. Five days after the beating, when the tenant could finally speak clearly enough so that his common-law wife could understand him, he told her he'd stolen some sugar from Loy Harrison and sold it to another bootlegger because Loy Harrison had refused to pay him his wages. When she confronted Loy Harrison about the beating, he said, "Them niggers done that."

As agents learned more about Loy Harrison's treatment of his black tenants, they saw that his penchant for violence wasn't a thing of his youth, that his behavior in 1921 was far from anomalous. Just in interviewing Moena Williams and her four adult brothers and sisters—all of whom had worked on Loy Harrison's farm at one time or another—agents discovered that he had physically attacked them at least five times in the previous three years. On a night in 1943, he hit Moena's eldest brother, who was drunk at the time, with a rock. Two years later, he knocked Moena's twenty-two-year-old sister, Grace, off the front porch of his house. Later he told her, "I'm sorry I slapped you, but if you ever tell anybody . . . I'm going to kill you." Soon thereafter, Grace fled in the middle of the night. "When I left the Harrison farm, I ran away without Mr. Harrison knowing," she told the FBI agent in Chattanooga. "I was afraid to tell him because I was afraid he would not let me go." And after returning from the army the winter before the lynching, Moena's thirty-two-year-old brother, Robert Elder, was walking on the road near Loy Harrison's farm when a group of men grabbed him and blindfolded him. Though he couldn't see anything through the blindfold, he could hear well enough to recognize Loy Harrison's voice saying, "All these damn niggers been to the army and come back and think themself something." After that, Robert Elder was struck on the head and remained unconscious until a group of blacks found him and took him to Moena's house. A few months later, when Robert Elder tried to leave the farm while still owing a debt—he planned to escape to Chattanooga like his sister, Grace—Loy Harrison snatched him from the bus stop and beat him with a lug wrench. After lying in bed incapacitated for three weeks, Robert Elder went back into the field to work off his debt.

In investigating Loy Harrison's attacks on his tenants, agents learned of an incident that had occurred less than one week before the lynching. On the morning of July 19, George Dorsey had asked to borrow Loy Harrison's red pickup truck to drive to the Oconee

County seat of Watkinsville to sign for his "rocking-chair pension," as the $20 checks paid to unemployed veterans in Georgia were known. Loy Harrison agreed to lend the truck on the condition that it was returned by noon, because he needed to go to Monroe that afternoon.

George took his brother, Charlie Boy, and his uncle, Robert Elder, along for the drive to Watkinsville. But instead of returning to Loy Harrison's farm immediately after finishing their business, the men bought liquor and drove around. They didn't turn toward home until nearly 3 P.M.

By then, Loy Harrison had found another ride to Monroe and was on his way back to the farm. He happened to be traveling past the Fanny Wright house at the exact moment George and Charlie Boy raced into the yard in his pickup truck. When George and Charlie Boy saw him, they jumped out of the truck and ran into the barnyard to hide behind the corncrib. But Loy Harrison had already spotted them.

In the few seconds it took Loy Harrison to reach the corncrib, each brother made his own plan. Charlie Boy darted across the road in the direction of Moore's Ford, then ran to a friend's house and begged him to drive him out of the area. The friend's truck wasn't working, so Charlie Boy ran off again. He was so frightened of being punished for keeping Loy Harrison's truck out too long that he didn't return to the farm for a week—not until the day after the lynching. When he did return, he told another tenant that Loy Harrison had fired five shots at him as he ran away.

After Charlie Boy fled, George Dorsey stepped out from the corncrib holding a rock. Loy Harrison grabbed a chain from the barn, began swinging it in the air, and ran toward George Dorsey. Later he got into his pickup truck and drove off, leaving George Dorsey lying in the dirt.

That evening, George and Mae visited their friends Gladys and Frank Taylor, who lived in a tenant house just down the road. They often walked to the Taylors' house in the evenings to listen to *Amos 'n' Andy*. *My nerves is all frayed*, the Kingfish would say. *Even the frayed part is frayed*. That Friday night, Gladys Taylor noticed that George Dorsey's pants were dirty and torn. When she asked him what had happened, he said Loy Harrison had thrown him down and stomped on his chest, then whipped him with a chain.

About the time agents began investigating Loy Harrison, rumors of their mistreatment of him started to circulate in Walton and Oconee counties. One rumor claimed they'd driven him around for fifty hours before taking him to a church, where they prayed for his soul. Another rumor claimed they'd driven him to Macon, where they showed him a man they suspected was the mob's leader. When Loy Harrison said he didn't recognize the man, they threatened to kill him. Loy Harrison was likely the author of these rumors; clearly he felt unfairly targeted by the FBI. Yet the rumors did nothing to quell agents' suspicions that Loy Harrison knew more than he was telling. In fact, once they'd learned the truth about Loy Harrison's background and temperament, they identified yet another suspicious point in his account of the lynching: his depiction of himself. In his version, he stands on the Moore's Ford Bridge, impotent as a group of white men jeopardize his livelihood by killing his tenants. That hardly reconciled with the legend of John Barfield, which traveled with Loy Harrison like a shadow, emerging when he fingered the scar on his arm and bragged of killing the federal revenue agent. That hardly seemed like the man who'd been beating and killing people since he was seventeen, a man who "feared no one"—and who was, in turn, feared by most in Walton and Oconee counties.

Now doubtful of Loy Harrison's account of the lynching, agents began scrutinizing his alibi for the day of the lynching, just as they were doing with the suspects in Hestertown. For instance, Loy Harrison maintained that he didn't decide to post bond for Roger Malcom until *after* talking with him at the jail. But agents learned that the deputy sheriffs, as well as the jail's inmates, had heard Loy Harrison tell Roger Malcom through the jail window that he'd post his bond and take him to his farm. He had, in fact, decided *before* talking with Roger Malcom.

Loy Harrison had also claimed that, while visiting the Monroe ice plant on the afternoon before the lynching, he'd talked only with the day and night manager there. But a black ice-plant employee named Lamar Howard saw Loy Harrison talking with a white Walton County man named James Verner there that afternoon. And two others, including a Monroe policeman, saw him talking with James Verner as well.

These two discrepancies not only revealed that Loy Harrison had "created" his alibi, they also revealed his motives for doing so. His first lie made it appear that he couldn't have known about, or participated in, the planning of the lynching. The second lie concealed his conversation with James Verner on the afternoon before the lynching. In fact, Loy Harrison not only denied talking with Verner at the ice plant, he denied even knowing him. But Loy Harrison's attempts to distance himself from James Verner only raised agents' suspicions.

When agents confronted James Verner, a former army sharp-shooter and gun dealer, it became clear that, just as some Hestertown suspects had matched their alibis, he and Loy Harrison had arranged their stories. Verner not only denied talking with Loy Harrison at the ice plant, he also emphatically denied knowing him. He said he spent most of the afternoon on July 25 driving from one beer joint in Walton County to another. Just before 8 P.M., he heard about the lynching at a filling station near the courthouse in Monroe and drove out to Moore's Ford with his girlfriend. He arrived while the coroner's inquest was in session. After watching for roughly a half hour, he said, he'd returned home.

Each time agents reinterviewed James Verner, he denied talking with Loy Harrison at the ice plant and denied having anything to do with the lynching. When agents asked to inspect the weapons he owned, he let agents test his sixteen-gauge double-barreled shotgun, his German Mauser pistol, and the .32 Smith & Wesson he kept in his car. None matched the bullet and casing specimens found at the crime scene or in the victim's bodies. James Verner also said he'd sold a German Luger several days before the lynching. Though he didn't know the name of the man who'd bought it from him, he knew he lived in the nearby town of Eatonton. With James Verner accompanying them, agents spent an afternoon in Eatonton searching for the man who'd bought the German Luger—a gun that fired the same type of 9mm bullets found at the crime scene. The search yielded nothing. Agents were never able to find the man to whom James Verner had sold the Luger. But they still considered Verner a strong suspect. His sharpshooter experience, his interactions with Loy Harrison, and his movements throughout Walton County on the day of the lynching certainly gave him the ability and the opportunity to have participated in the lynching.

The two lies within Loy Harrison's alibi—one regarding the time at which he'd decided to bond out Roger Malcom, and one regarding his conversation with James Verner at the ice plant—raised the possibility that Loy Harrison had somehow been involved in the planning of the lynching. This possibility grew even stronger when agents discovered a third discrepancy in his alibi. Both in his testimony to the GBI's Major Spence and to FBI agents, Loy Harrison claimed his car was alone on the road as he drove the four blacks to his farm that Thursday afternoon—alone, that is, until he reached the very last curve before the bridge. But Emerson Farmer, the twelve-year-old white boy who lived in the house closest to the bridge, told agents he was sitting on his porch that afternoon and saw Loy Harrison pass by on his way to the bridge. And he said Loy Harrison's car wasn't alone, but sandwiched between four other cars—two before, two behind. That information strongly suggested Loy Harrison was part of the mob, not a victim of it.

When agents interviewed twenty-two-year-old Ruby Dorsey, the wife of Charlie Boy Dorsey, she offered information that confirmed their suspicions. She told agents that on July 15, after Dorothy and Moena first asked him to bond out Roger Malcom from jail, Loy Harrison had told her that the reason he'd refused wasn't because he didn't think Roger Malcom would be a good tenant. He refused, he told her, because he believed "those folks in Hestertown might cause Roger some trouble. They might even take him away from me and something would happen to him after I bonded him out and before he could get over to my farm." That's why Ruby Dorsey was so surprised when Dorothy told her on July 25 that Loy Harrison had decided to post Roger's bond. "A funny feeling came to me," Ruby Dorsey told agents. "Why he suddenly change his mind?" But Dorothy and the rest of the family were happy, so Ruby kept her suspicions to herself. Her father had just died, and she had to leave the farm to make the trip to Greensboro, Georgia, for the funeral. She and Charlie Boy were still in Greensboro the next day when Loy Harrison and Moena drove up and delivered the news.

Ruby Dorsey told agents she believed Loy Harrison was "in on" the killing, and she said Moena and Jim Williams and Charlie Boy believed it as well. She said that sometimes when Moena was drunk, she'd walk up to Loy Harrison and say to his face, "I believe you helped kill my children."

But despite everything agents had learned, they hadn't been able to uncover anything more than a casual connection between Loy Harrison and the people of Hestertown. Such a casual relationship meant it was unlikely that, if Loy Harrison had participated in the lynching, he'd done so as revenge for Barnette Hester's stabbing. And if revenge wasn't Loy Harrison's motive, what was? Why would Loy Harrison want to lynch Roger Malcom?

CHAPTER TWELVE

On the afternoon of September 7, a procession of nearly fifty cars passed through downtown Monroe, traveled six miles east on the Atlanta–Athens highway, and turned onto the Mountain Lodge Road. The drivers followed the road past cotton fields, past the path that led to Mt. Enon Church, and past the little white house on the Fanny Wright place where the white man had been found hanging eight months before. At the fork, they took the road leading down to the river, parked, and walked along the old wagon trail to reach the killing place—just like the souvenir collectors who'd hurried to the Moore's Ford Bridge on the morning after the lynching. But, unlike the souvenir collectors, these people were black.

They were attendees at the Negro Baptist Convention in Atlanta, and they'd left the city en masse earlier that day to make the roughly fifty-mile journey to the scene of the crime. For more than a month, they'd heard about the lynching on the radio and read about it in newspapers. Now they gathered before the pine trees whose trunks were scarred by the bullets that had killed the victims. The trees had since been inscribed with four crude crosses, though whether they'd been carved in memory of the victims or as a sign of the Ku Klux Klan, no one knew. For several hours that afternoon, the sound of singing and praying traveled along the Apalachee River. Just before dark it ceased, and the procession of cars traveled up from the river and back to the highway to return to Atlanta. Though the *Walton Tribune* reported the Baptists were "quiet and orderly" during their time in the county, at least one white citizen in Monroe suspected they'd had guns hidden in the trunks of their cars.

By the time of the Baptists' visit, much of the cotton in the fields of Walton and Oconee counties had opened, and one week later, nearly every rural school had closed, signaling the height of the picking season. Harvest season was always an anxious time—so much depended on a good crop—but that September tensions ran particularly high. Heavy rain in the spring had delayed planting, while a dearth of rain in the early summer had produced meager cotton bolls, many of which had been destroyed by an unusually high weevil infestation. The bolls that were spared by the weevil had opened prematurely, thanks to the searing heat of July and August. That a farmer from Blasingame took the first bale of cotton to a local gin as early as August 22 was seen as a bad omen. Some farmers predicted only a half crop of cotton, maybe less.

And though September's cotton prices were at an almost unprecedented high (39¢ per pound), farmers worried the high prices wouldn't last through the harvest. Their worries turned out to be justified; in October, the price of cotton would plummet to 29¢ per pound, resulting in a loss of roughly $50 per bale. And despite the fact that wages for cotton pickers had skyrocketed from 50¢ per hundred pounds a few years before to between $2 and $3 per hundred pounds in 1946, there still weren't enough pickers in Walton and Oconee counties. The FBI agents had scared them off, farmers said.

As cotton fields all over Walton and Oconee counties turned white, citizens elsewhere in the nation continued to demand action in the Moore's Ford lynching via protest marches and mass rallies and in correspondence sent to the president and the attorney general—who had, by then, received several thousand letters from individuals, as well as hundreds of petitions and resolutions from civic groups. On September 19 the two months of sustained public outcry produced results: President Truman invited a delegation from the National Emergency Committee Against Mob Violence to address him at the White House.

NAACP executive secretary Walter White, who'd organized the emergency committee in the wake of the Moore's Ford lynching, opened the meeting at the White House that day by reviewing the year's most notable incidents of racial violence; if he hadn't selected only those incidents that had received widespread publicity in the white press, the review would have taken hours. As it was, the president sat quietly, his elbows resting on the arms of his chair, as White described the deaths of two black men and the destruction of the entire black business district in Columbia, Tennessee; detailed the blinding of Isaac Woodard in South Carolina; and then listed the year's six lynching victims: four killed in Georgia, one in Mississippi, one in Louisiana. "At least the excuse given for the torture and execution in Nazi concentration camps was that the victims were 'enemies' of the state," said White. "But recent victims of American lynchers were in numerous instances men who . . . fought for its preservation overseas. Instead of gratitude, they have been paid off in savagery."

By the time White concluded his speech, the president's face had drained of color. "My God," he said, his voice trembling. "I had no idea it was as terrible as that. We've got to do something!"

Before drawing the meeting to a close, President Truman pledged to create a national commission to study lynching and mob violence. One day later, he reiterated his belief in the need for such a commission in a memo to Attorney General Clark. "I have been very much alarmed at the increased racial feeling all over the country," he wrote. "I know you have been looking into the Tennessee and Georgia lynchings, but I think it is going to take something more than the handling of each individual case after it happens—it's going to require the inauguration of some sort of policy to prevent such happenings."

Though it would be months before President Truman followed through on his pledge, on that September day he made a surprising move for a native of Missouri, the son of "an unreconstructed rebel mother." Certainly when Truman became president after Franklin Roosevelt's death on April 12, 1945, the Southerners in Congress felt sure of his loyalty to their segregationist, states' rights philosophy. "Everything's going to be all right," one Democratic senator from South Carolina said, "the new president knows how to handle the niggers." But since assuming the presidency, Truman had become increasingly convinced of the federal government's responsibility to insure and protect the rights of all citizens—including blacks. No doubt he was motivated by a desire to win black votes, as well as the need for the nation to present a unified, democratic image in the world arena. But, as he'd explain years later, the factor that motivated him to finally take action was his outrage at the violence committed against black people in 1946. The attack on Isaac Woodard and the Moore's Ford lynching, he said, showed him "the lengths to which people would go."

As it happened, on the same day President Truman committed the federal government to a role in preventing lynchings, FBI director Hoover asked Attorney General Clark to pull his agents out of Walton County. The two months spent investigating the Moore's Ford lynching, Hoover informed Clark, had sapped the Bureau's resources and caused a huge backlog of cases. While agents had "some suspicions as to the identity of some of the participants in the mob action," the suspects had detailed alibis. And even if the FBI were to collect more evidence, he said, it "would only relate to a violation of a Georgia statute and would not establish any violation of a Federal Statute, since to date there has been no indication of any participation . . . by law enforcement officials or other officials in Georgia."

Though Hoover's request related specifically to the Moore's Ford lynching, it revealed his distaste for lynching investigations in general, a distaste that probably stemmed as much from his hatred of losing as it did from his racism. Given that the CRS had failed to secure a single conviction in a lynching case since its creation seven years before, Hoover had concluded that "the work of the [Justice] Department and the Bureau is completely ineffective, both as a deterrent and as a punitive force. Regardless of whether we like it, it is a fact that the Federal Statutes penalizing violations of civil liberties are inadequate weapons for efficient enforcement by the Department . . ."

But as much as Hoover was bothered by the failures themselves, he was far more distressed by the damage they caused to the FBI's otherwise strong conviction record. Always concerned about the Bureau's public image, Hoover felt strongly that the CRS's failure to win lynching convictions was sullying the FBI's reputation for "getting its man." Since neither the press nor the public understood the legal distinction between facts that justified federal prosecution for civil rights violations versus those that justified state prosecution for murder, he said, "there is a feeling and belief that the Bureau has failed to 'solve' many [civil rights] cases into which it has entered."

Hoover concluded his request to Clark on September 19 by saying, "I do not believe . . . that the Bureau should make inquiries or conduct investigations in the nature of 'fishing expeditions' on the mere possibility that there have been infringements of a Civil

Rights Statute." Hoover not only wanted his agents out of Walton County, he didn't want them assigned to lynching investigations in the future.

When Attorney General Clark presented Hoover's request for termination of the Moore's Ford lynching investigation to Assistant Attorney General Theron Caudle, who presided over the Justice Department's Criminal Division, of which the CRS was a part, Caudle replied that he was "thoroughly convinced we must not relax our efforts in this case." Because CRS lawyers hadn't yet received the FBI's investigative report in the Moore's Ford lynching case, he said, they couldn't responsibly conclude whether public officials had been involved, and therefore couldn't be certain there had been no violations of the federal civil rights statutes. And, more generally, while Hoover was inclined to forgo investigating lynchings because of their slim potential for success, Assistant Attorney General Caudle, as well as CRS head Turner Smith, believed the CRS had to continue to attempt to get justice. "Because of the seriousness of mob lawlessness, we feel firmly bound to exhaust the possibility of the existence of Federal jurisdiction," Caudle said. After all, if the federal government didn't pursue lynchers, no one would.

On October 3, 1946—just as Attorney General Clark was considering Hoover's request to terminate the Moore's Ford lynching investigation—the CRS's persistence finally paid off. A white Florida constable named Tom Crews, who'd beaten a black farmhand with a bullwhip, then forced him to jump into the Suwannee River, where he drowned, was convicted in federal court of violating Section 52, sentenced to one year in prison, and fined $1,000. Crews appealed his conviction, arguing that since his acts were those of "personal vengeance," rather than of "official character and authority," he did not "willfully" deprive his victim's federal rights—which was the same defense Sheriff Claude Screws had used to win his freedom one year earlier. But the Fifth Circuit Court of Appeals upheld Crews's conviction, and when the Supreme Court refused to hear the case on appeal, the CRS had earned its first secure victory in a lynching case.

Four days later, Attorney General Clark made his decision about the Moore's Ford lynching investigation. "Dear Edgar," he wrote to the FBI director, "I think our activity in Monroe, Georgia, case should continue until we find out who did it . . ."

So the agents continued to investigate in Walton and Oconee counties as the cotton was plucked from the stalks, transported to the gin, weighed, sold, and sent away on trains and trucks. And in mid-October, after spending nearly three months on the case, and after interviewing more than one thousand people, the agents learned information that made them realize that the story of the lynching they'd understood at the start wasn't the complete story. The owner of a store located on the highway between Monroe and Moore's Ford told agents he'd heard George Dorsey was lynched because he "and some other Negroes had been . . . associating with white girls." Another white man said he'd heard that "George Dorsey was killed because he was talking about going with white women." One customer at a store just off the Atlanta–Athens highway heard that George Dorsey had said that "as soon as Carmichael was elected governor, he was going to start going with the best-looking white woman in Oconee County and was going to start with Loy Harrison's wife." That man said the mob shouldn't have lynched Roger Malcom but definitely should've killed George Dorsey. Another man told agents he'd heard that "George Dorsey was killed by the mob because he waved and whistled at some white girls." Still another reported that he'd heard George Dorsey had been flirting with a white woman who was the wife of a cripple.

This last rumor sent agents back to the house closest to the Moore's Ford Bridge. It was there they'd learned from twelve-year-old Emerson Farmer that Loy Harrison's car had been sandwiched between four others as it passed by on the day of the lynching. That was important information, and agents had labeled Emerson Farmer a strong witness despite his youth. But when they returned to the Farmer house in October, it was not to question Emerson, but rather his father, a poor white sharecropper who was crippled as a result of childhood polio.

When agents asked Riden Farmer about his activities on the day of the lynching, he said he'd visited a friend that afternoon and returned home about 6:30 P.M. Shortly afterward, he said, he'd seen the sheriff's car and several others pass his house, and he and Emerson walked down to the bridge. They watched the coroner's inquest until Riden got sick, and then they walked home and went to bed.

When agents pressed him further, Riden Farmer explained that in January 1945, Loy Harrison had moved two of his tenant families from the Oconee County side of his farm to the Fanny Wright place. He'd put Moena's family—including Moena and Jim Williams; Charlie Boy and his wife, Ruby; and Moena's brother, Robert Elder—into the big two-story house. And he'd put the Adams family—a white family with five children, three girls and two boys—into the little white house next door. During that spring and summer, the two families helped each other in the fields and rode together on the wagon to Aycock's store—they were good neighbors to each other, Riden Farmer said. When George Dorsey returned from the army in late September 1945, nine-year-old Clinton Adams, the Adams family's eldest son, ran out to the bus stop to meet him.

But soon after George Dorsey returned home, Riden Farmer said, relations between the two families got "too friendly." One night, Riden Farmer saw George and Charlie Boy standing out on the road, talking to the eldest Adams girls: Ruth, who was seventeen, and Effie May, who was fifteen. Shortly afterward, Riden Farmer said, he saw Ruth and Effie May Adams dancing while George Dorsey played his guitar. And a few months later, in late January 1946, Riden Farmer said he learned that George Dorsey had spent three nights in the Adams home. The man of that house, George Adams, told Riden Farmer that George Dorsey had helped out during three days and nights when Adams was too ill to get out of bed. Nonetheless, Riden Farmer was outraged that a black man had stayed overnight in a white family's home—especially a black man like George Dorsey, whom he'd seen having "too close" contact with the eldest Adams girls, and who he'd heard had been having "sex relations" with them. When Riden Farmer chanced upon Moena Williams on the road after hearing of George Dorsey's overnight visits, he warned her to keep George away from the Adams girls. If she didn't, he said, George was "liable to get his neck broken." Or she "might wake up some morning and find him missing."

Instead, the Adams children woke up on the morning of February 5, 1946, to find their father missing. Ruth Adams looked everywhere, but she couldn't find him. Then the school bus arrived and shone its headlights into the wood house on the Fanny Wright place, and Ruth and her sister spotted their father hanging from the rafters.

Within an hour, Deputy Sheriffs Lewis Howard and Doc Sorrells arrived from Monroe, bringing the local justice of the peace with them. They cut down George Adams's body and carried it into the bedroom in the tiny house to examine it. They found no signs of struggle, no bruises or bullet holes—nothing to suggest George Adams had met with foul play. The coroner's jury declared the cause of death suicide, and the doctor issued his clinical verdict:

"Mr. Adams died by strangulation and neck broken. Been dead for several hours."

Since most of the white people who lived near Loy Harrison's farm had heard rumors about the "relations" between George Dorsey and the Adams girls—no doubt from Riden Farmer, who walked the roads with the aid of his crutch, spreading gossip from farm to farm—few were surprised by George Adams's suicide. They assumed what the manager of Aycock's store later told the FBI: George Adams killed himself because his daughters had been "promiscuous."

Several days after George Adams's death, Loy Harrison ordered the Adams family off his farm and moved Moena and Jim, Charlie Boy and Ruby, and Robert Elder out of the Fanny Wright house, and back to the concrete-block house near his own house, where he could supervise them closely. George Dorsey left the farm and went to work for a black farmer in Hestertown. When he returned after several weeks, asking to farm the Fanny Wright place, Loy Harrison agreed. Labor was short, and he needed the land cultivated. Besides, the Adams family was gone, so George Dorsey couldn't cause any more trouble with the two eldest girls.

But, Riden Farmer said, the trouble didn't end. He told agents that Moena's brother, Robert Elder, had driven by his house on two occasions that spring, stopping to yell "Hey, honey" to his daughters. On a third occasion, Riden Farmer claimed, Robert Elder had whistled at Farmer's wife. Further, Riden Farmer said he'd "heard it talked" that both George Dorsey and Robert Elder were bragging that they'd gone with white girls up North and would continue going with them. This time, instead of issuing a verbal warning to Moena, Riden Farmer detailed Robert Elder's transgression in a letter. A day after delivering the letter to Loy Harrison, Riden Farmer saw him on the road and told him that if Robert Elder ever harassed his family again, "he was going to find him as full of shots as would stick."

Agents' interrogation of Riden Farmer revealed his well-documented anger at George Dorsey, as well as at Charlie Boy and Robert Elder. But that discovery was secondary to the real value of Riden Farmer's testimony, which was that it exposed a "reason" for the lynching besides revenge for the stabbing of Barnette Hester. More specifically, Riden Farmer's testimony pointed to a motive for Loy Harrison's alleged participation in the lynching.

Loy Harrison, agents knew, had never needed a mob to discipline his tenants before; when there was trouble on his plantation, he meted out his own punishments—or forced other tenants to do so on his behalf. But the accusations about the black men on his farm presented a far more serious problem than Loy Harrison had likely ever encountered. These accusations had traveled, tarnishing Loy Harrison's image as a powerful landlord, and making it appear that he couldn't control his tenants. These accusations suggested he was allowing the worst possible transgressions—relations between black men and white girls—to occur on his farm. Perhaps Loy Harrison believed such accusations called for a communal response, an extreme response.

And so, perhaps Loy Harrison had known of the plot to lynch Roger Malcom and had viewed it as an opportunity. Perhaps he'd made sure George Dorsey was in the car that Thursday afternoon. Perhaps he hadn't been held at gunpoint but had raised his own gun and followed the leader's orders—"One, two, three." Or perhaps he'd shouted out the orders himself.

Yet if Loy Harrison had planned the lynching—or, at the very least, known of the plan—why did he agree to take Dorothy and Mae with him into Monroe that day? Did he intend for them to be lynched along with Roger Malcom and George Dorsey? And if

Moena hadn't decided at the last minute to stay home, would she have been lynched as well? Agents couldn't answer these questions. By mid-October, all they could say was that the man they'd once viewed as the lone eyewitness to the crime was now one of their chief suspects.

CHAPTER THIRTEEN

When agents turned to Dorothy and George's family in an effort to gather evidence of Loy Harrison's guilt, they had little success. Jim Williams would say no more than he suspected Loy Harrison was "in on" the lynching—and that he planned to leave the farm as soon as the cotton was gathered. Neither Charlie Boy Dorsey nor Robert Elder would say anything negative about Loy Harrison, even though each had recently been attacked by him. And, though agents knew from Ruby Dorsey that Moena Williams believed Loy Harrison had helped kill her children, when agents interviewed her, she insisted that Loy Harrison was "a good man" who treated her fairly. She said his attacks on her family were "strictly his own business." In fact, she was so "friendly and partial" to Loy Harrison that just six days after the lynching, she'd asked someone to write a letter to her sister Grace in Chattanooga, saying, "Mr. Loy said tell you . . . to come home for we all need you." (Grace, who recalled the beating from Loy Harrison every time her tongue brushed against the scar inside her mouth, declined.) Moena later relayed a warning from Loy Harrison to another black tenant on the farm, telling her that if she told the FBI anything, "Mr. Loy" would fill her "full of shots." One black newsman reported that "Mrs. Williams manifested a childlike faith in the integrity of Harrison." As agents saw it, she'd been threatened and coached too extensively to serve as an effective witness.

So had all of the other black people on Loy Harrison's farm. According to Ruby Dorsey, Loy Harrison had warned them that if they talked to the FBI, the FBI would tell his attorney what they told, and his attorney would tell him. Loy Harrison also told them that an illiterate young black girl who lived on the farm was an FBI informant and warned everyone to avoid her. As a last straw, he commanded all of his tenants, including Moena Williams and her family, to go to his lawyer's office and sign a statement that the FBI was "annoying them." Although only one tenant, a black man who made liquor for Loy Harrison, complied, the intimidation largely worked. Aside from Ruby Dorsey, who was able to speak more freely because she'd temporarily moved off the farm, the black people who worked for Loy Harrison couldn't or wouldn't give the FBI evidence that could incriminate him.

When agents sought information from other black people who lived throughout the area, they encountered a similar reticence. Much of it was due to the kind of fear Walter White had described to FBI director Hoover months before. As Boyzie Daniels, the man who'd led the voter registration efforts in Blasingame district, said, "We had some people just really scared to death in this county. They went through a painful shock of fearfulness." Even the "fearless and outspoken" undertaker Dan Young had grown frightened as the investigation wore on. He worried he was considered "a dangerous man" by the guilty parties, and though he owned property in Monroe and ran a successful business, he was considering moving. He had the luxury of such a decision. Most blacks in Walton County couldn't afford to move; or were bound by debt to a landlord; or feared the repercussions for their family if they left. And those with the means to leave were often hamstrung on the other end. One black woman in Walton County wrote to her daughter in Chicago immediately after the lynching, saying she was frightened and wanted to move. But because of the severe housing shortage in Chicago, her daughter—who was living in cramped conditions already—couldn't find her mother a place to stay.

Rosa Bell Ingram, Roger Malcom's aunt, who'd skipped his funeral out of fear for her safety, had no way to leave Walton County. So she did the next best thing: for months after the lynching, she didn't leave the farm where she worked. "At that time, I'll tell you the truth, us black folks were no more than rabbits," she says. "After that happened, it slowed us all up. Because we didn't know. We would talk to each other quietly. You know, *quietly*." Just as there were an infinite number of ways white people could punish blacks for voting, there were an infinite number of ways they could punish them for aiding—or even being seen with—the FBI. They could kill them or their families; beat them; have them arrested on trumped-up charges; or cheat them at the cotton settle. Thus, when black people told agents they "didn't know nothing" or changed their stories again and again, it was due as much to an instinct for survival as a failure of nerve. Even when agents sought black people's help in gathering information about the double lynching that had occurred in Walton County thirty-five years earlier, they encountered resistance. "The FBI said they were here to protect us," says Boyzie Daniels. "I said, 'You're here to protect us, but you're not carrying us in a pocket. They can do a heap of trouble before y'all can get here.'" Said another black woman: "We didn't know who might come out of the swamp and put a bullet in us." After all, Isaac Brooks, the black man who'd helped clean the bodies at Almand Funeral Home, hadn't been seen since the FBI had entered the county, and most black people assumed something had been done to him. In the days after the lynching, they'd made the "stark realization that to squawk to the authorities means certain death."

And yet some black people in Blasingame did talk to the FBI. Elizabeth Toler told agents she'd seen Weldon Hester drive through Hestertown at 6:30 P.M. on the day of the lynching. Jimmy Brown told agents he'd overheard Alvin Adcock tell his wife about the lynching and later offered the FBI the blood-stained pair of pants for testing. These people, and several others, overcame their fear and aided the FBI because they knew Roger Malcom. And while some believed his rage may have been misdirected, uncontrolled, or heightened by an afternoon of drinking liquor, it was something they understood. Roger Malcom had lashed out against the conditions they all struggled against. They not only sympathized with him, they empathized with him.

The fact that the FBI encountered no such similar cooperation from the black people who lived near Moore's Ford Bridge revealed that, while the black people who knew George and Mae Murray Dorsey, and Dorothy Malcom, were horrified they'd been lynched, they didn't have the same empathy for them that black people in Hestertown had for Roger Malcom. In their eyes, George, Mae, and Dorothy had not been punished because they'd lashed out against the extreme unfairness of being black in rural Georgia; they'd been punished because they were "low-class blacks."

Long before the lynching, agents discovered, Moena and her family had acquired less than favorable reputations among both black and white people. In 1940, after sharecropping for two years in the next county south, they'd been kicked off their landlord's farm. When agents interviewed the landlord, he said he'd ordered the family to leave because they drank too much. He also said Moena was undependable, and George had a "big mouth." After that, the family moved to a farm near Watkinsville in Oconee County. But, two years later, they were again forced off. This time, the white woman who ran the farm said the loud music and foul language coming from Moena's house each weekend scared her. "They was awful. Soon as they got in with all the niggers around there, they started ripping and roaring," says a white man who lived near that farm. "That old Dorothy—she wasn't bigger than a bar of soap. But she'd go up and down the road cursing and fighting, one bottle in each hand. I never did fool around with them because I mighta had to kill them."

Many black people who lived near that farm seemed to feel likewise, though for slightly different reasons. After Dorothy bragged to a black woman named Lizzie Lou Vinson about going with white men, Lizzie Lou Vinson never visited her again. "I told my sister not to fool with Dorothy and them, because they were running around with men—white men," says Lizzie Lou Vinson. "Them folks wouldn't do to mess with." "Dorothy wasn't the best type of black person. She didn't just go with white, she went with anyone. We called her trash," says Edward Jackson, the man who drove Moena, Jim, and Charlie Boy to the funeral. "It's like if you take a branch from a pecan tree and root it. It's still a pecan tree. She came from that type of family."

When the white woman who ran the farm near Watkinsville begged Loy Harrison to take Moena's family off her hands, he agreed. And at that point, the family had no choice but to go to work for him; given their reputations, few landlords were willing to take them on. So in 1942 they moved onto Loy Harrison's farm and promptly began the same behavior that had got them thrown off the other farms: drinking and fighting. "My momma used to call them a rough set of folks," said a black woman who lived near Loy Harrison's farm. "Folks said, 'They ought to run them back where they come from.'"

Because Jim Williams sold liquor, and because, as Ruby Dorsey says, "there was mighty few that didn't drink," there were always parties at Moena's house. And in 1945, when the family moved across the river to the Fanny Wright house, the parties became legendary.

"All the people on the road here would go down to the Fanny

Wright house on the weekends," says John Pope, a young black man who lived near Aycock's store. "That house would be full—sometimes more than forty people."

"There would be a crowd down there and we'd dance," says Roy Jackson, a black man who went to the Fanny Wright house regularly that fall. "It was the onliest fun we had."

In one room, people gathered to play Georgia Skin, groaning or grinning when the dealer flipped the cards. In another room, people danced to records or to live music. They ate catfish and barbecue—cooked and sold by Moena—and drank bootleg liquor—supplied by Loy Harrison via Jim Williams. Years later, one woman would remember passing the Fanny Wright house on her way to night meetings at Mt. Enon Baptist Church. "We'd see a whole bunch of cars, but no lights on in the house," she says. "That's the reason we call it an outlaw house."

Sometimes at parties, Moena got drunk and laid into Jim Williams for running off with another woman many years before. The woman had been married to George before he went into the army. "You never did hear George say nothing about it," says Ruby Dorsey. "Treated Mr. Jim just as nice as could be. But when Miss Moena got high, she'd throw it up to him." Sometimes Moena called Ruby Dorsey a "red son of a bitch" because she was lighter-skinned than Moena and her children.

"Moena was all right until she got to drinking. Then she said things. She used to cuss most everyone out. The whole family was bad about drinking," says Ruby Dorsey. "Jim Williams had to keep the trunk where he kept the liquor locked, or else Moena would drink it all."

But despite the frequent fights at the Fanny Wright parties—Ruby Dorsey once cut a man who came at her and sent him to the hospital—the parties themselves weren't considered a problem by the white people who lived nearby. As one white man said, "All black folks party at dark. Like a dog they stroll at night. Like a dog, they'd be running around. They got drunk and the law wouldn't bother them as long as they stayed around the house and drank and fought there."

But then, in September 1945, George Dorsey returned from the army. And, says Roy Jackson, the parties suddenly became a problem—because Ruth and Effie May Adams began attending them.

At first, Roy Jackson and John Pope continued going to the Fanny Wright house on Saturday nights, but kept their distance from the two white girls. "I didn't even sit in the room where they was at," says John Pope. "I never did mess with them—period." Like most black people in Walton County, John Pope and Roy Jackson were keenly aware that in three of the county's four recorded lynchings, the victims were lynched after being accused of contact with a white woman. In 1890, Jim Harmon had been lynched for allegedly putting his "large, rough hand" on a white woman's face while she slept. In 1911, Tom Allen was lynched for allegedly raping a white woman. In 1913, General Boyd was lynched for allegedly entering a white woman's room at night. And, in 1939, a black man named J. D. Vaughn was nearly lynched for allegedly raping a white woman. He was protected by state patrol officers from a mob gathered outside the courthouse in Monroe, only to be later executed in Georgia's electric chair. Most recently, a black man in Monroe had been beaten for "going with a white woman" and lost his sight permanently as a result.

That's why, Roy Jackson says, when he saw George Dorsey getting friendly with the Adams girls, he had to stop going to the parties at the Fanny Wright house. "He'd get 'bout half-drunk and get to hugging on these gals and getting up against them," Roy Jackson says. "All of us who had sense stopped going. We could see there was going to be trouble."

But even those black people who didn't frequent the parties at the Fanny Wright house suspected that George and Charlie Boy Dorsey were having more contact with the Adams girls than was prudent—or safe. "Every evening they'd be out there on the road," says a black woman who lived near Moore's Ford. "I'd just stand there looking at them. Mrs. Adams come by my house one time and told me, 'George might have gone with white girls in the army, but he can't do it here.' "

When George Adams was found hanging in the wood house on the Fanny Wright place on that morning in February 1946, the black people who lived near Loy Harrison's farm assumed, like many of the whites, that he'd died because of his daughters' promiscuity. But they didn't believe it was suicide. They'd heard of the Ku Klux Klan killing "sorry white people" before, and they believed a group of white men—members of the Klan or sympathizers with its cause—had killed George Adams because he'd allowed his daughters to have sex with black men. "You know they mad when they get mad with the girls' daddy," says Roy Jackson. "You know that man didn't kill his self."

And after George Dorsey and the others were lynched, many black people who lived near Loy Harrison's farm again reached the same conclusions as their white neighbors. One black tenant on Loy Harrison's farm told the FBI that George Dorsey "had appeared closer to the Adams girls than Negro boys should and . . . this was a reason why George was killed."

Roy Jackson saw himself as an outlaw. Since returning from the army, he'd stayed out of work, driving the roads of Walton and Oconee counties, drinking and selling whiskey and gambling. He carried a pistol hidden in the bib of his overalls. One Sunday morning he used it to beat a man during services at Mt. Enon Church and got arrested for "disturbing divine worship." Another day, he shot a friend during a fight over a woman. But Roy Jackson never messed with white girls. "I knew better," he says, "and George should have too."

Roy Jackson had been angry at George Dorsey before he'd been lynched, and he would stay angry for long afterward. "He went ahead and did what he want, even though he knew it would cause trouble," says Roy Jackson. "It was already hard enough on black folks." So when the FBI came knocking on his door, asking for his help, telling him he was their big break, Roy Jackson did what many of the white people in the county had done: he lied.

describes lie after story
Tab

From their interviews with people who lived near Moore's Ford, agents had gotten a tip that Roy Jackson, along with a pair of brothers named Willie and Mahlon Thrasher, had tried to cross the Moore's Ford Bridge on the afternoon of the lynching, but turned around when they saw the mob. This was exactly the kind of lead they'd hoped for throughout the entire investigation. Three eyewitnesses could give them what they lacked: the ability to place specific men at the lynching scene. Three eyewitnesses could probably crack the case.

When agents asked Roy Jackson to describe his activities on July 25, 1946, he was reluctant at first, but finally revealed that he'd bought whiskey from a black man who worked for a white man in Oconee County, then returned to his tenant house near Aycock's store. He said he had indeed crossed Moore's Ford Bridge that afternoon, but hadn't seen anything unusual. Despite Roy Jackson's claim that he'd seen nothing, agents considered him an excellent witness prospect. In their report, they'd thereafter refer to him as Confidential Informant T-6.

Meanwhile, the two black men who were with Roy Jackson on July 25, Mahlon and Willie Thrasher, gave agents different accounts of the threesome's activities that day. Mahlon Thrasher told agents they'd gone to buy a goat—not whiskey. About 5 P.M., he said, they'd returned to his mother's house to prepare the goat for barbecuing. While there, they saw two cars come from the direction of Good Hope and head toward Moore's Ford. Both cars, Mahlon Thrasher told agents, were loaded with white men. The first car was a 1938 or 1939 black Chevrolet, and the second was a gray 1939 Ford.

Willie Thrasher, when interviewed separately, told agents that the first car was a dove-colored 1940 or 1941 Chevrolet sedan, and the second was a 1940 or 1941 black Ford. He then said that while driving past the Fanny Wright house a short while later, he and Roy Jackson had seen two 1941 Ford sedans drive up from the Moore's Ford Bridge. Both cars, he said, were dark-colored, and the second one was definitely black.

To verify Roy Jackson's story, agents tried to locate the black man who'd sold him liquor on the afternoon of the lynching. After spending weeks interviewing, they concluded the black man didn't exist. That part of Roy Jackson's testimony was "a fictitious story." After spending weeks pursuing the leads from the Thrasher brothers, agents similarly concluded that much of the brothers' information was false. And yet, despite the unreliable testimony offered by Roy Jackson and the Thrashers, agents continued to hold out hope. "We thought we could convey the seriousness of the crime to them and stir up their ire," says agent Louis Hutchinson. "We thought if we riled them up and then took them to a place away from the neighborhood—to a schoolroom or a library—where they could feel comfortable, that maybe they would start talking."

So one afternoon, several agents drove Roy Jackson and the Thrasher brothers to the federal courthouse in Athens, put them in a room, and "riled them up." Then they went into another room to listen to the men's conversation, which was being recorded by a hidden microphone. After a while, the agents heard only silence. They returned to the room to find all three men dozing with their heads on the table.

"They put us in the room where we could talk and they could hear every word we say," says Roy Jackson. "We know the trick when we went there. We wouldn't say nothing."

Dan Young had already paid Roy Jackson a visit, asking him to tell the FBI what he knew. "He said I be safe," says Roy Jackson. "That was his line, but I didn't pay him no attention."

Roy Jackson was an admirer of Loy Harrison's. And as Loy Harrison often said, "It's a damn fool that can't tell a lie."

The agents' big break fell through at the end of October, yet they continued on in Walton County. They were there when Loy Harrison sold the Fanny Wright place because, he said, it was too risky to have blacks on the other side of the river. They were there on November 5, when Eugene Talmadge won the general election for governor of Georgia, though he'd been too sick to attend the state Democratic convention one month before. They were there on November 12 when a primary election was held to fill several council seats in Monroe. Unlike the July 17 election, no black people voted in Monroe that November day—because the city fathers had declared the election a Democratic White Primary.

And the FBI agents were still in Walton County when radio stations carried the news that a federal grand jury would soon be convened in Athens, Georgia, in the matter of the Moore's Ford lynching.

CHAPTER FOURTEEN

On the morning of Monday, December 2, 1946, twenty-one white men and two black men arrived at the federal courthouse in Athens, Georgia, to serve on the first grand jury convened there in years. The twenty-three jurors ranged in age from thirty-one to sixty-eight and included thirteen farmers, two merchants, two coal dealers, a clerk, a barber, a laundry manager, a cotton gin operator, a banker, and a retiree. They'd been selected randomly from the tax receivers' list of the Middle District of Georgia, which included three counties in addition to Walton. That two black men were among the jurors wasn't unusual. Since 1935, when the U.S. Supreme Court reversed the conviction of Clarence Norris—one of the nine "Scottsboro boys" accused of raping two white women in Alabama in 1931—because blacks had been systematically excluded from the jury that convicted him, the constitutionally mandated inclusion of blacks on federal juries had become more regularly, though far from uniformly, enforced. *History given*

That morning, after assembling in the main courtroom, the jurors took an oath to "fearlessly and fairly" inquire into all things brought before them, indicting no one from "envy, hatred, or malice," nor failing to indict anyone out of "fear, favor, or affection." Then federal judge T. Hoyt Davis entered the room and launched into his charge. Not once during his instructions did he mention the word *lynching*; instead, he informed the jurors that they'd be looking into an "occurrence" in Walton County. The closest he came to discussing the violation of civil rights statutes—the basis of any federal prosecution of a lynching—was to say that "in commission of an offense where the major violation might fall within jurisdiction of state courts, there still might be violation of certain U.S. criminal statutes."

A former U.S. attorney for the Middle District of Georgia, Hoyt Davis had worked with CRS lawyers to prosecute the civil rights case against Sheriff Screws and his fellow Georgia lawmen. Named a federal judge by President Franklin Roosevelt soon afterward, he was on the bench for only a short time when the Primus King case came before him in October 1945. One month after hearing the case, he'd made the ruling that codified the right of all Georgians to vote in the state's primary elections, prompting more blacks to vote in the state on July 17, 1946, than had ever voted in any other election in the state's history. The Primus King ruling had no doubt cost Judge Davis friends; nonetheless, he'd obviously felt his duty as a federal judge—his duty to justly interpret the Constitution and federal law—trumped the political and social repercussions. That December morning in the Athens courthouse, Judge Davis made it clear that he'd adhere to the same strict interpretation of the Constitution in presiding over the grand jury investigation into the Moore's Ford lynching case. "State and federal courts function within their prescribed jurisdictions," Judge Davis told the jurors. "If there is no jurisdiction, that is the end of my inquiry." But before concluding, he added a crucial caveat: in the event the grand jury wasn't able to indict for federal violations, it could turn over the evidence it had obtained to state prosecutors, so they might pursue state charges. Lynchers had rarely, if ever, been prosecuted for murder, but the fact that the possibility existed gave the grand jury the ability to serve a double duty.

In theory, the twenty-three men had been called to the courthouse that day because the Fifth Amendment of the Constitution provides that no one can be prosecuted for a federal felony without first being indicted by a federal grand jury. By requiring grand juries to indict in so-called infamous crimes (crimes in which the punishment exceeds a one-year prison sentence), the Constitution's framers meant for grand juries to act both as a shield—protecting citizens from unwarranted prosecutions—and as a sword—authorizing the government's prosecution of suspected criminals.

In practice, however, the federal grand jury could do far more than act as a judicial gatekeeper; it could ferret out wrongdoing. Because, while a federal grand jury has to show probable cause in order to *indict* an offender, it doesn't have to show probable cause in order to *investigate* a suspected crime. And given that the federal grand jury possesses an unparalleled ability to summon witnesses and compel them to testify, it can, at times, serve as one of the federal government's most powerful investigative tools. One scholar deemed it "the greatest legal engine ever invented for the discovery of evidence." Though the potential power of federal grand juries in the South was often blunted by jurors' unwillingness to indict whites for crimes against blacks, they still represented one of the best options the federal government had for pursuing lynching investigations.

So, although the twenty-three jurors assembled in the courtroom that December morning were restricted to returning indictments that alleged violations of federal civil rights statutes, as Judge Davis explained, the jurors themselves weren't similarly restricted in the scope of their inquiry. In the case of the Moore's Ford lynching, they could seek evidence of both murder and civil rights violations; they could, as Attorney General Clark had written to FBI director Hoover two months earlier, try to find out "who did it." In this way, the grand jury probe would serve both as an extension and a summation of the FBI's four-month-long investigation in Walton and Oconee counties.

After Judge Davis delivered his instructions that morning, the jurors climbed to the third floor of the courthouse, entered the grand jury room, and spent the rest of the afternoon clearing the docket of routine indictments in order to begin inquiry on the Moore's Ford lynching the following day. Once the grand jury had adjourned for the day, the two federal lawyers presenting the government's case in the Moore's Ford lynching, John Kelley Jr. and John Cowart, issued the last of their 106 subpoenas.

Both John Kelley, a CRS lawyer from Justice Department headquarters in Washington, D.C., and John Cowart, the U.S. attorney for the Middle District of Georgia, had spent the previous month studying the FBI's summary report. Hoover had sought to save his agents the work of compiling such a report, telling Assistant Attorney General Caudle that it wasn't necessary because the investigation had uncovered no federal violations. But Caudle refused to let Hoover off the hook. "In arranging to present this case it is of great importance that the various witnesses be selected with the utmost care, and . . . that a careful plan be worked out in advance as to the order in which the witnesses should appear," Caudle said. "A summary report is virtually indispensable in making these preparations, and I very much hope that the Bureau will cooperate with us."

Hoover cooperated. He not only ordered his agents to condense roughly 10,000 pages of investigative reports into a 353-page summary document, but he also suggested a detailed strategy for presenting the case to the grand jury. Reiterating the assumptions the Justice Department had made in late July, Hoover said, "It appears that one possible theory of Federal jurisdiction in this case lies in the possibility that some member of the Sheriff's office at Monroe, Georgia, may have been implicated in this killing either directly or indirectly." The first goal of the grand jury, Hoover advised, should be to determine if the sheriff's office was, in fact, implicated. "Witnesses before the Grand Jury could be questioned as to any possible notice given by [Deputy Sheriff] Lewis Howard that Roger Malcom was being released on bond," he said. Further, "the Sheriff and his deputies might be called before the Grand Jury . . . [to explain] a number of matters which they have never explained satisfactorily."

If evidence against the sheriff's office could be developed in the grand jury room, Hoover continued, it would automatically suggest probable cause of federal civil rights violations. That suggestion, in turn, would allow federal lawyers to secure federal warrants allowing them to search the homes, barns, and cars belonging to the lynching suspects. "If some of the suspects' guns could be obtained in this way," Hoover concluded, "it is possible that a positive identification might be made by the Bureau's Laboratory." That could mean everything. As FBI agent Louis Hutchinson had said months earlier, "one good handgun ID" would crack the case.

Hoover's plan was complicated. But the machinations he described were necessary, given the vicious circle of federal jurisdiction in lynching cases. Unless the federal government could prove there was probable cause that a federal crime had been committed as part of a lynching, it lacked the legal right to secure search warrants. Yet, without the benefit of federal search warrants, determining whether public officials had been involved was difficult—and that difficulty, in turn, made determining whether a federal crime had been committed nearly impossible.

That's why the federal grand jury was such a crucial tool. When agents tried to interview suspects and witnesses in the cotton field or on the front porches of farmhouses, those suspects and witnesses were free to refuse to answer, or to say they'd forgotten, or to lie—and many did. But, because the Fifth Amendment doesn't apply to grand jury testimony, the 106 witnesses summoned to the grand jury would have no right to refuse to answer questions. And if they were "falsely forgetful" or if they lied under oath, they could be charged with contempt or perjury. Even a witness who claimed he couldn't testify without incriminating himself could be compelled to do so through a grant of immunity assuring him his testimony wouldn't be used against him in court. Once protected with an immunity order, a witness had to testify—or else risk being found in contempt and jailed. No witness, further, was allowed to be accompanied by legal counsel inside the grand jury room.

In short, a farmer from Walton or Oconee County subpoenaed to testify at the grand jury would find himself facing a very different situation from the one he'd faced for four months. He would be locked in a room with the federal lawyers and grand jurors—for minutes or for hours, depending on their fancy. He'd be questioned, and his answers would be scrutinized. He'd be intimidated and pressured. And he—or some of his fellow witnesses—would, the federal lawyers hoped, break down or get tangled in lies. When the breakdowns and entanglements occurred, the federal lawyers planned to exploit them.

At 9 A.M. Wednesday, with the temperature in Athens hovering at an unusually frigid twenty-five degrees, the twenty-three jurors arrived at the courthouse once again, this time joined by more than sixty witnesses. After the witnesses appeared before Judge Davis to hear instructions on their rights and duties, and to take an oath to answer all questions truthfully, they separated by race and retreated to their respective waiting rooms. In the White waiting room were several farmers from Blasingame, including Barnette Hester—though neither his father, his brother Weldon, nor any of his close relatives accompanied him. The chief of police from Monroe was also waiting, as was a former white inmate of the Walton County jail. Riden and Emerson Farmer were there. And so was Loy Harrison. He'd transported the only black witnesses subpoenaed to appear that day: Moena and Jim Williams, Charlie Boy and Ruby Dorsey, and Robert Elder, who waited in the Colored waiting room down the hall.

When the bailiff called the first witness, Barnette Hester rose from his seat. He was pale and gaunt; after his release from the hospital in late July, he'd been readmitted at the end of August and had remained in the hospital through mid-October. Underneath his shirt was a long scar that ran diagonally across the lower left side of his chest. The scar was flat on this day, but periodically it swelled and burst as it had on election day, making infection a continuing and serious threat to his life.

Barnette Hester limped into the grand jury room holding the drainage bag attached to a tube in his chest. After only twenty-five minutes, the doors opened and he limped back out. When a reporter asked him what he'd told the grand jury, he said he'd told them he was wounded by Roger Malcom when he tried to stop a quarrel between Roger and Dorothy. That Barnette Hester was detained so briefly inside indicated that the federal lawyers saw little chance of convincing—or forcing—him to tell what he knew.

When the bailiff called the next witness, Loy Harrison rose from his seat in the waiting room and strode into the smoke-filled grand jury room as the newsmen milling in the hallway scribbled the same descriptions of him they'd used in the days following the lynching: "big," "florid," "prosperous farmer." Though the grand jury room was off-limits to reporters, most could guess what was transpiring inside: the lawyers were prodding Loy Harrison about the conflicts in his alibi and pressuring him to name the men in the mob. After an hour and a half, Loy Harrison emerged from the room with several jurors to drink from the water fountain. One reporter noticed beads of perspiration on his brow, in spite of the day's frigid temperatures. "However," the reporter noted, "he did not look worried in the least, and laughingly spoke to some of the witnesses who were cooling their heels." Loy Harrison, the reporter concluded, had "the attitude of a man who knows he has the close-lipped confidence of his white neighbors, and is even more sure of the Negroes called there to testify."

Once Loy Harrison had exchanged pleasantries with the other white witnesses and returned to the grand jury room, the reporters stalked the hall, looking for material. The white witnesses, many dressed in overalls or khaki farm clothes, eyed them warily. Not a single one was willing to talk—none, that is, until a seventy-two-year-old Walton County gun dealer named Tom Long entered the courthouse. Several reporters were settling in to interview him when Ray Flanagan, a member of the Walton County sheriff's office, jumped up from his seat and ran at them.

"Get out and stay out!" he yelled, pushing the reporters toward the stairs. "I don't care if Truman said you could stay."

Federal marshals quickly removed Ray Flanagan from the courthouse until it was his turn to testify. Just the same, his sentiments were shared by most of the white witnesses in the courthouse. To them, the grand jury had taken up where the FBI had left off. It was yet another federal intrusion into local matters.

At 1 P.M., after Loy Harrison had spent three and one-half hours inside the grand jury room, the federal lawyers adjourned for the day. Moena and Jim Williams, Charlie Boy and Ruby Dorsey, and Robert Elder hurried outside. When a black newsman saw them waiting on the courthouse steps, he seized the opportunity to conduct an interview. According to the reporter, Moena, Jim, Charlie Boy, and Ruby "asserted they knew nothing of the lynchers," and said "they believed everything Mr. Harrison told them." After the reporter raised doubts about Loy Harrison, "they rushed to defend" him. When the reporter asked more pointed questions, Moena and her family got "close-lipped." Within minutes, the black reporter had concluded what FBI agents had months before: Moena and her family had been both coached and threatened by Loy Harrison. Indeed, when interviewed by a white reporter earlier that day, Moena Williams had been so afraid that she'd whispered her answers. She'd said Dorothy had gone to Monroe with Loy Harrison to get Roger Malcom that Thursday "just because she wanted to see him," and her son George, and his wife, Mae, had gone to buy meat. She said she hadn't been near the Moore's Ford Bridge since the lynching. She didn't want to go there.

When Loy Harrison emerged from the courthouse, the newsman's opportunity ended. He quickly snapped a picture, then watched as the black people followed Loy Harrison to his car.

The next morning, the federal lawyers called Loy Harrison back into the grand jury room and kept him there for six hours before releasing him.

Leaving the courthouse that afternoon, Loy Harrison took the moral high ground. "I told them what I knew. That's all I could tell 'em," he said. "I can't invent facts just to please 'em."

CHAPTER FIFTEEN

When the jurors and witnesses arrived in Athens on Monday, December 9, to begin the second week of the grand jury investigation, their minds were likely not on the Moore's Ford lynching. Over the weekend, the worst hotel fire in the nation's history had swept through the fifteen-story Winecoff Hotel in Atlanta. One hundred and twenty people had died—some by plunging from their windows, some by burning to death or suffocating in their rooms. Many of the wounded were sent to Atlanta's Piedmont Hospital, where Governor-elect Eugene Talmadge was getting treatment for his chronic stomach trouble.

On each morning of the previous week, more and more witnesses had crowded the hall on the courthouse's third floor, and each afternoon most of them left without having testified. By Friday, federal lawyers had questioned Moena Williams and her family, the Monroe chief of police, and several of the Blasingame farmers believed to have attended the July 16 meeting at Towler's Woods. Though early estimates had predicted the grand jury would last a week or so, it now appeared it would go until mid-December, maybe until Christmas. The lawyers still had at least sixty witnesses to interrogate.

The fire in Atlanta had drawn the reporters away from Athens; none were at the courthouse to record the witnesses called on Monday, or for several days following. But during the next few days, the bailiff called Boyzie Daniels's name, and he rose from his seat in the Colored waiting room, walked past the white people milling about

in the hall, and entered the grand jury room. Like all of the witnesses, he'd waited for days to testify. He'd sat in the waiting room
and watched Moena Williams shake and cry, knowing neither she
nor any of her family were going to tell what they knew. "You knew
they wasn't gonna say nothing, but it was requested and required
for them to be at court," he'd later comment. "What were they
gonna say? He was a good Mr. Harrison. They was eating his meat
and bread, and they didn't want it stopped." Boyzie Daniels had
watched nineteen-year-old Lamar Howard sit silently in a corner.
He, and everyone he knew, had heard Lamar Howard had seen
something that had to do with the lynching at the Monroe ice plant.

Boyzie Daniels had had a lot of time to think while he waited. He
wondered why Dan Young, who'd prepared the victims' bodies for
burial and who knew so much, hadn't been subpoenaed. And he
wondered why Mama Dora, Roger Malcom's grandmother, hadn't
been brought from Chicago to testify. Their absences made him
question whether the federal lawyers were really trying to solve the
crime—just as he'd questioned the FBI's intent. But in spite of his
doubt, he believed it was his moral duty to tell the truth. He'd
recently become the pastor at Chestnut Grove Church—in whose
cemetery Roger Malcom was buried—and he believed what he told
his congregation, what the Bible said: "It would have to come to
light what was in the dark." Boyzie Daniels walked into the grand
jury room with a smile, "because if you can't tell people what you
know to be true," he says, "you're a slave in your own country."

Inside, Boyzie Daniels told the jurors and lawyers that he'd
driven to Monroe on the day of the lynching to buy supplies for his
wife, who was preparing to can peaches. He said he'd seen the four
lynching victims on the street downtown, and they'd greeted him.
Then he said that on his way home from Monroe, he'd seen a white
farmer from Blasingame named Roy Peters speed by him in a car.

Four other men were with Roy Peters in the car, Boyzie Daniels said, but he couldn't identify them.

After he was dismissed, Boyzie Daniels returned to the Colored waiting room to wait for the black woman he'd transported from Monroe that morning to finish her testimony before the grand jury. A short while later, the bailiff came to the door of the room and told Boyzie Daniels that the woman had been released, and asked him to take her out of the courthouse immediately.

"We went on out the door of the courthouse and she was shaking with fear," says Boyzie Daniels. On the way to his car, she told him she needed to stop in a store. She went in while he waited outside. After fifteen minutes, he went in, and the store clerk told him a woman had just run out the back door.

Boyzie Daniels didn't know what the woman had told the grand jury. He waited a little longer for her to reappear, and then he drove back to Monroe alone.

One day later, after the grand jury had adjourned for the afternoon, the two federal lawyers placed a telephone call to CRS chief Turner Smith in Washington, D.C. Evidently their nine-hour interrogation of Loy Harrison, as well as their questioning of roughly thirty other witnesses, had yielded no evidence against any member of the mob, nor any evidence of federal civil rights violations. The lawyers told CRS chief Smith they planned to conclude the grand jury by the end of the week.

But then, one day later, the lawyers called Smith and told him they were "about to get somewhere with the case." After that phone call, Smith, in turn, alerted his superior, Assistant Attorney General Caudle. "If this new development will stand up and the members of the mob identified," Smith said, "I think it would provide sufficient legal basis for a Federal case."

The "new development" was the discovery that Deputy Sheriff Lewis Howard had placed Major Jones, the black trusty at the Walton County jail, into a locked cell on the jail's second floor on three nights following Roger Malcom's stabbing of Barnette Hester. What made this information so crucial was that Lewis Howard didn't *normally* lock Major Jones into a cell on the second floor. Normally he slept on the jail's sleeping porch, which was on the first floor—and which was unlocked.

According to the FBI's report, Major Jones had first been interviewed about two months earlier, on October 10. At that time, he told agents he'd seen George, Dorothy, and Mae on his way to do an errand on the afternoon of the lynching. He'd said, "Thought you were going to get that boy out of jail," and Mae Murray had called back, "We are going to get him. We're going to get him at five o'clock." During that same interview, Major Jones had also reported that Lewis Howard had altered his sleeping arrangements on the nights of July 15, 16, and 17. Even more important, Major Jones explained the reason for the change: Lewis Howard expected a mob to come and take Roger Malcom out of jail, and he didn't want the mob to "mistakenly get Major Jones" instead.

The testimony from Major Jones revealed two key facts. One, Lewis Howard knew there were threats on Roger Malcom's life before he was lynched—despite the fact that he and the other members of the sheriff's office had told the U.S. attorneys on July 26 that there'd been no indication of trouble, "not a bit." And two, in the face of the threats Lewis Howard had acted to protect Major Jones, but did nothing to protect the man who was the target. He didn't arrange for Roger Malcom to be moved to a jail in Atlanta, as had been done in 1939, when "feeling" ran high against J. D. Vaughn, a black man charged with raping a white woman. He didn't ask his fellow lawmen to provide increased security at the jail. He didn't move Roger Malcom to a locked cell on the second floor. And despite being aware of threats on Roger Malcom's life, he didn't prevent him from being released on bond on July 25.

Major Jones's testimony to FBI agents on October 10 didn't necessarily provide proof that Lewis Howard had violated Section 52, the color-of-law statute—largely because the *Screws* case had raised the issue of "willfulness." But it clearly provided probable cause of a federal violation. And yet it appears the agents who recorded Major Jones's testimony on October 10 didn't grasp its relevance. There's no indication that they enclosed it in a teletype marked URGENT to FBI director Hoover. And they didn't move Major Jones to a safe location. Instead, they waited nearly a month and interviewed him again.

During the second interview, Major Jones told agents that Lewis Howard had learned he'd told the FBI about the alteration in his sleeping arrangements, and that, since then, he'd been barred from leaving the jail yard. Major Jones confided to agents that he was "extremely afraid of the possibility of the Howards harming him bodily." Yet, once again, it appears agents failed either to notify anyone in D.C. about their discovery, or to take action to protect Major Jones's life and his valuable testimony.

This inaction seems even more problematic given that Major Jones's testimony was corroborated by several other witnesses. A black woman who worked at the jail told agents that, after the stabbing, Mrs. Lewis Howard told her she was worried, because a crowd was coming to the jail "to get the boy [Roger Malcom] out and mob him." And various jail inmates, black and white, told agents they'd heard Lewis Howard tell Roger Malcom that he better pray, because if Barnette Hester died, "his time wouldn't be long." Given the likelihood that, at the very least, Lewis Howard knew of threats to Roger Malcom's life and failed to take action either to protect him or to pursue the authors of those threats, why didn't the agents convey the information about Lewis Howard to the CRS lawyers back in October? And why didn't they aggressively investigate him throughout the last two months of their investigation?

Perhaps agents hadn't taken Major Jones's testimony seriously—because he was black, or because he was a convicted criminal. Or perhaps they had taken it seriously, but believed it proved only that Lewis Howard had known about the Towler's Woods meeting, not that he'd actually participated in the lynching. And because the agents were after the "triggermen," perhaps they'd forgone pursuing Lewis Howard further. An examination of a five-hundred-page excerpt of the FBI's reports, including the summary, shows that only twenty pages relate to the sheriff's office. Clearly, the agents spent the bulk of their time in Walton County investigating civilians suspected of murder—even though the federal government would have no case against those civilians unless there was evidence of a public official's involvement in the lynching. This represented a mistake not only on the part of the field agents; it represented a lapse in supervision on the part of the U.S. attorney's office and the CRS. Whether this lapse resulted from an apathy born of racism, as Walter White accused, or mere administrative disorganization, the effect was the same.

On December 11, when the federal lawyers learned of Major Jones's testimony, they must have greeted it with mixed emotions. Had they known the information months earlier, they could have pursued obtaining search warrants based on probable cause of a federal violation. They could have directed the FBI agents to focus their energy on marshaling evidence against the sheriff's office, rather than spreading their efforts countywide. They could have had a fighting chance at getting indictments against at least some members of the Walton County sheriff's office. And those indictments could've provided the hairline crack that might have broken the case wide open.

But the crucial information came to the lawyers' attention too late for any of this. In an attempt to salvage its potential, on December 12 the lawyers ordered Major Jones to be transported from the Walton County jail to the Athens jail in preparation for testifying. When Lewis Howard learned of the move, he promptly instructed Major Jones to perjure himself to the grand jury, to tell them he'd been locked in an upstairs cell on those three July nights because he was sick. In threatening Major Jones, Lewis Howard allegedly committed a federal crime, the intimidation of a federal witness. Clearly he was worried.

On December 16, the grand jury handed down its first indictment. But Lewis Howard needn't have worried. The indictment was against Alvin Adcock, the man seen driving through Hestertown with Weldon Hester on the evening of the lynching and later spotted taking a double-barreled shotgun from his car. In his testimony before the grand jury, Alvin Adcock swore that he hadn't left home on the day of the lynching except to attend the revival at Union Chapel Church. He also swore that he hadn't visited the lynching scene the following day. When several witnesses—in addition to the FBI agents, who'd been scrutinizing the grand jury transcripts each day in an effort to discover such lies—testified that Alvin Adcock had, in fact, done both, he was indicted on two counts of perjury. His father, Powell Adcock, who was also a suspect in the lynching, posted a $2,000 bond, and Alvin Adcock went free.

The indictment didn't make headlines. By then, most newspapers had relegated news of the grand jury to the back pages. And anyway, the indictment was a token; the perjury charges didn't implicate Alvin Adcock in the lynching. The best thing about the indictment, U.S. Attorney Cowart told CRS chief Smith, was the effect it could have on the thirty or so witnesses who had yet to appear in front of the grand jury. And so the lawyers pushed on. During the next three days they interrogated Weldon Hester, Jack Malcom, Hughlon Peters, and a score of other Hestertown residents. They questioned James Verner. They finally got to twelve-year-old Emerson Farmer, who'd been coming to Athens each day with his father, waiting to tell what he'd seen. And on December 18, they questioned several members of the Walton County sheriff's office.

But in spite of the "tangible break" represented by Major Jones's testimony, and the perjury indictment against Alvin Adcock, the lawyers soon concluded the case was "pretty well washed out." At 3:55 P.M. on December 19—nearly five months to the day after the Moore's Ford lynching—the grand jury foreman read from a prepared statement. "We the grand jury have carefully and patiently during the past three weeks investigated the killing of four Negroes in Walton County, Ga., which occurred on July 25, 1946. Numerous witnesses called as a result of the extensive four-month investigation by the Federal Bureau of Investigation have been questioned exhaustively," he said. "The members of this body are unanimous in reporting that we have been unable to establish the identity of any person or persons participating in the murders or in any violation of the civil rights statutes of the United States." Twenty-five FBI agents, four months of investigation, 2,790 people interviewed, 106 people subpoenaed before the grand jury—and then no indictments. The federal government had responded to the worst incident of racial violence since the end of World War II with the most massive lynching investigation in the country's history. And yet, there was still no justice.

NAACP special counsel Thurgood Marshall couldn't contain his frustration at the news. He wrote a letter to Attorney General Clark, asking him to investigate his department. "The FBI has established for itself an uncomparable [*sic*] record for ferreting out persons violating our federal laws," he wrote. This "extends from the prosecution of vicious spies and saboteurs . . . to nondescript hoodlums who steal automobiles and drive them across state lines. On the other hand, the FBI has been unable to identify or bring to trial persons charged with federal statutes where Negroes are the victims."

In a memo to colleague Walter White, Marshall wrote, "I . . . have no faith in either Mr. Hoover or his investigators . . . and there is no use in my saying I do." And later he'd elaborate even further: "To my mind it is unbelievable that the FBI couldn't find a member of that mob. . . . With them on the spot the next day and having been down there with that many men, that they can't find one member of the mob . . . to me it is unbelievable."

In the face of the criticism, FBI director Hoover pointed to the challenges of the case: there was almost no physical evidence, almost no cooperation from witnesses, and no confessions from the guilty parties. These three things—essential to the solving of any homicide—simply didn't exist in Walton County. "That was a case in which the phrase I used, the 'iron curtain,' is typical," said Hoover. "The arrogance of the . . . white population was unbelievable, and the fear of the Negroes was almost unbelievable."

In the wake of the grand jury's failure to indict, the words the famed liberal editor of the *Atlanta Constitution*, Ralph McGill, had written just four days after the lynching offered the only consolation for some: "Even though they [the lynchers] never come to justice, they will have to live with themselves. They will wonder to themselves how it was that they, who some mother nursed and cared for to rear them to manhood, dreaming dreams for them, managed to come to do murder. They will begin to realize that they have taken human life and are cursed of God. They must live with that uncomfortable fact. It will become an intolerable load which will, in some fashion, break them all."

One day after the grand jury returned no indictments in the case of the Moore's Ford lynching, Governor-elect Eugene Talmadge lapsed into a coma at Atlanta's Piedmont Hospital. Just before dawn on December 21 he died. The immediate cause of death was acute hepatitis, which had caused his liver to fail, and his stomach and intestinal tract to bleed. The long-term cause was cirrhosis: a lifetime of drinking. And too, many said it was the 1946 gubernatorial campaign that had killed Eugene Talmadge. As he'd traveled from one town to another that spring and summer, warning that the federal government and the "niggers" were destroying Georgia, he had, in the end, destroyed himself.

At the news of Talmadge's death, Governor Ellis Arnall ordered the flag at the state capitol lowered to half-staff and ordered the Christmas lights—which were lit for the first time since the beginning of World War II—turned off. The next day, when Talmadge's body lay in state under the capitol's gold dome—surrounded by flowers and a wreath marked KKKK (Knights of the Ku Klux Klan)—more than ten thousand people passed by to pay their respects. Mingled with their grief was worry: Who would be Georgia's next governor?

Eugene Talmadge's closest supporters, aware of his failing health, had already answered that question. They'd devised a sort of insurance policy before the general election in November by asking people to vote for Eugene's thirty-three-year-old son, Herman, as a write-in candidate. At Ole Gene's death, his supporters claimed the candidate with the next-highest ballot count should be governor. And since Herman Talmadge had received nearly seven hundred write-in votes during the general election, he should be the one to succeed his father, they said. Though nowhere did the state constitution mandate that if an elected official died before taking office, the candidate with the next highest number of votes would automatically replace him, Herman Talmadge took his case to the Georgia General Assembly. At 2 A.M. January 15, he would be declared governor under a cloud of fraud and deception that was his seeming birthright.

Long before then, the FBI agents had cleared their files and belongings from the Monroe Hotel and driven back to their homes in Charlotte, Charleston, Birmingham, New Orleans, Knoxville, and Atlanta. They were gone by the time of the cotton settle, when it became clear that poor weather and the FBI investigation had not, despite farmers' grim predictions, ruined the harvest after all. Cotton yields were lower in 1946 than in 1945, but prices were higher. The crop in Walton County fetched more than $3.6 million.

The agents were gone by the time Charlie Boy and Ruby Dorsey heard Dorothy's voice float through the screen door at the concrete-block house on Loy Harrison's farm, and by the time they heard George's hard-heeled army shoes on the steps. Soon after hearing those sounds, Charlie Boy left the farm and returned in a truck belonging to a white farmer who lived in the next county south. He and Ruby Dorsey, and Moena and Jim Williams, loaded their few belongings onto the truck and drove off to live and work on that man's farm—even though Loy Harrison had offered each a $100 bonus to stay with him for another year.

The agents were gone from Monroe by the time Mama Dora spent her first Christmas in Chicago—so far from home, and without her grandson for the first time in twenty-two years. That fall, Mattie Louise, Roger's first wife, had left Georgia for Ohio and taken Roger Jr. with her. Mama Dora couldn't know it, but she'd never see him again.

The agents were gone by the time Isaac Brooks, the black employee at Almand Funeral Home, returned to Monroe, and revealed why he'd disappeared after the lynching. He said E. L. Almand had paid for him to go to Detroit to visit his sister. It was the first paid vacation he'd had in thirty-two years of working for the white funeral home, and his stepdaughter, Mary Alice Avery, believed it was an effort to "get rid of" him during the FBI's investigation. "Isaac seen too much," she says. "He was troubled, really troubled. He started drinking and talking. I believe he was going to have a breakdown." That winter, when Isaac Brooks came back from Detroit, he was calmer. "He probably seen things up there that were more peaceful than small-town Monroe," says Mary Alice Avery.

And the FBI agents were gone by the day the calendar flipped to 1947, and two white men appeared at the Monroe ice plant, looking for the nineteen-year-old black man named Lamar Howard.

CHAPTER SIXTEEN

Lamar Howard was sitting in the manager's office at the ice plant that afternoon when James Verner and his brother, Tom, walked in. He knew both men well; his family had worked for their sister for years, and he'd often seen them around her farm. Lamar Howard started to greet the brothers, but didn't have the chance. Tom Verner rushed at him, snatched his cap, threw it on the floor, then slapped him. James Verner put his face close to Lamar Howard's. "What," he demanded, "did you tell 'em down at Athens?"

Two weeks before, Lamar Howard had traveled to Athens, waited in the Colored waiting room, and entered the grand jury room when his name was called. He hadn't wanted to go, but he'd been subpoenaed and had no choice. Inside the room, he told jurors what he'd told the FBI agents who'd interviewed him at the ice plant one week after the lynching. He said James Verner had brought two guns into the ice plant the day before the Moore's Ford lynching; one was a .32-caliber Smith & Wesson revolver, and the other was a German Luger. He also said James Verner had visited the ice plant just a few hours before the lynching. This time he'd stood out front, talking with Loy Harrison.

When he could get the words out, Lamar Howard answered James Verner's question: "I didn't tell them anything. I didn't know anything to tell them."

James Verner hit him, then demanded again to know what he'd told the grand jury. When Lamar Howard again said he'd told nothing, both brothers closed in on him. At thirty-six and twenty-six, they towered over Howard, who, at nineteen, was slight and boyish.

Then the door to the office opened, and Lamar Howard saw the ice-plant manager standing there. Roughly one year before, the manager had hired Lamar and taught him how to make ice—fill a big metal can with water, blow through a tube to prevent bubbles. The ice Lamar Howard made was always clear, never cloudy or frosty. "I had learned it real good," he says. The manager had told him so. And so, that afternoon, when Lamar Howard saw his boss in the doorway, he assumed he'd come to protect him.

"Don't beat him up in here," the manager told the Verner brothers. "Take him out back."

In the cow stall out back of the ice plant, James Verner brought out a .38-caliber pistol, pulled back the hammer, pointed it at Lamar Howard, and asked, "Did you tell 'em about us bringing those guns over here and cleaning 'em?"

"I didn't tell them anything about any guns," said Lamar Howard.

"Did you tell 'em we cleaned those guns the same day of the lynchings?" James Verner asked.

"No," said Lamar Howard.

The brothers started clubbing him with the butt of the pistol. When they paused briefly, one remarked to the other that Lamar had the hardest head he'd ever seen.

Fifteen minutes later, the Verners pushed Lamar Howard out of the stall and into his car. On the drive home, he held his left eye open with his fingers, but it didn't help, because the blood running from his forehead clouded his vision.

That evening, Lamar Howard's family took him to the Walton

County Hospital, where a nurse phoned Deputy Sheriff Lewis Howard. He informed her that since the assault had occurred within city limits, it wasn't in his jurisdiction. The nurse called the city police, but after several hours passed without an officer arriving, Lamar Howard's entire family fled to a house seven miles outside of Monroe, where they hoped they'd be safe through the night.

When undertaker Dan Young learned of the beating the next day, he notified his brother-in-law, C. A. Scott, and after nightfall, Scott sent two *Atlanta Daily World* employees to Monroe. Their photographs, which later ran large on the newspaper's front page, showcase Lamar Howard's injuries: his left eye is swollen shut; his right cheek is cut; his lips are puffy and bruised; and his sweatshirt is speckled with blood. "I looked like Joe Louis," Lamar Howard would say years later. He also looked eerily like the victims of the Moore's Ford lynching, whose bodies had been photographed in Dan Young's funeral home five months before.

Late that night, the newsmen laid Lamar Howard on the backseat of their car and drove him out of Monroe. "I'm sort of a bully and I'd never be scared, but on those country roads with the lights shining behind you . . . ," says William Fowlkes, one of the *Atlanta Daily World* reporters who traveled to Monroe that night, "I knew something could happen just like that."

After spending a few days in an Atlanta hospital, Lamar Howard was strong enough to get into a car provided by the Citizens Defense League, which had formed in the wake of the lynchings, and travel to the FBI's Atlanta office, where he told agents of his beating. Soon afterward, an anonymous caller telephoned the office to say that if the FBI attempted to arrest the Verner brothers, they wouldn't leave Walton County alive. When agents relayed the threat to Hoover, he responded by ordering agents to apprehend the Verner brothers immediately—in broad daylight and in public.

"I wanted to show that there was at least an authority of law that they could not deny," Hoover would later say.

On the morning of January 5, agents arrested James and Tom Verner and took them to the federal courthouse in Athens, where they were arraigned on charges of intimidating a federal witness. The brothers posted bond and were released, only to be rearrested several days later—this time on state charges of assault and battery.

The state arrests were significant; that Walton County was bringing charges against white men for a crime committed against a black man was a rare occurrence. But the federal arrests were an occasion for hope. Because the Verners' attack was inextricably linked to the Moore's Ford lynching—as Lamar Howard's account indicates, he'd been beaten in retaliation for his grand jury testimony—their arrest offered a second chance at solving the lynching case. And this second chance was, in many ways, a better chance, for the FBI now had clear jurisdiction and a living witness. The front-page headlines of the *Chicago Defender* declared, "Brothers Hold Key to Monroe Case; Pressure on Two Can Crack Lynch Mystery." In a strange way, the beating of Lamar Howard on New Year's Day, 1947, was a backhanded stroke of luck, an act of violence that created an opportunity for justice when it seemed there was none.

On February 24, 1947, four days after Georgia governor Herman Talmadge signed a white primary bill into law—"If I couldn't keep Papa from dying, at least I could keep him from dying in vain," he said—a capacity crowd of nearly two hundred white people and twenty black people filled Monroe's stately courthouse to witness what many were calling the trial of the year. The state had dropped charges against Tom Verner, who was slated for army reenlistment, but retained the charges against James Verner. If convicted of assault and battery, he faced six months in jail or twelve months in a public works camp, and a $1,000 fine.

Lamar Howard was the prosecution's first witness. When he took the stand and testified that James Verner had beaten him at the ice plant on New Year's Day, he felt everyone looking at him—the whites on the floor, the blacks in the gallery above. He was scared, and though nearly two months had passed since the Verners had clubbed him with a pistol, his head hurt. But as the morning wore on, each succeeding witness strengthened Lamar Howard's testimony. Monroe's police chief testified that James Verner had told him, "Yes, I beat him and I'll beat the hell out of him again." And Tom Verner testified that he'd watched his brother beat Lamar Howard and admitted he'd noticed his brother's knuckles were bloody afterward.

The county district attorney rested his case just after noon, confident of a quick conviction. Everyone in the courtroom, even those who'd come to support James Verner, assumed there was a slim chance for anything but a guilty verdict—the facts were so clear, the evidence so overwhelming. But as soon as James Verner's lawyer took the floor, that assumption was proven premature. On the stand, the ice-plant manager—the white man Lamar Howard had believed would rescue him—testified that no beating had occurred in his office that day and that he'd never told the Verner brothers to move the beating to the back of the ice plant. And James Verner admitted on the stand that he'd hit Lamar Howard "eight or ten times pretty hard, knocked him down twice," but said he'd done so because Lamar Howard had run him off the road in his car. The beating was an act of self-defense, he said, not an act of revenge; it was the punishment Lamar Howard deserved. In closing, the defense lawyer urged jurors to think seriously before taking a "nigger's word" against the testimony of several "fine white gentlemen."

As the trial drew to a close, the county district attorney tried to recover the case by appealing to jurors' concern for Monroe's national reputation. The Moore's Ford lynching had already scarred the town's name, he implied. A "not guilty" verdict in such an egregious attack would only give Northern liberals and the Northern press more fodder for their attacks. But his strategy failed. The jurors were obviously less concerned with Monroe's national reputation than with maintaining the system of white supremacy. At 6 P.M., twelve white men filed into the courtroom and pronounced James Verner "not guilty." As a victory cry rose up from the white crowd, Lamar Howard fled the courthouse, returning to Atlanta in the safety of a state patrol car.

Even as a Walton County jury failed to find James Verner guilty, the FBI agents who'd returned to Monroe in early January, just weeks after they thought they'd left for good, began preparing a federal case against him. They spent little time marshaling evidence against Tom Verner, who'd been stationed in Germany during July 1946 and thus wasn't a suspect in the lynching. Instead, they focused on James Verner, the former army sharpshooter and gun dealer who'd been a strong suspect in the lynching from early on.

That winter, agents learned that James Verner's attack on Lamar Howard was hardly his first attack of the kind; he'd knocked a black man down in 1945 for the same offense of which he accused Lamar Howard: running him off the road. And they learned that, more recently, James Verner had been among the white men who'd whipped Albert Hunter on the night before election day in Walton County.

Most important, after obtaining a federal search warrant to search James Verner's room, agents found not only the .38-caliber pistol used in the assault on Lamar Howard, but also a German

Luger. Back in September 1946, James Verner had told agents he'd sold the Luger several days before the lynching. Now it was clear he had not. This was a crucial discovery, because both a .38-caliber Smith & Wesson revolver and a German Luger had been among the weapons used to kill Roger and Dorothy Malcom and George and Mae Murray Dorsey on July 25, 1946.

Such a discovery would seem to have justified the formal opening of a state murder investigation. But a jury in Walton County had just found James Verner not guilty of assaulting Lamar Howard despite an airtight case against him. It was unthinkable that he'd ever be convicted of murder.

On June 2, 1947, nearly four months after he'd testified in court in Monroe, Lamar Howard again left the safety of Atlanta—where the Citizens Defense League had gotten him a job at the Butler Street YMCA, just off Auburn Avenue—to testify about his beating at the ice plant. During the trial, which was held in Judge Davis's courtroom in the same federal courthouse where the grand jury had convened six months earlier, Tom Verner testified he took no part in the beating. James Verner supported his brother's feigned innocence and, once again, testified that he'd beaten Lamar Howard as punishment for running him off the road. Tom Verner was immediately acquitted and, after jurors failed to come to a consensus on James Verner's guilt, Judge Davis declared a mistrial. James Verner was released on bond, free until a new trial date was set. Lamar Howard returned to Atlanta, where his headaches continued, and where he remained bitter for a long time. He changed his name to Lamar Jones, but when people learned he was the one beaten at the ice plant, they gave him the nickname Monroe.

Despite clear jurisdiction, physical evidence, and a living witness—three things the federal lawyers had lacked in the original lynching case—James Verner went unpunished. The efforts of the federal government, ultimately, were no match for a jury selected from a white community that didn't view attacks on black people as crimes. That had been proven with the Verners' trials, as it had been proven one month before in Greenville, South Carolina, when a local jury had found thirty-one white men charged with lynching a black man named Willie Earle not guilty—even though twenty-six of those men had admitted to the FBI that they'd been members of the lynch mob.

Following the release of James Verner, even NAACP secretary Walter White lost hope. When a private detective offered his services to solve the Moore's Ford lynching case, White declined, saying, "We have no more money to spend on the Walton County lynchings." It was a far cry from his attitude one year before, when he'd dispatched an investigator to Monroe, pledged a $10,000 reward, and lobbied lawmakers and the president for action. "We had better get them when they've overplayed their hand to the limit," he'd written to NAACP branch presidents then. He'd believed the lynchers made a tactical error. Their brutality would shock most Americans out of their indifference, he'd said, and once that happened, there was no way the crime could go unpunished.

The crime had now gone unpunished. And yet Walter White and his liberal allies took comfort, because nearly four weeks after the federal government failed to win convictions against the Verner brothers, an American president addressed the NAACP's annual conference for the first time in history. "I should like to talk to you briefly about civil rights and human freedom," President Truman said as he stood at the foot of the Lincoln Memorial on June 29, 1947. "It is my deep conviction that we have reached a turning point in the long history of our country's efforts to guarantee freedom and equality to all our citizens. Recent events in the United

States and abroad have made us realize that it is more important today than ever before to insure that all Americans enjoy these rights.

"And when I say all Americans—I mean all Americans."

Then, with a crowd of ten thousand gathered before him, and a worldwide radio audience listening in, the president continued. "The extension of civil rights today means, not protection of the people *against* the government, but protection of the people *by* the government. We must make the federal government a friendly, vigilant defender of the rights and equalities of all Americans," he said. "And again I mean all Americans." In closing, he added, "We must and shall guarantee the civil rights of all our citizens."

After the speech, President Truman sought out Walter White. "I said what I did because I mean every word of it," the president told him, "and I am going to prove that I do mean it."

Already the president had followed through on the pledge he'd made during his meeting with Walter White at the White House on September 19, 1946, with the issue of Executive Order #9808, which created the President's Committee on Civil Rights. The order charged the committee's fifteen members—two blacks, two Southern white liberals, and eleven Northern white liberals—with conducting a thorough investigation of the state of civil rights in the nation. Only twice before had such a national civil rights review been undertaken: once during the creation of the Bill of Rights, and once during the Civil War.

Four months after Truman's June address to the NAACP, the President's Committee on Civil Rights issued a report containing nearly three dozen recommendations for improving the state of civil rights in America. When, on February 2, 1948, President Truman sent a special message to Congress asking it to enact several of the report's recommendations, he became the first American president to put civil rights at the forefront of the national agenda. The President seemed to take the report's title, which was *To Secure These Rights*, to heart. He called for the abolition of the poll tax; desegregation of the armed forces and interstate travel; a permanent Fair Employment Practices Commission to prevent racial discrimination in federal jobs; and a federal antilynching law that would hold both public officials *and* private individuals responsible.

What black people and white liberals saw as the "conversion" of President Truman in early 1948, politicians and elected officials in the white South saw as treason. The president has "run a political dagger into our backs and now he is trying to drink our blood," said one Mississippi congressman. The president's civil rights message will "destroy the South 'beyond hope of redemption,'" Mississippi senator James Eastland claimed. "Mr. Truman's unwarranted attack upon our Southern civilization has made me sick at heart," Georgia's junior senator, Richard Russell, told a constituent.

Though faced with attacks—and eventual mutiny—from the Southern wing of the Democratic Party during an election year in which he was campaigning for the nation's highest elected office for the first time, President Truman refused to back down. "When the mob gangs can take four people out and shoot them in the back, and everybody in the country is acquainted with who did the shooting and nothing is done about it, that country is in a pretty bad fix," he said. "I am going to try to remedy it, and if that ends up in my failure to be elected, that failure will be in a good cause."

But this was still the sound of the future. Though the president was able to desegregate the armed forces by executive order in 1948, it would be years before the other planks in his civil rights message became law. And one never did. There is still no federal law against lynching in the United States today.

The consolation is that lynching generally declined in the years following 1946, a result of the rise of black political power, the transformation of the South from a largely agrarian society to one industrially based, a lessening of the prevailing isolation of rural communities, and an increasing knowledge on the part of lynchers that they'd face investigation, if not punishment. In 1947, there was one lynching; in 1948, two; in 1949, three; and in 1950, there were two. In 1952, the country finally celebrated its first lynchless year. There would be bad years after that—1955 and 1964, for example—but the trend was set. The Tuskegee Institute, which had recorded the nation's lynchings since 1882, stopped counting in 1968.

But in 1947, and in the years that directly followed, the black people of Walton and Oconee counties couldn't know these things. What they knew was that 1946 had dashed their hopes. First the election for governor was lost in a swirl of deception and violence. Then both the Moore's Ford lynching and the attack on Lamar Howard went unpunished. Then, in 1947, a string of arsons left every black church and school in the Walton County town of Loganville burnt to the ground. And in 1948 it wasn't any safer for black people to vote than in 1946. Though Herman Talmadge had been dethroned by the Georgia Supreme Court in March 1947, after the justices ruled his election unconstitutional, he ran for governor again in 1948. And when he won, he'd call his victory "the restoration," vowing to keep his father's pledge to bar blacks from Georgia's polls.

And what the black people of Walton and Oconee counties also knew was that the men who'd lynched Roger and Dorothy Malcom, and George and Mae Murray Dorsey, continued to live freely while they continued to work for them; to borrow money from and be cheated by them; to step around them on the sidewalks downtown; to be arrested by them; to be beaten by them; to fear them; and to never know for sure who had been in the mob that Thursday afternoon in July. The black people of Walton and Oconee counties had no access to the facts of the Moore's Ford lynching; the grand jury proceedings were never transcribed, since there'd been no indictments, and the FBI report was filed in D.C., unreachable. The only thing the black people knew for sure was that the lynchers hadn't been punished by any law on earth, and never would be.

So they looked to God for justice, because they believed what Atlanta newspaper editor Ralph McGill had written in the days following the lynching: "God is not mocked, even if law is." When the infant child of a white family in Hestertown burned to death in a washbasin full of scalding water, it was God punishing the community. When two young white men in Blasingame were electrocuted by loose wires, it was God's punishment again. When several white farmers who lived near the Moore's Ford Bridge committed suicide, it was their guilt that drove them to it. And years later, when men suspected of participating in the lynching flailed on their deathbeds, yelling, "Get them niggers off me. Get them off," that was Roger and Dorothy, and George and Mae, strangling them. It was God whupping them.

In 1949, the federal government dropped all charges against both Alvin Adcock, the man indicted for perjury by the grand jury in Athens, and James Verner, the man indicted for attacking Lamar Howard. One year later, a novel titled *Reprisal* was published, and despite the author's insistence that the town of Hainesville, Georgia, which served as the book's setting, was "completely imaginary," the citizens of Monroe and Walton counties knew differently. In *Reprisal*'s cast of characters they recognized the four lynching victims, as well as Barnette Hester, Loy Harrison, James Verner, the deputy sheriffs, and undertaker Dan Young. And with an uneasy sense of déjà vu, they discovered that the book's version of the lynching bore a striking resemblance to the account Loy Harrison had given newspaper reporters and the GBI one day after the Moore's Ford lynching—though it offered more details. In *Reprisal*, the Loy Harrison character says the men in the lynch mob were drunk, their breath laced with liquor and their eyes narrowed and red. He explains that when they dragged the George Dorsey character from the car, he held out his roped hands in a "queer, pleading gesture" and said, "I ain't done nothin', boss." He describes the screams of the two black women as "chattering that sounded like a fear-crazed monkey." He says that, near the end, the Dorothy Malcom character "seemed to go completely mad," her "teeth snapping blindly, a whitish foam on her lips." Meanwhile, the Mae Murray Dorsey character prayed with her face pressed against the trunk of a pine tree. Then they were all shot: "One, two, three." In Walton and Oconee counties, the publication of *Reprisal* raised fears of renewed interest in the Moore's Ford lynching. But since the book was fiction—since the town's name was Hainesville, not Monroe, after all—the fears soon subsided. Just the same, *Reprisal*, like the lynching itself, was nothing to be talked about openly.

In 1954, three years after the five-year statute of limitations for federal civil rights convictions in the Moore's Ford lynching case ran out, the FBI transferred several frayed lengths of rope and a handful of bullets and shells from its headquarters in Washington, D.C., to the headquarters of the Georgia Bureau of Investigation in Atlanta. After that, nothing happened in the case until 1991, when fifty-five-year-old Clinton Adams—the eldest son of the family that had once lived in the little white house at the edge of the Fanny Wright place—told an FBI agent what he'd seen on July 25, 1946, while hiding in the woods near the Moore's Ford Bridge.

Early that July afternoon, Clinton Adams said, he and his friend Emerson Farmer, who lived in the house closest to the Moore's Ford Bridge, had led the Farmers' cow into a honeysuckle patch at the edge of a small field just above the Apalachee River. It was a hot day, but in the honeysuckle it was cool and shady, and after tying up the cow to graze, the boys dropped into the grass to play. They were still playing hours later when they heard the screams.

Without a word, both boys ran to the edge of the woods that lay between the field and the river. From there, they could see out to the road, where a group of white men was pulling some blacks out of Loy Harrison's car.

At first, Clinton Adams wasn't frightened. "We just fell down on our belly and started watching," he says. "We was going to watch them get whipped." Then, when he saw the guns and realized it wasn't just a whipping, it was too late to run. So he and Emerson Farmer hid themselves as best they could and settled in to watch and wait.

The white men pushed the blacks down the hill that sloped off the road, then dragged them along the old wagon trail that ran parallel to the riverbank. When they stopped in a clearing roughly 140 feet from where the boys lay hiding, Clinton Adams spotted four white men he recognized in the mob. He saw Loy Harrison, the farmer for whom his family had worked for three years. He saw Andrew and Frank Ford, a pair of brothers who worked for Loy Harrison. And he saw Emmett Harper, a wealthy Walton County landowner. They all carried guns, and they all had their hands on the blacks, pushing and shoving them.

When Clinton Adams spotted George and Dorothy Dorsey, he could barely keep from crying out. The previous winter, when Clinton Adams's father had taken sick, George had cut and hauled wood for them, cared for their horses and hogs. And after Clinton's father had killed himself, George had been nice to Clinton. George Dorsey was a friend anyone would have been proud to have, and Dorothy was a good person too, he thought. Clinton Adams watched through the trees as the white men forced George and Dorothy, and two other blacks he didn't know, to line up in a row.

The four men Clinton Adams recognized fired the first shots, then the blacks fell to the ground, hanging on to each other and making the most eerie sounds Clinton Adams had ever heard, "like an animal caught in a trap." Then all the men—there were roughly twelve—started firing. They shot into the air, into the trees, into the ground. When they stepped close to the bodies and shot down at them, Clinton Adams again fought the urge to cry out. There were so many gunshots that it sounded like a fire in a canebrake, he says.

When the shooting finally stopped, it got so quiet that Clinton Adams could hear his heart beating in his throat. After the men walked back to the road, some walked across the bridge, got into cars, and drove away. Others stood around, talking and laughing. Loy Harrison stayed the longest, and only after he left did Clinton Adams finally stand up. When he did, he could see gun smoke hanging in the air above the wagon trail, and blood bubbling out of the bodies. He ran out of the woods and across the road to Emerson Farmer's house, where he saddled his horse and raced home.

One year before, he would have had a short ride home, just to the little white house at the edge of the Fanny Wright farm, next to the big house where George Dorsey lived. But in February, after his father had been found hanging in the wood house, Clinton Adams's family had been forced to move to a farm six miles away, in Good Hope. Clinton often rode the family's old white horse back to visit Emerson Farmer, his best friend. That's what he'd been doing that afternoon, he says.

When Clinton Adams got home and told his mother what he'd seen, she didn't say much. "At that time it was a dead nigger," he says. "Nobody paid it no attention." Still, the next morning, she hitched up their wagon and took Clinton and his brother and sisters to Moore's Ford. They walked along the wagon trail with the other souvenir hunters, peering at the bullet holes in the tree trunks and the bloodstains on the ground. There, in the dirt, Clinton Adams found something that reminded him of George Dorsey: a tooth. "George had a big old mouth," Clinton Adams says. "He could swallow a basketball." He wanted to keep the tooth as a souvenir, but his mother ordered him to throw it down.

A few days later, when Walton County deputy sheriffs Lewis Howard and Doc Sorrells paid his family a visit, Clinton Adams told them he'd seen the lynching. Immediately, Lewis Howard told him never to mention it again. "If you tell this," he said, "them people could come kill your brother, your mama, and your sister, even you." Though he was only ten years old, Clinton Adams understood. "As long as I kept my mouth shut," he says, "I didn't have nothing to fear."

When the FBI came into the county, Clinton Adams says, they didn't force him to tell what he'd seen. They didn't even interview him, he says, because "they didn't question no children." For the next ten years, as Clinton Adams helped his family scratch out a living—his only reprieve the rainy days when he could attend school, and the weekly trips he made to Monroe—he told no one what he'd seen at Moore's Ford. He never even discussed it with Emerson Farmer. And yet Loy Harrison talked freely to him. He told Clinton he'd had all the blacks killed because "that damn George thought he was better than any white man." Just as Clinton Adams kept silent about what he'd seen at the Moore's Ford Bridge, he kept silent about what he heard. Yet Lewis Howard and Doc Sorrells continued to watch him closely, he says, and in 1955, when he returned to Walton County after serving in the army, Doc Sorrells told him to leave.

"Well, Doc," nineteen-year-old Clinton Adams said, "I ain't never said nothing to nobody and don't have no intentions of saying nothing."

"Yeah," Doc Sorrells said, "but some people don't know that."

So Clinton Adams got a job with a traveling carnival and met a girl named Marjorie. She was the first person he told what he'd seen at Moore's Ford, and afterward he said he'd understand if she left him. In 1959, they got married, and when their first child was born in 1960, Clinton Adams quit the carnival and got a job driving trucks in Augusta, Georgia. They were just settling into life in Augusta when a police officer stopped him on the road one day.

"We know all about you, Adams, and what you've been doing. It's time for you to move on," he said. "We don't want you too comfortable in any one place. We're afraid of what you might say."

Augusta lay more than one hundred miles from Walton County, yet the police officer knew Clinton Adams had witnessed the Moore's Ford lynching. That day, Clinton Adams went home and told Marjorie they had to leave. But just as they were getting settled in another town, Clinton Adams rushed home to tell Marjorie they had to move once again. Later, driving away in the car, she asked him, "Will we ever be able to stay in one place?"

"Not if *they* have their way, we won't," he said.

Insurance agents and encyclopedia salesmen, factory managers and fellow hunters—again and again they let Clinton Adams know they were in the Ku Klux Klan, and the Klan was watching him. And so even as the Adams family continued to grow—Clinton and Marjorie had six children by 1970—they continued on the run, moving as many as twelve times in some years, moving all over Indiana, Illinois, Georgia, and Florida. In the daylight hours, Clinton Adams remained constantly on guard, constantly looking over his shoulder, he says. At night, he suffered nightmares, his mind constantly replaying the sight of the smoke hanging in the air, and the blood bubbling out of the four bodies at Moore's Ford.

By 1989, Clinton Adams was fifty-three years old and working at a dairy farm in the Florida panhandle. Early on the morning of November 9, he went to feed the cows and found the feed mixer full of water from a heavy rain the night before. He stepped inside to bail out the water, and a few minutes later, while he was still inside, the mixer suddenly kicked on. The rotating blades caught hold of Clinton Adams's boot, then dragged in his body. Before the mixer was finally shut off, he'd lost his left leg just below the kneecap.

After weeks in the hospital, Clinton Adams was fitted with an artificial leg that allowed him to walk, but prevented him from performing the physical labor that had always been his livelihood. Even worse, without the ability to constantly find jobs in different locations, Clinton Adams could no longer dodge the Klan. "Honey," he told Marjorie one night after his accident, "I can't run no more. I've got to tell somebody." On July 17, 1991, after forty-five years of silence about the Moore's Ford lynching, he went to the FBI office in Panama City, Florida, and revealed his secret.

That July day, Clinton Adams described not only the lynching itself, but the burden of witnessing it. "Everywhere you go they had an eye on you and they was watching you," he told Special Agent

Jim Procopio. "I can't describe to you how these things has haunted me over the years." The agent listened and asked questions, struggling to follow the bends and twists in Clinton Adams's memory. At the end of the interview, he thanked Clinton Adams for coming forward. "The murder is solved as far as we're concerned, being you're an eyewitness," said Agent Procopio. "You have solved a forty-five-year-old case that was never solved."

But solved doesn't mean proven, because, as Agent Procopio quickly discovered, the four men Clinton Adams accused of participating in the lynching—Loy Harrison, Andrew and Frank Ford, and Emmett Harper—were dead by 1991. And former Walton County deputy sheriffs Doc Sorrells and Lewis Howard, the men Adams accused of pressuring him to keep silent, were also dead. Without living suspects to investigate and potentially prosecute, Agent Procopio had no rationale to investigate further. "Back then I was working a lot of other cases," says Agent Procopio, who retired from the Bureau in 1997. "This was a diversion." So he passed on the story to a reporter at the *Atlanta Journal-Constitution*, and nearly a year later an article based on Clinton Adams's account of the lynching appeared on the newspaper's front page under the headline "Murder at Moore's Ford."

Less than two months after the article's publication, Clinton Adams's story was featured on *Dateline NBC*. For the benefit of the *Dateline* reporter and viewers, Adams stood in the tall grass by the Moore's Ford Bridge and used his cane to point to the spot where he and Emerson Farmer had hidden that July afternoon in 1946. Later, sitting in his new home outside Bonifay, Florida—bought with a portion of the $2-million insurance settlement he'd received as a result of his farm accident—he explained why he'd waited so long to come forward. "I could have done it before," he said. "But if I had, and something happened to one of my children, then I would have had to live with that." Explaining why he finally did reveal his secret, he said, "I didn't do it for any glory, because there's none in it. I didn't do it for any money, because there's no money in it. And I'm not trying to be no hero. I just want to live my life with my family. That's all I want."

But Clinton Adams did become a kind of hero. Soon after his appearance on *Dateline*, he was invited to appear alongside Mamie Till-Mobley, the mother of Emmett Till, and Myrlie Evers Williams, the wife of slain civil rights leader Medgar Evers, on an episode of *Oprah* devoted to unsolved hate crimes. Once again he told the story of the Moore's Ford lynching and described how witnessing it had ruined his life.

"So, could you go back to Walton County now?" Oprah Winfrey asked.

Yes, Clinton Adams said, but he wouldn't be comfortable doing so. "There's a lot of people there," he said, "and they—they feel a lot of hate."

"Still?" Oprah Winfrey asked.

"Yes. Because if you don't think so, you go down and talk about it a little bit and you'll find out."

"Don't think I will," Oprah Winfrey said, and she and the studio audience laughed.

In the wake of his national media appearances, Clinton Adams was formally commended by the Georgia House of Representatives for his "courage, honesty, and willingness to pursue justice." Because, although his confession didn't lead to justice—for the men he named were dead, unpunishable—it produced something that some viewed as nearly as valuable: an authoritative account of the lynching. Many had told stories of the lynching and many still would, but none could be believed like Clinton Adams. Only he, an eyewitness, could say Loy Harrison held a gun and fired again and again. Only he could say three other white men were also guilty. And only he could tell a story that was whole and complete, a story whose villains had names. Only Clinton Adams could rise above the rumors and gossip and uncertainty and finally provide closure.

The desire for closure, which is as strong a desire as exists, led many people—FBI agents, reporters, lawmakers, citizens—to accept Clinton Adams's account of the lynching without rigorously investigating it. And that same desire for closure allows many to continue to believe it, even in the face of serious conflicts.

By the time Clinton Adams came forward in 1991, Emerson Farmer was, like the four men Adams named as shooters, and the two deputy sheriffs, unavailable to refute his story. After being convicted of a string of burglaries as a teenager, Emerson Farmer had left Walton County for the north-Georgia mountains. Then, in 1980, at the age of forty-five, he'd abruptly disappeared. His disappearance remained a mystery until April 1989—roughly six months before Clinton Adams suffered his devastating farm accident—when his remains were discovered in a trash pit six miles northwest of the town of Blairsville, Georgia. As was later revealed during a murder trial, he'd been fatally shot by his sister-in-law—with whom he'd fathered children—after he'd allegedly beat her son. Then she and his wife had dumped his body in the trash pit and reported him missing.

Emerson Farmer himself wasn't available in 1991, but his testimony was. Clinton Adams told Agent Procopio that "Emerson was never questioned [by the FBI]. Emerson is the kind of person that he wouldn't tell anything." But he was wrong on both accounts. Emerson Farmer was indeed questioned by the FBI in 1946. And what he told them directly conflicts with Clinton Adams's account of the lynching.

According to the FBI's report, Emerson Farmer spent the afternoon of July 25, 1946, sitting on his porch. Late in the day, he saw five cars pass—Loy Harrison's car in the middle—and shortly afterward, he heard a blast of gunfire coming from Moore's Ford. He didn't leave the porch until long after the shooting had ceased, when he and his father walked down to the bridge to watch the coroner's inquest. Agents reinterviewed Emerson Farmer several times throughout their four-month investigation. According to sources familiar with the FBI's complete investigative report, not once did he mention that Clinton Adams was visiting him that afternoon, or that they'd taken a cow to graze in the woods near Moore's Ford. Neither Emerson Farmer's father nor his mother mentioned Clinton Adams when interviewed by agents. And though Emerson Farmer's younger brother and sister, Ralph and Della Farmer, were too young to be interviewed in 1946, when interviewed in 1998, both said they were home on the afternoon of the lynching, and they're certain Clinton Adams wasn't visiting them.

Further, Frank and Gladys Taylor, the black couple who'd listened to *Amos 'n' Andy* with George and Mae Murray Dorsey the summer before they were lynched, remember that the Farmers' cow was grazing in their pasture on the afternoon of the lynching— not in the woods near the Moore's Ford Bridge, as Clinton Adams claims. "I know the Farmers' cow was with our cow," says Gladys Taylor. Given that the Taylors lived between the Farmers' house and Good Hope, where Clinton Adams lived in July 1946, he would've had to pass their house to get home that day. Yet, while the Taylors saw many cars pass on July 25, they did not see Clinton Adams racing home on his horse.

Neither did anyone who lived near the Moore's Ford Bridge, according to the FBI's 1946 report, which investigators say doesn't mention Clinton Adams's name once in roughly ten thousand pages. Certainly it's possible he escaped agents' notice, but given that they interviewed roughly three thousand people—including nearly a dozen children—during four months in Walton County, it's unlikely his name would never have come to their attention. Clinton Adams's absence from the FBI report—a document that does, in contrast, mention his elder sisters, Ruth and Effie May, as well as the death of their father—in conjunction with the fact that his story conflicts with Emerson Farmer's, raises the possibility that his account of the lynching isn't altogether accurate. Perhaps Clinton Adams was so terrorized by the atmosphere surrounding the lynching that he imagined he witnessed it, and now truly believes he did. Or perhaps he pieced together his "eyewitness account" from rumors, gossip, newspaper articles, and conversations with Loy Harrison, Emerson Farmer, and others. Certainly, Adams's statement that the lynching sounded like a "fire in a canebrake" is an exact repeat of Riden Farmer's comment on the day after the lynching. And his statement that the black women's screams sounded "like an animal caught in a trap" echoes imagery used in *Reprisal*. Perhaps he waited until everyone who could contradict him was dead—or so he thought, given he didn't know the FBI's 1946 report existed. Perhaps he came forward as a way of banishing fear, of claiming power, or of re-creating himself as a hero. But since these possibilities are as unprovable as Adams's story itself, the only thing to do is what agents did with Loy Harrison's alibi in 1946: examine it point by point.

"One thing for sure," says Clinton Adams, "I have consistently told the same story every time I've been interviewed. It is burned into my memory." But a close comparison of the statements made by Adams in his testimony to Agent Procopio; during his interviews with members of the media; and in *The Secret Inside*, a 1999 book written and published by his wife, reveals troubling inconsistencies. The most glaring pertains to the number of lynchers he saw at Moore's Ford on July 25. In 1991, Clinton Adams told Agent Procopio there were roughly twelve men in the mob, and that four men fired the initial shots. But in his wife's book, he claims there were sixteen to eighteen men in the mob, and that one man fired the first shots. In 1991, he told the FBI that he'd heard that a white farmer used his tractor to block the road leading to Moore's Ford. But, in *The Secret Inside*, he claims he himself saw the man's tractor blocking the road. During an interview in 1999, he said he picked up a tooth on the day after the lynching; in the book, he says it was his sister who did so.

An examination of Adams's claims regarding his life after the lynching also raises questions. In her book, Marjorie Adams writes that Clinton took her to meet the family of George Dorsey and Dorothy Malcom in Georgia in 1959. Given that Jim Williams died in 1947 or 1948, and Moena, Charlie Boy, and Ruby Dorsey moved to Shelby, North Carolina—where Moena's first husband, Columbus Dorsey, lived—in 1949, it's unlikely such a visit could have taken place. Further, Clinton Adams claims that the Ku Klux Klan tailed him throughout his life because of what he'd witnessed at Moore's Ford. But, according to the FBI's 1946 report, there was no active Klan chapter in the area in 1946, and no evidence that the mob at Moore's Ford was organized by the Klan—though it's certain some of the men in the mob were past, or even future, members. Moreover, by 1946 and thereafter, the Klan wasn't organized enough or resourceful enough to effect the kind of multistate surveillance Clinton Adams describes. And though Adams has talked extensively about his fear of the Klan, he worked for a Klan member named Billy Perkins for several years in the 1980s. In fact, Billy Perkins, the owner of a dairy near Walton County, laughed out loud when he saw the 1992 article in the *Atlanta Journal-Constitution*. "Clinton says in the article that he was always being followed by the Klan," Billy Perkins says. "I was in the Klan. I still have my robe over there at the house. If he were frightened of the Klan, why would he want to work for me?" In the same vein, Clinton Adams has made several statements about his mortal fear of returning to Walton County. But he and his family have visited the county several times throughout the years and have lived in the area for months at a time.

On some occasions, Clinton Adams has claimed he harbored guilt for being unable to save George and Dorothy on July 25, 1946, and has said he contacted the FBI to get the story off his chest. But during other interviews Adams has said he contacted the FBI not because he wanted to pursue justice long-deferred, but because the lawyer he hired to sue the dairy farm warned him to air old secrets in the interest of building an airtight legal case. As Adams says, "The lawyer said, 'You better talk to the FBI.'" Had he never lost his leg, he says, he would've taken his story to the grave. When asked whether he's bothered by the possibility that some of the lynchers—some he recognized—might still be living, Adams says, "It don't bother me one bit. I don't dwell on it." And despite having professed affection for George Dorsey in Marjorie's book and in several earlier interviews, in a 1999 interview Adams called George "that nigger lived beside us" and said, "He wasn't like no big brother." Adams "didn't have much associating" with him.

By 1999, Clinton Adams was wishing he'd never said anything about the Moore's Ford lynching. He'd become so tired of reporters asking him to tell his story that he'd instituted a price for interviews: $1,000 per hour. "If that doesn't make it end," he said, "I'll raise the price." But when Adams did get talking, he again contradicted himself. Though he claimed in 1991 that he recognized only *four* men at the Moore's Ford Bridge that afternoon, he claimed in 1999 that he recognized *seven*. He'd only told four names to the FBI, he said, because he's saving the rest to give to his grandchildren, so they can publish the story and make money off it.

"When it's published, it will tell the whole thing. I try to stay as close to the truth, right on the truth, as I can remember. Because there's only one story," he says. "Of course there will be holes in it, but I intend for that."

When confronted with the conflicts in his testimony, Clinton Adams says, "God is my witness. That is the truth." But Adams's story—like every story of the Moore's Ford lynching—gets blurrier the closer one looks. The closer one looks, the more one realizes that his account may be no more accurate than Loy Harrison's, that the closure it provides may well be false. But many people in Walton and Oconee counties didn't look closely at his story when it broke in 1992. Those whose relatives or friends were implicated by his story simply rejected it outright. The relatives of Andrew and Frank Ford hired a lawyer to try to pursue a suit against Clinton Adams, and the son of Emmett Harper publicly denied his father's guilt. Randall Whitehead, a friend of Loy Harrison's who lives near the Moore's Ford Bridge, called Clinton Adams's story "the biggest lie ever been told," and Jamey Harrison, the grandson of Loy Harrison, says he thinks Clinton Adams's allegations are unfair. He says there's no doubt his grandfather was once a member of the Klan, and there's no doubt he hit his tenants, but there's never been any proof he was involved in the lynching. "He was a good man. He was my hero," says Jamey Harrison, who inherited six hundred acres of Loy Harrison's land after he died of a heart attack in 1987. "It bothers me that they want to make these black people out to be martyrs."

The sons of former deputy sheriffs Lewis Howard and Doc Sorrells responded to Clinton Adams's allegations against their fathers by declaring them absolutely untrue. Their fathers, they say, would've never urged Clinton Adams to keep silent if he'd seen the lynching. And they would never have had the time to watch over him to ensure he stayed silent. Barney Howard, the son of Lewis Howard, says he never once heard his father mention Clinton Adams; he hadn't even heard Clinton Adams's name before seeing it in the *Atlanta Journal-Constitution*. And Marvin Sorrells, the son of Doc Sorrells, says Adams's claims aren't "worthy of dignifying with a response." According to him, the failure to solve the lynching was a "great tragedy" in his father's life. "My daddy just said, 'If the FBI left us alone, we'd have brought them to court and convicted them,' " he says.

Beyond his personal disagreement with Clinton Adams's story, Marvin Sorrells, who is Walton County's senior superior court judge, doubts the benefits of "bringing up" the lynching. "If all it's going to do is stir up old memories, it can't do anything but hurt folks. Who wants to talk about Nagasaki and Hiroshima? Who wants to talk about Dachau?" he says. "Well, probably those things need to be kept alive, but this thing, I don't see anything positive to come from it." In a similar spirit, William Gregg, a member of the Walton County Board of Commissioners, called the lynching a "skeleton in the closet that doesn't need to be brought back out." And one Monroe insurance salesman said he would "just as soon not fool around" with the issue of the lynching. "Most people I know could care less about it," he said. "I've got other issues that I'm trying to work on . . . to try to help Monroe and Walton County be a better place to live."

Indeed, in the weeks, months, and years following the publication of Clinton Adams's story, many white citizens of Walton and Oconee counties did what their forebears had done in 1946. They criticized the attention paid to the Moore's Ford lynching and said that the lynching wasn't news. It was just a murder, the act of a "wanton few"—not an incident of collective violence. Some said and continue to say that the lynching resulted from a bootlegging feud. "The whole thing was economic," says Barney Howard. "One black guy was bootlegging for Loy Harrison and then decided to work for someone else."

The fact that neither the Moore's Ford lynching nor the county's three previous recorded lynchings are documented in the official history, *Wayfarers in Walton*, proves the county succeeded at officially forgetting its legacy of lynching—at least until Clinton Adams resurfaced. Much to the dismay of those who hoped that talk of the Moore's Ford lynching would die out within a few months of Clinton Adams's revelation, as it had in the wake of the publication of *Reprisal*, the talk continued. Historians began to mention the lynching in articles and books about postwar Georgia, and several documentarians spent time in the county filming footage and interviewing people.

In July 1997, when a small group of black and white citizens from Walton, Oconee, and surrounding counties met at First African Baptist Church in Monroe, it became clear that talk about the lynching wouldn't end anytime soon—and maybe not ever. The gathering of teachers, lawyers, businesspeople, and laborers named themselves the Moore's Ford Memorial Committee. Just as the members of the newly formed Walton County Civic League had vowed on a spring day in 1946 to register every eligible black person in the county in time for the July 17 primary election, the members of the newly formed Moore's Ford Memorial Committee vowed that summer day to unearth the lynching and publicly memorialize its victims. And then to begin healing the community.

On the afternoon of May 16, 1998, a crowd of one hundred black and white people gathered in the auditorium of Carver Middle School on Good Hope Road, on the outskirts of downtown Monroe. The people came from Atlanta and Athens, and from Oconee and Walton counties. Some were pushed in strollers, and others in wheelchairs. Some knew nothing about the Moore's Ford lynching, except that it had happened. Others had lived through it and still didn't know much. Many who came to the cool, dark auditorium were doing something they'd never believed was possible: attending a public memorial service for Roger and Dorothy Malcom, and George and Mae Murray Dorsey.

A white pastor from a church in Oconee County offered the service's opening invocation, and then a white man named Richard Rusk—founder of the Moore's Ford Memorial Committee, and son of the late Dean Rusk, a former U.S. secretary of state—took the podium. He asked the crowd to recall the atmosphere of fear and reprisal that had silenced two entire counties fifty-two years before. He asked the crowd to remember nineteen-year-old Lamar Howard, who'd been beaten for his testimony to the grand jury, and to honor Clinton Adams, whom the committee had taken as their inspiration. (Clinton and Marjorie Adams were not in attendance that day, though Marjorie Adams claims in her book that they were.) And Rich Rusk urged people to support the healing mission of the Moore's Ford Memorial Committee, which extended to all those affected by the lynching. "As we reach out to the Malcoms and Dorseys, we need to reach out further to another set of victims, and these are the descendants and the family members of the men who did these killings back in 1946," Rich Rusk said. "There are hundreds of such people in our two counties, and for every one of those who takes a secret pride, I can assure you there are ten or twenty that are absolutely ashamed about what happened."

After that, there were songs by church choirs, black and white, and then a black man named Robert Howard, who'd learned about the lynchings in 1968 when Dan Young showed him the photographs taken of the bodies in his funeral home, stepped to the podium. When he spoke the name of each victim, a family member came forward to light a candle. George Dorsey Jr., the youngest son of Charlie Boy and Ruby Dorsey, lit two candles for George and Dorothy, the uncle and aunt he'd never known. "I really can't say it all," he said. "All I can say is thank you."

Betty Foster, who was seven years old at the time of the lynching, stepped forward to light a candle for her second cousin, Mae Murray Dorsey. "I'm proud to be able to speak for the family," she said. "Everybody connected with the Moore's Ford lynching has been afraid to say anything these many years."

Fifty-four-year-old Roger Malcom Hayes Sr., who was two years old when Roger Malcom was lynched, lit a candle for the father he had no memory of. He'd been adopted by a family in Toledo, Ohio, when he was four and had known since he was six that his father had been lynched—though until he read the *Atlanta Journal-Constitution* article in 1992, he thought his father had been hung, not shot, to death. "Praise the Lord," he said, as he stepped to the podium. "That's my greeting. I'm a Holy Ghost–filled preacher."

Then Robert Howard took the podium again and announced the afternoon's surprise guest: Mrs. Moena Williams, mother of George Dorsey and Dorothy Malcom. "Because of threats, Miss Moena didn't get to go to her children's funeral in 1946," said

Robert Howard. "But . . . we made sure she'd be here today." The crowd offered a collective gasp as a shrunken black woman was pushed onstage in a wheelchair. Moena Williams had been forty-six in 1946; she was now ninety-eight. Her mind gone, she stared blankly out at the audience as two red roses were placed into her lap. She couldn't appreciate the symbolism of the moment, but the audience members could. Some sat in stunned silence, others wept.

When the memorial service ended a short while later, the crowd filed out of the auditorium and into cars and buses for the procession to Moore's Ford. On July 25, 1946, a fine red dust had risen from the dirt roads leading to the bridge, as the members of the lynch mob hurried to get there before Loy Harrison. But on May 16, 1998, the cars moved slowly along the smooth, paved roads. In 1946, the drivers passed miles of cotton fields. On this day in 1998, the drivers passed fields of pine trees planted in rows, and just as many fields of stumps, where the trees had been cut, stacked onto trucks, and delivered to paper mills. Farther south, near Blasingame district, there were still working farms, though they were large operations, not the one- and two-horse farms of a half century before. One man planted cotton by the road, but it was for nostalgia, not profit. Near the Moore's Ford Bridge, farming had almost completely disappeared by the 1970s. The landowners had converted their cotton fields into timber or horse farms, or sold them to housing developments. The sharecroppers, tenant farmers, and field hands, who owned no land to convert or sell, had moved to Athens or Atlanta, or into Monroe, where many had found work at the sewing factory and the chicken plant.

Nearly eight miles out of Monroe, the procession came to the fork in the road where the Fanny Wright house sits. In 1946, the road cut so close, it nearly came in the front door. But the road had been paved and rerouted, and now the Fanny Wright house sits at the crest of a sweeping carpet of grass, its dark green roof and shutters resplendent against freshly painted white clapboard. On this May day in 1998, there was no evidence that the house had ever fallen into disrepair, that it had ever been occupied by a family of black farmhands. There was no evidence of the little white house where the Adams family had lived for a year before being forced to leave. No doubt that little house had fallen to the ground or folded in upon itself and then been dismantled, providing a winter month's worth of firewood.

Had the cars turned left at the fork that afternoon, they'd soon have passed the turn-off to Mt. Enon Church, where the sound of singing could still be heard on the one or two Sundays each month when services were held. On those Sundays, cars lined the rutted road to the church; no one walked to Mt. Enon anymore, because almost no black people lived near the Moore's Ford Bridge. Farther on lay the Atlanta–Athens highway, now known as Highway 78, now a busy four-lane thoroughfare.

But the procession turned right at the fork and headed down toward the Apalachee River. Had it been 1946, they'd have driven past the house where Emerson Farmer sat on the porch and watched Loy Harrison's car pass, sandwiched between four other cars, on the day of the lynching. That house was gone, replaced by a field of grazing horses. Across the road, several For Sale signs advertised the houses nestled back in the trees, back near the spot where Clinton Adams said he was hiding that July afternoon.

In 1946, the road led down a hill to a narrow wooden bridge whose boards knocked—the sound echoing off the water—when a car passed over. In 1998, the road curved before reaching a wide cement bridge. Thick gray paint blotched the bridge; in honor of the day's event, the sheriffs of Walton and Oconee counties had given orders for the racist graffiti usually found scrawled there—"to meny nigers crosed this bridge"—to be concealed. Below the bridge, the Apalachee River gurgled. In fifty years, it hadn't silted up or become polluted. Its banks were still lined with mountain laurel and wild rhododendron, and with stalks of river cane.

The procession ended on the Walton County side of the Moore's Ford Bridge, near the spot where Loy Harrison said the mob ambushed his car. Those in the crowd who were able left the paved road and walked down through tall grass and thistle, and trash and beer bottles, to stand on the power-line trail that follows the road Loy Harrison took on July 25, 1946. The trail leads to the riverbank, where the stone foundation that once anchored the old bridge remains, marking the spot where the lynchers dragged their victims from Loy Harrison's car. Turning toward the thick woods just downriver, people squinted, trying to detect a trace of the old wagon trail. Several walked into the woods, looking for bullet holes in tree trunks, looking for the clearing. They soon gave up and walked back onto the road to gather at the entrance to the bridge.

After songs and prayers, Chris Culbreath, a black city councilman from Monroe, took the podium. "It is my belief that our collective communities in Oconee and Walton counties got stuck at this bridge on July twenty-fifth, 1946," he said, his deep, booming voice amplified by the river. "We got stuck in fear, we got stuck in hate. We got stuck in hopelessness."

Then, looking up to the sky, he addressed the four victims: "We are here to take this red clay of Georgia that has been stained by your blood and mold it into a brick of brotherhood. And then we shall take those bricks and build a nation where . . . every living thing is respected."

Under the glaring sun, people fanned themselves and sipped water from paper cups. The heat of the day and the improbability of such an event made some a little faint.

"The healing process has been delayed for fifty years by fear and a code of silence," a black preacher said. "Let us dedicate this river bridge to the memory of the lynching, and designate May sixteenth as a Day of Healing."

Then the people in the crowd linked hands and began to walk across the bridge singing "We Shall Overcome." Some lingered halfway, tossing rose petals into the water and waiting until they'd floated out of sight. But soon everyone reached the other side of the river.

Later that evening, when a local television news station aired a report about the memorial service, a woman in Athens caught a fleeting glimpse of her mother slumped in a wheelchair onstage at Carver Middle School. Within a few days, it became clear that the Moore's Ford committee had made a mistake. The Moena Williams they'd brought to the memorial service was not the mother of George and Dorothy Dorsey. Investigation later revealed that she'd died of cervical cancer in Shelby, North Carolina, on November 15, 1955. She was fifty-five years old; her children had been dead for nine years. Moena Williams, the mother of George and Dorothy Dorsey, had been buried at Pine Grove Church near Shelby. In 1989, a tornado destroyed the church and cemetery, and the tin marker that had once identified her grave went missing. But, as late as 1998, one church member still remembered reading Moena Williams's obituary aloud at her funeral in 1955. "No one ever put flowers on her grave," the woman said. "I've always wondered, where was her people?"

The mistake about Moena Williams, however embarrassing,

didn't stop the Moore's Ford Memorial Committee from continuing its efforts. On a Sunday afternoon seven months later, cars
streamed into the grass parking lot of Mount Perry Missionary
Baptist Church. Reporters and photographers stood in the churchyard, just as they had before George and Dorothy's funeral on July
28, 1946. Inside, when the preacher stepped to the lectern, more
people filled the pews than had that Sunday in 1946, and more than
half of them were white.

After the service, the people followed the preacher and the committee members to the far side of the cemetery, to a double grave
that had been identified by a black woman who'd attended the joint
funeral in 1946. The crowd watched as members of the Moore's
Ford Memorial Committee unveiled a granite grave marker bearing the birth and death dates of Dorothy Malcom and George
Dorsey, and the words "May Your Suffering Be Redeemed in
Brotherly Love."

Undertaker Dan Young wasn't there to witness the marking of
the graves he'd prepared a half century before. He'd died eleven
years before, his body laid out by employees at his funeral home—
which had, by then, moved from the Corner to elegant quarters on
Monroe's main street. But Boyzie Daniels, the young black man
who'd struggled to register black voters in Blasingame in 1946, was
in the cemetery that day. After he'd testified at the grand jury, a man
had visited him and warned he'd be beaten like Lamar Howard if he
didn't leave town. Boyzie Daniels didn't leave town, and he wasn't
beaten. He said he'd tried to keep the lynching investigation going,
even after the FBI left. But when he'd preached about the lynching
at Chestnut Grove Church in the first years after 1946, he'd felt as
alone as he had when he'd urged blacks to vote. "The people would
become more depressed and more nervous and more shaky," he

says. "It got to where they were willing to let it alone, put it in the hands of the Lord. Nobody was willing to suffer for it." He said he was glad something was finally being done. It gave him hope.

Neither Charlie Boy Dorsey nor Robert Elder was there to see George and Dorothy's graves marked that Sunday in 1998. Charlie Boy had died in 1985 in Shelby, North Carolina, and Robert Elder had died years before in Chattanooga, Tennessee—where he'd finally moved, despite Loy Harrison's attempts to prevent him from leaving his farm. But Ruby Dorsey was in the crowd. That Sunday she saw her brother- and sister-in-law's graves for the first time; she'd missed their funeral in 1946 because she was in Greensboro, Georgia, preparing for her father's funeral. She and her three sons still lived in Greensboro, where they'd moved after a few difficult years in Shelby. Charlie Boy had got violent after his brother and sister were killed, she says. Moena had got worse too. When she ran out of liquor, she drank rubbing alcohol. The last time Ruby Dorsey had seen Charlie Boy was in 1970; the last time she'd seen Moena was in 1951. Ruby Dorsey said she'd told the FBI as much as she could in 1946, but she'd never told them about the shotgun she found near Loy Harrison's barn a few months after the lynching. "What I should have done was steal one of the bullets from that gun," she says. "But I was living on his place, and I was scared." Fifty-two years after the lynching, Ruby Dorsey still believed as strongly as she had in 1946 that Loy Harrison was "in on it."

After leaving Mount Perry, the crowd traveled on to Monroe and drove through downtown, past the courthouse with its four-sided clock tower, and the Walton County Medical Center, which had replaced the tiny hospital where Barnette Hester had been taken the night he was stabbed. Just beyond a sign advertising B & B Small Engine Repair, the procession turned off the road and parked in front of a thick grove of trees. Only after the people stepped out of their cars did they glimpse the gray headstones and realize that the trees concealed the old Zion Hill cemetery. Moving closer, they saw that only a few of the stones stood upright; the rest were upended, lying on their sides, cracked, and separated from the graves they'd once marked. Then they saw the body-sized depressions in the ground: sunken graves. And, stepping over the drainage ditch that had been run through the center of the cemetery, and walking to the far edge, they discovered that B & B Small Engine Repair had been built on top of graves.

When Mae Murray was buried on July 28, 1946, a black church sat alongside Zion Hill cemetery. But the Zion Hill congregation had sold the land under the church in the 1950s and moved across town to larger quarters. And once the church moved, the cemetery was forgotten, left to disappear behind trees and vines that grew thicker with each year. Workers at the office complex just across the parking lot said that before the Moore's Ford committee spent months cutting back the brush and vines, they hadn't known there was a cemetery there.

Since no one had been able to identify the grave where Mae Murray was buried, the committee had placed her marker near the graves of her relatives. After unveiling it that afternoon, they went on to the cemetery at Chestnut Grove Church, where they unveiled the last marker at a grave identified by Roger Malcom's cousin, who'd passed it on his way to school each morning. By sundown on December 13, 1998, the graves of the four victims of the Moore's Ford lynching were marked, their shared death date—July 25, 1946—written into granite.

Six months after that, a crowd gathered on Highway 78 six miles east of Monroe, at the place where Loy Harrison turned off on July 25, 1946. There, the Moore's Ford committee unveiled a state historical marker titled "Moore's Ford Lynching."

It is the only historical marker in Georgia that commemorates a lynching, and it says that George and Mae Murray Dorsey, and Roger and Dorothy Malcom, were brutally beaten and shot by an unmasked mob following an argument between Roger Malcom and a local white farmer. It says that their unsolved murders played a crucial role in both President Truman's commitment to civil rights legislation and the ensuing modern civil rights movement. And it says that in 1998 a memorial service was held at the Moore's Ford Bridge to honor the victims.

Most of all, it says that the Moore's Ford lynching is a historical fact.

But it isn't only history.

As the Moore's Ford Memorial Committee focused on commemoration and healing, Roy Jackson lay in a hospital bed in a four-room house in one of Monroe's black neighborhoods, saying he was still angry at George Dorsey for ruining the parties at the Fanny Wright house, and for getting too close to the eldest Adams girls. "He knew there was gonna be trouble when he did it," said Roy Jackson, "and he went ahead and did it."

Roy Jackson—the man FBI agents had hoped would supply their big break in 1946—was eighty-four years old and dying of cancer in 1998. Though he kept his pistol handy, as he'd done all his life, he was too weak to use it. And perhaps Roy Jackson was too weak to resist when an FBI agent from the bureau in Athens, Georgia, pulled a chair up to his bedside and asked him the same question agents had asked him in 1946. Because he finally answered. He said he and the Thrasher brothers bought liquor up in Oconee County on the afternoon before the lynching. On the way home, they tried to cross the Moore's Ford Bridge, but stopped suddenly when they saw the mob. "I seen the white folks and them colored folks standing there," said Roy Jackson. "I took off and backed up. On my left-hand side, I hit a stump. I took off and went around the road, come across the river further down, hit Walton County, and come right there at Moore's Ford and give out of gas. We sat there about an hour. ∴ . . And all them cars were coming by. About fifty, seventy-five cars."

Roy Jackson's voice was gravelly from age, and from the cancer that was killing him. At times he talked loudly, and at other times his statements sounded more like questions. "Mr. Lewis Howard, I seen him down there. I seen Mr. Carl Aycock. I seen Mr. Doc Sorrells," he said. "But they was so many it was hard to see. There were cars just like somebody going to a funeral."

When the FBI agent asked if any of the men Roy Jackson saw were still alive, he told them the names of two white men, one living in Walton County and one in Oconee County. By the time agents interviewed the two white men, Roy Jackson was dead. After both men denied involvement in the lynching, the agents' inquiry ended—making Roy Jackson's testimony one more unconfirmable story of the Moore's Ford lynching.

More than a year later, Georgia governor Roy Barnes responded to calls for action from the state's black lawmakers by ordering the GBI to conduct a full reinvestigation of the Moore's Ford lynching. By then, the handful of bullets and few lengths of rope transferred to GBI headquarters in 1954 had disappeared. The only evidence available was the FBI's 1946 report. After agents from the GBI's Athens bureau spent a week poring over the ten-thousand-page report, they identified only three suspects listed in the report who were still living. Loy Harrison was gone, of course. Weldon Hester had died of a brain aneurysm in 1958. Alvin Adcock had died in 1953, four years after the perjury charges against him were dropped. And James Verner was dead, as well. Nearly twenty other men who'd been suspects in the FBI's 1946 investigation lay buried in the cemetery behind Union Chapel Methodist Church, and in cemeteries throughout Walton and Oconee counties.

But there were three suspects from the 1946 investigation who were still living, so the agents drove out to Blasingame district to interview them. One woman refused to let them inside her house to talk to her husband. He's too sick, she said. Since the agents didn't have a warrant, they couldn't press any further.

But Jack Malcom did agree to talk briefly with agents. In 1946, he'd been labeled a suspect after he'd given conflicting alibis for the day of the lynching—first saying he hadn't left home, then admitting to going to Monroe before receiving a visit from Hughlon Peters at roughly 7:30 P.M. That he'd returned from the army just one day before the lynching had raised agents' suspicions that he was the sidekick Loy Harrison said held a gun on him at the Moore's Ford Bridge. Late in 1999, Jack Malcom stood in front of his house in Blasingame district, and recalled standing there with an FBI agent a half century before. "What he try to tell me was that I was at Moore's Ford," he said. "I was not. I was at home. I said, 'Whatever you're saying, you're a damn liar, and the truth ain't in you.'"

At seventy-eight, Jack Malcom was thin and frail. Standing in his front yard, he spread his arms wide and talked about the first Hesters and Malcoms to settle on the surrounding land. He talked about his grandfather, who fought in the Civil War, and about his own service in World War II, when he was wounded in his left ear. He talked a lot about the man who pushed the button that dropped the atomic bomb on Nagasaki—what he'd have to reckon with in the afterlife. When asked if he'd participated in the Moore's Ford lynching, Jack Malcom said: "Somebody done the work, but I have no idea who. It's that simple. I got a witness that knows I wasn't there: God."

When agents knocked on the door of Hughlon Peters's house on Hestertown Road, he also agreed to answer their questions. Back in 1946, he'd told agents that on July 25, after returning from the hospital at about 1 P.M., he'd remained home until 5 P.M., when he'd driven to visit Jack Malcom. This conflicted with Jack Malcom's claim that Hughlon Peters didn't visit him until 7:30 P.M. That, coupled with Hughlon Peters's claim that he'd first heard about the lynching on the radio at 7 or 8 A.M. the following morning, had made Hughlon Peters a suspect.

When interviewed in 1999, seventy-seven-year-old Hughlon Peters sat in a chair and said, "I'll be dogged if I know about that killing." After pausing, he went on, "Don't know nothing about it. I wasn't up there then. I didn't know."

Asked why he was named as a suspect, he shook his head. "Never even been to Moore's Ford then," he said. "Didn't know they killed them till they done killed them." But, when pressed, he admitted, "I know a lot of Hesters were in it. I just heard it—that is all I'll say."

Hughlon Peters had grown hard of hearing in the years since 1946. When he turned to question his wife, whose father, Melvin Hester, had been a suspect in the lynching, he shouted, "I don't think the Hesters killed anybody at Moore's Ford, did they?" He had seemingly forgotten that, just minutes before, he said he knew a lot of Hesters were "in it." His wife shook her head, and they both went back to watching TV.

After the interviews with Jack Malcom and Hughlon Peters, there were few leads for the agents to follow. They attempted to find the GBI and FBI agents who'd worked the case in 1946, but located only former FBI agent Louis Hutchinson, who'd recorded his memories of the investigation, including the failure of the lead about Roy Jackson and the Thrashers to break the case, in his autobiography. Agents took no more action on the Moore's Ford lynching case until April 2001, when a white man contacted the editor of the *Walton Tribune* and named five men he claimed took part in the lynching. "It was a family secret hidden for so long," said the man, a Walton County citizen in his twenties who declined to be identified. "But I've heard the same story from three different people— they did it, and they know they did it." One of the man's family members had even described how "he jerked the boy who did the stabbing out of the car and roughed him up."

When the GBI investigated the five men, they discovered that three were dead, and none had been mentioned in the FBI's 1946 report. They contacted the two men who were living, but got nowhere; one man was sixty-seven years old, which meant he would have been twelve at the time of the lynching.

In June 2001, nearly fifty-five years after then Georgia governor Ellis Arnall offered a $10,000 reward for information leading to the arrest and conviction of those responsible for the Moore's Ford lynching, Georgia governor Roy Barnes offered a new reward of $17,000, which the Georgia Association of Black Elected Officials immediately bumped up to $25,000. Echoing Governor Arnall's sentiments of more than a half century earlier, Governor Barnes issued a statement saying, "This was an unspeakable crime, and we owe it to the families of those murdered to find out who did this."

Just a month before the governor announced his reward, a white man named Thomas Blanton Jr. was found guilty of first-degree murder and given four life sentences for his role in the 1963 bombing of the Sixteenth Street church in Birmingham, Alabama, that claimed the lives of four black girls. And several years before, in 1994, a white man named Byron De La Beckwith, who assassinated civil rights leader Medgar Evers in Mississippi in 1963, was convicted of murder—after being found innocent during two trials in

1964. Many wanted the state of Georgia to mount a similar effort to get justice in the Moore's Ford lynching.

But the convictions of Beckwith and Blanton were won with evidence; in Beckwith's case, prosecutors discovered his confession in a book that had been out of print for twenty years. They also recovered the murder weapon, the transcript of Beckwith's first trial, part of a police report, and several crime scene photos. In Blanton's case, the jury convicted largely on the basis of surreptitious recordings made by the FBI in 1963. The Moore's Ford lynching occurred nearly two decades before these crimes, and not a scrap of physical evidence remains. Even if someone were to confess to taking part in the lynching, it's likely the confession would be unprovable. Even if a suspected murder weapon were found in an attic or a basement, there are no bullets from the crime scene to compare it with. The Moore's Ford lynching, in short, is not a case to be solved. There will be no justice.

In the absence of justice, people all over Walton and Oconee counties continue to do what they've done since the first days after the lynching: tell stories.

Roger Malcom's picture is taped to the wall in Mattie Louise Campbell's house in a Monroe housing project, in the front room where she spends her days lying on a couch, looking out the window, and selling sodas and Popsicles to the neighborhood children who knock softly on her front door and put coins into her lined palm. She's had three husbands since she married Roger Malcom in 1943, but he remains her one true love, she says.

The fall after he was lynched, Mattie Louise stayed in Hestertown for the cotton harvest. When the other pickers gossiped in the field, she pricked her ears. "I did everything I could to try to find out who was in the lynching," she says. "I would have made a good undercover cop. I went with a bunch of people to get drunk, and I listened." But after the cotton settle, she gave up. "It was taking too much out of me," she says. "I was losing friends. I had to watch my back." When another man asked her to marry him, she moved out to Toledo, Ohio, and took Roger Jr. with her. But a few months later, she says, she found her new husband in bed with a preacher's wife. She left him, rented a room, found a job as a waitress, and began drinking. She'd drink before her shift, and afterward. Then she'd drink to go to sleep. She needed it to numb her grief. "I was a mean black girl, especially after they killed my husband," she says. "I hate so much, my hair stand on end."

When the couple who rented her the room offered to adopt Roger Jr., she let them. "I did not want him raised in Georgia, with people picking at him like they picked at me," she says. "Our colored would have been picking at him if the white didn't." She left Roger Jr. in Toledo—where he became Roger Malcom Hayes Sr.—and went to Florida, then on to Atlanta, where she worked as a maid for a Jewish woman whose family had perished in the Holocaust. That woman, she says, was a role model. Years later, when Mattie Louise became a Christian, she was able to forgive. She realized Satan was in the lynchers, that the devil had made them do what they did. "You got to forgive," she says. "That's the only way you can live in this world." But, lying on the couch in her front room, smoking her last cigarette down to the nub, Mattie Louise makes it clear she hasn't forgiven Dorothy. "It was that whore's fault," she says. "One whore, nothing else."

And when members of the Moore's Ford Memorial Committee visit to invite her to attend their events, Mattie Louise usually declines. She'd like them to give her money instead. So would her son. "I'm interested in justice," he says, "but money, too. It's like hot coffee spilled—how much is a life worth?" If he ever has the time to pursue it, Roger Malcom Hayes Sr. says he'll solicit damages from Walton and Oconee Counties.

Fifteen miles from Mattie Louise's house, in a trailer outside the tiny town of Statham, Georgia, Ruth Adams looks at the FBI's 1946 report, which documents the claims that she and her sister "had sex relations" with George Dorsey, and calls it a lie. "I never did know about any parties down at the Fanny Wright house," she says. "Far as going to their parties, I never did. I ain't never been to a party but once in my life. Everybody that knows me know I didn't go to no parties."

Ruth Adams says she rarely even visited the Fanny Wright house during the year her family lived in the little white house next door. "I went over there one time when there wasn't no one there but Moena and maybe Ruby," she says. "I'll say it was two or three times. Moena was always good to me. I felt comfortable with her. And Dorothy was just like any other gal, friendly and respectable."

When her father took sick during the winter before the lynching, Ruth Adams says, it was she who cut wood and kept the stove going—not George Dorsey. Despite the claims of both Riden Farmer and her younger brother, Clinton Adams, she says George Dorsey never once set foot in their house. "My daddy wouldn't help a black person lying in the road," she says. "He . . . didn't like black people. That's why I tell you George did not go in my house. Ruby and Moena brought something to eat and visited thirty or forty minutes when my daddy's corpse was laid out. If he'd known, he'd gotten up out of the casket and kicked them out."

But amid all her denials, Ruth Adams does say that one afternoon during the fall of 1945, she was sweeping the front yard of their little house when George Dorsey walked up the road wearing his uniform.

"Hey, look up at me," she recalls George Dorsey saying. "Why don't you and me go to New York?"

She picked up her broom and went around to the backyard. "I hated him for doing that," she says. "I thought he was getting out of his place. I thought he was sticking himself where he shouldn't. I thought he should have been punished."

After that day, Ruth Adams never talked to George Dorsey again. "I'd see him coming up the road and I'd turn around and go in the house," she says. "Because we had nothing to say. I didn't think he had the right to be walking in the road and just pop off like that. He's a nice-looking black man in a uniform. But he wasn't that good-looking to me. In the sight of God's eye, he was as good as a white man, but God gave him the knowledge to stay in his place. And, back then, if they caught you associating with blacks, they'd kill you."

A half century after the Moore's Ford lynching, Ruth Adams sits in her house, an old woman in failing health, saying, "I feel so sorry about what happened to George and the others. Believe me, I've cried about the way them blacks was killed.

"But," she says, "he had it coming to him for what he did to me."

Outside Monroe, past the abandoned mill and the railroad tracks—where passenger trains no longer travel between Monroe and Atlanta—and past Towler's Woods, where so many couples used to park at night that a nearby farmer would shoot off his gun to get some peace, the road is lined with gas stations and beauty parlors and clapboard and brick houses. There's a country store where old white farmers meet in the afternoons to play cards. There is Union Chapel Methodist Church, and down the road, Brown's Hill Baptist Church—where Roger Malcom never attended services that Sunday afternoon. On Hestertown Road, the tenant house where Roger and Dorothy Malcom once lived is gone, and only widows remain in the modest homes that once sheltered the growing families of Hestertown—who were known as some of the best, and cruelest, cotton farmers in Walton County. The widow of Weldon Hester says she never did know her husband to be mean to Roger Malcom. She says Weldon Hester wasn't a suspect in 1946, and he didn't go to Athens to testify at the grand jury. The widow of suspect Clarence Hester, who died in 1987, says he couldn't have been involved in the lynching because he was at church that day. She doesn't know anything about the lynching, but she does remember that Roger Malcom killed Barnette Hester in July 1946. "That nigger killed Barnette," says the widow of Clarence Hester. "He sure did suffer."

Other white people in Hestertown also remember that Roger Malcom killed Barnette Hester that summer. But, contrary to their memories, Barnette Hester didn't die in 1946. He lived thirty-six more years, until the night of July 1, 1982, when he lay down in his bed in the farmhouse where he'd spent his entire life, and never got up.

On the morning of the day Barnette Hester was stabbed, his baby daughter, Linda Lemonds, had just taken her first steps. Now she is fifty-seven years old, and a grandmother. She says she was never told much about the lynching, but she saw the effects of the stabbing all her life. Every so often her father's side would swell and burst, and she or her mother—because her older brother, Nelson, committed suicide in 1961—would run to him with a basin and catch the liquid spilling from his wound. Her father underwent several operations, but he never really healed. It wasn't only that he was physically sick, she says. He was depressed. "Before he was stabbed, he drank on Saturday nights with the other men in Hestertown," she says. "But in the years after he got stabbed, he would drink all week. Then he'd be sick in the bed for a week. My mother would say, 'I just wish old Roger hadn't stabbed him.'"

Linda Lemonds remembers that when her father drank, he

sometimes mentioned Loy Harrison's name. Otherwise, he never said anything about the lynching or his stabbing. "He never acted like he was angry or talked mean about black people or mistreated them," she says. "He'd take his truck into Monroe to hire cotton pickers, and they'd jump on. They weren't scared of him."

Like Roger Malcom Hayes Sr., the son of Roger Malcom, Linda Lemonds learned much of what she knows about the lynching from the 1992 *Atlanta Journal-Constitution* article, which reported the rumors of her father's "relations" with Dorothy Malcom. Linda Lemonds believes the rumors could be true and wonders if she might have a half brother or a half sister, had things turned out differently. She would've liked that, because she's the only one left from the family now.

Linda Lemonds lives five miles from Hestertown and works part-time for the post office. When she's driving the roads of Walton County delivering mail, she thinks about sin and repentance. She wonders what her father knew about the lynching, and if he asked for forgiveness before he died. A devout Christian, she worries that those who participated in the lynching—some of whom were her neighbors and relatives—are being punished in the afterlife. The thought of their suffering causes her grief, and yet she sees no alternative. "These people committed a murder, and I don't know that they ever realized it was a bad thing," she says. "At the time, they had no remorse. The whole community let it go by."

She pauses, then says, "I know it was a great wrong."

NOTES

A Guide to Abbreviations in Notes

AB *Athens Banner* (Athens, Georgia)

AC *Atlanta Constitution* (Atlanta, Georgia)

ADW *Atlanta Daily World* (Atlanta, Georgia)

AJ *Atlanta Journal* (Atlanta, Georgia)

CD *Chicago Defender* (Chicago, Illinois)

CRS Documents relating to FBI File 144–19M-14 (Monroe, Ga., lynching case), Civil Rights Section (now Civil Rights Division), United States Department of Justice, Washington, D.C.; available through the Freedom of Information Act

F1 FBI File 44–136 (Unknown Subjects; Roger Malcom, et al., Victims); covers period between 10/24/46 and 11/24/46

F2 FBI File 44–136 (Unknown Subjects; Roger Malcom, et al., Victims); covers period between 11/18/46 and 11/25/46

F3 FBI File 144–19M-14 (Monroe, Ga., lynching case), Record Group 60, Civil Rights Division Classified Subject Files, 1930–1987, National Archives II, Washington, D.C. (citations listed by box number, section number, and page; e.g., 506, 15, p. 7)

F4 FBI File 44–144–44–106 (Georgia Election File), file #5920, unfiled archives, Georgia Historical Society, Savannah, Georgia (citations listed by file number)

F5 Transcript of FBI agent James T. Procopio's interview with Clinton U. Adams, Port Panama City, Florida, 7/17/91

NAACP Papers of the National Association for the Advancement of Colored People, Manuscript Division, Library of Congress, Washington, D.C. (citations listed by group number, series, and container; e.g., NAACP, II, A, 407)

NM   Papers of the National Association for the Advancement of Colored People, part 7, "The Anti-Lynching Campaign," series A, microfilm (citations listed by frame number; e.g., 28SF588)

PC   *Pittsburgh Courier* (Pittsburgh, Pennsylvania)

PCCR   Files of the President's Committee on Civil Rights, Harry S. Truman Library, Independence, Missouri (citations listed by record group, box number, page number; e.g., 220, 14, p. 42)

WN   *Walton News* (Walton County, Georgia)

WT   *Walton Tribune* (Walton County, Georgia)

Specific dates of interviews are listed when someone was interviewed only once. No date in the citation means the person was interviewed numerous times.

During the course of researching *Fire in a Canebrake*, the author was given a partial copy of FBI File 44–136, the report of the FBI's 1946 investigation into the Moore's Ford lynching. Since the copy wasn't obtained through the Freedom of Information Act (FOIA), it wasn't censored; it includes names of suspects, witnesses, and informants, as well as their corresponding testimony. The author's request for the full copy of the FBI's 1946 report through FOIA was declined. As there is no statute of limitations on the crime of murder, the Justice Department's position is that releasing the report could jeopardize the potential for Georgia to one day prosecute the lynchers.

CHAPTER ONE

3 Then he ran away: This account of the stabbing is drawn from the testimony of Bob Hester, Grady Malcom, Wayman Malcom, and Barnette Hester, F2, pp. 1–2, 241, 259, 262, 265; also from interviews with Linda Lemonds.

3 "bleeding to death": F2, p. 241.

6 Mother of Governors: WT, 11/13/46, p. 1.

7 wasn't segregated by race: WN, 3/5/46, p. 4.

7 would live out the week: F2, p. 4.

CHAPTER TWO

9 instead of going to church: Interview with Boyzie Daniels.

9 "leave you in the fall anyway": F3, 506, 15, pp. 5–6.

10 if a few white men hadn't restrained him: F1, p. 23.

11 "as sure as you're born": F2, pp. 151–52.

11 suspected they were having sexual relations: Ibid.

12 thought Dorothy was "fast": F3, 506, 15, pp. 3–4.

12 "other hands know about this mess": *Los Angeles Tribune*, 8/17/46, n.p.

12 easier access to Dorothy: "Investigation into the lynching of Roger Malcom, George Dorsey, veterans, together with their wives, Willie Mae and Dorothy, near Macon, Georgia, July 25, 1946," NAACP, II, A, 407.

12 "didn't pay me no attention": Interview with Allene Brown.

13 "and now I know it": F2, p. 151.

13 "SOB Roger walk this road again": F2, p. 255.

13 "kill him now": F3, 506, 15, p. 7.

14 "let the others do it": F2, p. 29.

14 holding his intestines: Phone interview with Barney Howard, 11/30/00.

CHAPTER THREE

18 bootleg liquor for the crowd: F1, p. 30.

18 trouble with the landlord: F2, p. 139.

19 averaged roughly one hundred acres: U.S. Bureau of the Census, *United States Census of Agriculture: 1945*, vol. 1; *Statistics for Counties*, pt. 17, *Georgia* (Washington, 1946), p. 39.

20 had moved away: U.S. Bureau of the Census, *Fifteenth Census of the United States: 1930*, vol. 3; *Population*, pt. 1, *Alabama-Missouri* (Washington, 1932), p. 541; U.S. Bureau of the Census, *Sixteenth Census of the United States: 1940*, vol. 2; *Population*, pt. 2, *Florida-Iowa* (Washington, 1943), p. 343.

20 "work it off on my farm": Interview with Hershel Dillard, 5/28/99.

20 "and they'd arrest you": Interview with George Marshall, 2/11/99.

21 if he brought him to the farm: Interview with Ruby Dorsey.

22 no schooling at all: "Enlisted Record and Report of Separation, Honorable Discharge," NAACP, II, A, 407.

23 lynched from it in 1911: AC, 6/28/11, p. 8.

24 only black man who owned commercial property: *Sixteenth Census*, p. 281.

25 black lawyer from Atlanta to represent him: Eugene Martin to Walter White, 8/24/46, NAACP, II, A, 407.

25 "He was strong and fearless": Interview with William Fowlkes, 2/3/99.

25 it was standard statewide: Donald L. Grant, *The Way It Was in the South: The Black Experience in Georgia* (New York, 1993), p. 200.

25 as *Brown v. Board of Education of Topeka:* John Egerton, *Speak Now Against the Day: The Generation Before the Civil Rights Movement in the South* (Chapel Hill, N.C., 1995), p. 380.

26 homeland "war for democracy": Jennifer Elizabeth Brooks, "From Hitler and Tojo to Talmadge and Jim Crow: WWII Veterans and the Remaking of Southern Political Tradition" (Ph.D. diss., University of Tennessee, Knoxville, 1997), p. 164.

27 backlash from her white supporters: Frederick Allen, *Atlanta Rising: The Invention of an International City, 1946–96* (Atlanta, 1996), p. 2.

27 "was to have been nothing": William Anderson, *The Wild Man from Sugar Creek: The Political Career of Eugene Talmadge* (Baton Rouge, 1975), pp. 219–20.

28 worked by people who didn't own them: *Census of Agriculture*, 1945, p. 212.

29 they owed him $48: F1, p. 190.

29 for attempting similar escapes: F1, p. 23.

29 "not be permitted to move away": Ibid.

30 "got to refigure the whole thing": Interview with James Barrow, 4/12/99.

31 primary election on July 17, 1946: WT, 7/12/46, p. 1.

31 ever before registered in Walton County: WT, 7/12/46, p. 1

31 only 40,000 and 50,000 respectively: Stephen G. N. Tuck, *Beyond Atlanta: The Struggle for Racial Equality in Georgia, 1940–1980* (Athens, Ga., 2001), p. 7.

CHAPTER FOUR

33 vigil at the hospital: F2, p. 242.

33 would somehow get through to him: Interview with Linda Lemonds.

33 maybe killed her: F2, p. 245.

34 "didn't want no trouble": Interview with Naomi Studdard, 12/9/99.

35 "and hold office in the South": Tuck, *Beyond Atlanta*, p. 43.

35 fourth term as governor: Anderson, *Wild Man*, p. 222.

35 "son of a bitch that can win": Ibid., p. 217.

35 a street in his hometown: Grant, *Way It Was*, p. 351.

36 "Southern traditions and segregation laws": AC, 7/12/46, quoted in Calvin McLeod Logue, *Eugene Talmadge: Rhetoric and Response* (New York, 1989), p. 216.

37 into white neighborhoods: Egerton, *Speak Now*, p. 383.

37 "drunk with their own power": AC, 6/28/46, quoted in Logue, *Rhetoric*, p. 226.

38 even the laws that prohibited intermarriage: *Savannah Morning News*, 6/4/46, quoted in Logue, *Rhetoric*, p. 226.

38 puff big cigars and smile wide: Allen, *Atlanta Rising*, p. 11.

38 "white people on buses": WN, 7/3/46, p. 1.

39 "you'll smell it, too": Ibid.

40 "bloodshed in Georgia": WSB-Atlanta radio broadcast, 7/6/46, quoted in Brooks, "From Hitler and Tojo," p. 312.

40 "do anything he wished": WT, 7/12/46, pp. 1, 5.

41 "hell-bent on halting the future": Anderson, *Wild Man*, p. 214.

41 to offer final instructions: Interview with Boyzie Daniels.

41 "do not take this ballot to the polls": WN, 7/24/46, p. 1.

42 it would be by accident: Anderson, *Wild Man*, p. 230.

42 to get some peace: F1, p. 183.

42 feared what this group of white men intended: F2, p. 22.

42 white men did park their cars: F1, p. 189.

43 one of the girls was so distraught: F2, pp. 32–33.

43 on a June night in 1911: AB, 6/28/11, p. 1.

44 no leader stepped forward: F2, p. 17.

CHAPTER FIVE

45 "here's five dollars": Interview with Boyzie Daniels.

47 "more orderly election": WT, 7/26/46, p. 2.

47 three black people were killed: F1, p. 12.

47 "brought the Negro into our primary": AJ, 7/18/46, p. 12.

48 "any race I ever won": AJ, 7/20/46, p. 1.

48 "I'm real tired": Ibid.

49 "your right to register and vote": Subpoena included in report of discrimination against Negro voters in Clay County, Ga., F4, File 44–116.

50 purged from voting lists throughout Georgia: F4, various.

50 to discuss the possibility: F4, File 44–127.

50 "improperly marked": WT, 7/19/46, p. 1.

51 threatening notes folded inside: F4, various.

51 only black man to vote in his district: AJ, 7/26/46, p. 20.

51 a hose, a pistol, and sticks: F2, p. 327.

52 "as fair as any election": F1, p. 124.

52 "damn foots across that road": F2, pp. 340–41.

52 voted in Blasingame: Tom O'Connor, *PM*, 7/28/46, NM, 28SF590.

52 while Carmichael got 39: WT, 7/19/46, p. 1.

53 altered the election's outcome: Joseph L. Bernd, "White Supremacy and the Disfranchisement of Blacks in Georgia, 1946," *Georgia Historical Quarterly*, winter 1982, p. 492.

53 "overestimated the amount of democracy": Eugene Martin to Walter White, 7/24/46, NAACP, II, A, 412.

54 "anywhere he might go": WT, 9/6/46, p. 2.

54 each day Loy Harrison had said no: F2, p. 6.

54 "thought he was going to die": Interview with Dolphus Norington, 2/12/99.

55 "a free man anymore": F2, p. 93.

55 wristwatch to use in jail: F3, 506, 15, p. 9.

55 "get out of here alive": Interview with Mattie Louise Campbell.

CHAPTER SIX

57 sat up in his bed: F2, p. 4.

57 Barnette would live: Ibid.

57 he could go free: F2, p. 243.

58 ironing for Loy Harrison's wife: F2, p. 139.

58 Again, Roger Malcom's muffled reply: F2, p. 115.

59 on his way home: F2, p. 116.

59 "get him at five o'clock": F2, p. 108.

59 ten cents' worth of penny candy: F2, p. 136.

59 Spot in the lead: F2, p. 137.

59 he called hello back: Interview with Boyzie Daniels.
60 met them there with his car: F2, p. 119.
60 "his wife's people": F2, p. 106.
60 black sharecroppers lived: Interview with Ruby Butler.
61 drove toward his farm: F2, p. 120.
61 "Stick 'em up," they said: F2, p. 121.
62 "the SOB that we want": Ibid.
62 "expertlike, prettylike": WN, 7/31/46, p. 1.
62 "take you along too, Charlie": F2, p. 121.
62 "This is our party": Ibid.
62 "Get those bitches too": Ibid.
63 "What could I do?": WN, 7/31/46, p. 1.
63 "know what to do with him": F2, p. 122.
64 "What should I do?": F2, p. 134.
64 routes between Monroe and his farm: F2, p. 124.
64 for news from the sheriff: F2, p. 140.
65 walked down with his twelve-year-old son: F2, p. 62.
65 while he joined the others: F2, p. 323.
65 left forearm were fractured: Coroner's report of Moore's Ford lynching, filed 7/26/46, Walton County Clerk of Court; also F2, p. 11.
66 vomited into the bushes: F2, p. 62.
66 "one Chevrolet car": Coroner's report.
66 "gun shots (many times)": Certificate of Death for Mae Murray Dorsey, File No. 177, Vital Records Service, Georgia Department of Human Resources.
66 after they'd fallen to the ground: F2, p. 11.
66 the first souvenir: O'Connor, *PM*, 7/30/46, NM, 28SF602.
67 already made burial arrangements: F2, p. 141.
67 "They were friends": Interview with Ed Almand III, 6/2/99.
67 wring a chicken's neck: Phone interview with Mary Alice Avery, 4/28/99.
68 hurried back inside: Ibid.
68 clearing black people off the streets: CD, 8/3/46, p. 6.
68 close up for the night: Interview with Hazel Sims, 3/19/99.
68 "something else could happen": Interview with John Culbreath, 1/12/98.
69 in the interest of protection: PC, 8/3/46, p. 4.
69 didn't drop below seventy-four degrees: AJ, 7/26/46, p. 1.
69 weak and disoriented, dreamy: F2, p. 259.
69 "do anything to Roger": Interview with Alberta Brown, 8/20/98.

CHAPTER SEVEN

73   to the bottom of a pond: AC, 7/11/1890, p. 1.

73   knucklebones on display: Grace Elizabeth Hale, *Making Whiteness: The Culture of Segregation in the South, 1890–1940* (New York, 1998), pp. 213–14.

73   out from the county jail: AC, 6/30/05, p. 1.

73   inclined to commit similar "crimes": AC, 6/28/11, p. 8.

73   sold briskly in Monroe: AB, 6/28/11, p. 1.

74   "tooth would be something": Phone interview with Don Garrett, 3/6/99.

74   fire in a canebrake: F2, p. 67.

74   perforated with bullet holes: *Louisville Courier-Journal*, 7/28/46, News Clippings File 1943–48, Division of Social Science Research, Carver Research Foundation, Tuskegee Institute (Tuskegee, 1971), 233F335.

74   "Lynchings at Dawn and Noon": AB, 7/28/11, p. 1.

74–75 "men from adjacent counties": AC, 6/29/11, p. 6.

75   within the county's borders for four days: AB, 11/25/13, p. 1.

75   telephone call from Georgia: Walter White, *A Man Called White* (Athens, 1995), p. 323.

76   of the victims were black: Jessie Parkhurst Guzman, ed., "Lynchings by Year and Race," in Allen D. Grimshaw, ed., *Racial Violence in the United States* (Chicago, 1969), pp. 58–59.

77   authorized to "go out and kill niggers": Roy Wilkins, introduction to Walter White, *Rope and Faggot* (New York, 1969), p. ii.

78   fighting with a bus driver: Egerton, *Speak Now*, pp. 362–63.

78   "Talmadge and Ku Klux Klan": Walter White to Tom Clark, 7/26/46, NM, 28SF571.

78   "but democracy itself": Walter White to Harry Truman, 7/26/46, NM, 28SF571.

78   incorrect surname for George Dorsey: Press Service of the National Association for the Advancement of Colored People, "Bulletin," 7/26/46, NM, 28SF443.

79   as quickly as possible: Walter White, "Memorandum From the Secretary," 7/26/46, NM, 28SF531.

80   "talked all over the place": AJ, 7/27/46, p. 5.

80   "I just needed a farmhand": AJ, 7/27/46, pp. 1, 5.

80   try to take revenge: AJ, 7/29/46, p. 4.

81   No, they said, not a bit: O'Connor, *PM*, 7/28/46, NM, 28SF588.

81 "Four Negroes lynched!": WT, 8/2/46, p. 1.
82 "riddled by sixty bullets": *News of the World*, 7:15 P.M., 7/26/46, National Broadcasting Corporation archives, Library of Congress, RWB 4385 A1.
82 had policies worth only $25 each: O'Connor, *PM*, 7/28/46, NM, 28SF594.
82 charged the city $140: Eugene Martin to Walter White, 8/8/46, NM, 28SF398.
82 "don't leave much face": O'Connor, *PM*, 7/28/46, NM, 28SF588.
82 knocked him off his feet: Interview with Dolphus Norington, 2/12/99.
83 time for a good-night kiss: Interview with Livingston O'Kelley, 12/10/99.
83 "they'll kill more": Interview with Annie Maud Dowdy, 6/3/99.

CHAPTER EIGHT

85 "they looked like ants": Interview with Glenn Sims, 12/10/99.
85 "to protect 'Negro balloting'": ADW, 7/30/46, p. 1.
85 "induced to go near": AC, 6/29/11, p. 6.
86 didn't want to see the place: AJ, 12/3/46, p. 1.
86 "mute evidence in human form": CD, 8/3/46, p. 2.
86 done to her child: Karla F. C. Holloway, *Passed On: African American Mourning Stories* (Durham, 2002), p. 130.
87 fired at close range: CD, 8/3/46, p. 2.
89 "tragedy . . . had never occurred": Ibid.
89 work for them once again: Oliver Harrington, untitled and undated report, NM, 28SF578.
90 "four of us in hell together": Ibid.
91 white men had done: PC, 8/3/46, p. 1.
91 "twenty pounds heavier": AJ, 7/28/46, p. 1.
92 "first confined to jail": AJ, 7/27/46, p. 1.
92 "an idea who it is": *The New York Times*, 7/28/46, p. 1.
92 "to take place in our state": Ibid., p. 1.
92 "incensed over this atrocity": AJ, 7/29/46, p. 1.
92 deemed the lynching "regrettable": Ibid.
92 "can't cope with them": AJ, 7/28/46, p. 1.
93 confronted him several days later: WT, 8/2/46, p. 2.
93 autopsy order from a Walton County judge: Judge Henry H. West, Superior Court, Walton County, untitled memo, 7/27/46, Walton County Clerk's Office, Monroe, Ga.

93 in the body's lower region: Interview with Louis Hutchinson, 7/14/99.

94 fruits of the night's labor: F2, p. 11.

95 "lynching is on the loose": ADW, 7/27/46, p. 1.

CHAPTER NINE

97 preside over the afternoon funeral: O'Connor, *PM*, 7/29/46, NM, 28SF594.

98 twice in recent history: Ibid., 28SF593.

98 "They ain't nowhere": PC, 8/3/46, n.p.

100 "to make sure he couldn't go": Interview with Ed Jackson, 5/25/99.

100 "why everyone was so scared": Ibid.

101 finished high school: F2, p. 153.

101 to appear at the funeral: Interview with Rosa Bell Ingram, 3/18/99.

102 "me and everyone else": CD, 8/17/46, p. 12.

103 "love could go a long way": Interview with Mattie Louise Campbell.

104 "get yourself killed, nigger": Ibid.

105 thanks to a $773 check: Eugene Martin to Walter White, 8/19/46, NAACP, II, A, 412.

105 take much with her to Chicago: F1, pp. 33–34.

105 kept it for himself: F2, p. 127.

106 because of what had happened: Interview with Annie Dorsey, 4/10/99.

106 owing him $300: F2, p. 259.

106 owing $17: F1, p. 56.

106 "Try and do something": Letter from [name withheld] to Tom Clark, 7/28/46, CRS.

106 "down the street any moore": Letter from Miss Vinita Ann, 8/21/46, F3, 506, 15, p. 11.

106 "the same thing is waiting for him": Letter from [name withheld] to Tom Clark, 7/28/46, CRS.

107 "here in our own United States": Letter from [name withheld] to Tom Clark, 7/30/46, CRS.

107 "at the mercy of lynch law": Letter from [name withheld] to Tom Clark, 7/28/46, CRS.

107 one every two minutes: CD, 8/10/46, p. 4.

107 "order for all its citizens": Letter from [name withheld] to Tom Clark, 7/28/46, CRS.

107 "Use it": Letter from [name withheld] to Tom Clark, 7/29/46, CRS.

107 less than 1 percent of lynchers: Robert L. Zangrando, Introduction, "The Anti-Lynching Campaign, 1912–1955," Part 7, Series A, The Papers of the National Association for the Advancement of Colored People (microfilm), p. xvii.

109 no violation of federal rights: Robert Carr and Nancy Wechsler, "Background Notes on the Lynching Problem," PCCR, 220, 6, pp. 9–10.

110 *willfully* deny his civil rights: Ibid., p. 14–15.

110 "Screws had willfully used his authority": Ibid., p. 17.

110 "crime committed against a Negro": Ibid., p. 16.

111 "their civil rights had not been violated": O'Connor, *PM*, 7/28/46, NM, 28SF589.

112 "blasted America into doing something": CD, 8/17/46, p. 14.

113 ratcheted up nationwide outrage: AJ, 7/30/46, p. 1.

113 "Mania Grips Dixie": CD, 8/10/46, p. 1.

113 largest mass meeting held in a decade: CD, 8/3/46, p. 6.

113 "those responsible for these horrible crimes": Petitions from the American Youth for Democracy, 8/13/46, CRS.

113 "prosecution of the criminals": AJ, 7/30/46, p. 1.

114 "some State officer had tipped off the mob": Theron Caudle to Tom Clark, 9/26/46, quoted in John Thomas Elliff, "The United States Department of Justice and Individual Rights, 1937–1962" (Ph.D. diss., Harvard University, 1967), p. 234.

114 one of the nation's midsized cities: Ibid., p. 232.

114 "The FBI": WT, 9/13/46, p. 1.

CHAPTER TEN

115 in his own way: F3, 506, 15, p. 7.

115 "reprisal against Roger Malcom": F2, p. 260.

116 denied the conversation had taken place: F2, p. 243.

116 "into the ground": Ibid.

116 "The obvious motive for the lynching": F2, p. 14.

116 "happen to the Malcom boy": O'Connor, *PM*, 7/29/46, NM, 28SF594.

118 "not that I know of": F2, pp. 157–58.

119 laughed out his car window: F2, pp. 159–60 .

119 ringleader in the beatings: F1, p. 190.

120 called out Weldon Hester's name: F2, p. 170.

120 licked his lips continuously: F2, p. 164.

120 that it was human blood: F2, p. 163.

121   left the house at any time: F2, pp. 200–203.

122   to visit Jack Malcom: F2, pp. 204–5.

122   alerting them of agents' plans: F1, pp. 205–8.

123   "I'd kill him": F1, p. 197.

123   "such information in their possession": F2, p. 15.

123   "all they want is a white woman": O'Connor, *PM*, 8/5/46, NM, 29SF611.

123   "killed the two women": *Louisville Kentucky-Courier*, 7/28/46, Tuskegee News Clippings File, 233F335.

124   "In broad daylight": J. J. Holley to Richard Russell, 7/31/46, Richard B. Russell Library for Political Research and Studies, University of Georgia, Box 201, Folder 4.

124   "intensify sectional and racial hatred": Richard Russell to J. J. Holley, 8/5/46, ibid.

124   anyone arrested in the lynching: F1, p. 194.

125   "Town Where Four Negroes Were Slain": WT, 9/13/46, p. 1.

125   "who know so little about it": WT, 8/2/46, p. 2.

125   "without bearing a crop": O'Connor, *PM*, 8/5/46, NM, 29SF611.

126   "just a killing": Mrs. W. T. Brightwell to Richard Russell, 7/31/46, Richard B. Russell Library for Political Research and Studies, University of Georgia, Box 201, Folder 4.

127   "should not be so difficult": CD, 9/17/46, p. 7.

127   "few signs of a manhunt": Edward B. Smith, Scripps-Howard News Service, 8/12/46, n.p.

128   "punishment of the mobsters": *Indianapolis Times*, 8/13/46, n.p.

128   "struck back at Hester's son": *Daily Worker*, 8/5/46, p. 1, Tuskegee News Clippings File, 233F338.

128   "world's best human bloodhounds": CD, 9/21/46, p. 2.

129   could they be sent to Walton County?: Walter White to J. Edgar Hoover, 8/21/46, NAACP, II, A, 267.

129   employed three black agents: Gail Williams O'Brien, *The Color of the Law: Race, Violence, and Justice in the Post–World War II South* (Durham, N.C., 1999), p. 195.

129   "they would talk to a Negro agent": Testimony of J. Edgar Hoover, 3/20/47, PCCR, 220, 14, p. 78.

130   "didn't believe a word of it": Interview with Boyzie Daniels.

130   "enforcement of civil rights": Testimony of Thurgood Marshall, 4/17/47, PCCR, 220, 14, p. 118.

130 "on behalf of the criminals": Walter White to Robert Carter, 8/21/46, NAACP, II, A, 267.

130 "in no time at all": letter from [name withheld] to Tom Clark, 8/7/46, CRS.

130 "done the horrible deed": letter from [name withheld] to Tom Clark, 8/14/46, CRS.

131 abandoned the lead: F1, p. 19.

131 and a 9mm revolver: F2, p. 11.

132 lead went cold right there: F1, p. 113.

132 to the lab for analysis: Interview with Louis Hutchinson, 7/14/99.

133 "Hell, yes," he said: PC, 8/3/46, p. 1.

CHAPTER ELEVEN

135 "not sticking to the main road": William H. Fitelson, "The Murders at Monroe," *The New Republic*, 9/2/46, p. 259.

135 "going to kill himself": Interview with Ruby Dorsey.

136 "just like they was family": Interview with Anne Harrison Manders, 9/5/99.

136 drove over the Moore's Ford Bridge: F1, p. 37.

137 show him he meant business: Phone interview with Jack Ward, 10/12/99.

137 "all the nigger hands I can get": O'Connor, *PM*, 7/28/46, NM, 28SF594.

138 dropped all the charges in 1923: Cases 734, 760, and 765, Superior Court docket, Oconee County, Oconee County Courthouse, Ga.

139 "he did not tell the truth": Case for Appeal, "The State, Respondent, against John Barfield, alias Loy Harrison, Appellant," Supreme Court of South Carolina, November 1923.

139 he'd served prison sentences: F2, p. 126.

140 hadn't been discovered yet: F3, 507, 17, p. 2.

140 Roughly one-third of all crimes: Author's survey of Walton and Oconee Counties' Superior Court docket books, Walton County Clerk's Office, Monroe, Ga.

141 "big man go to Mr. Loy": Interview with Roy Jackson.

141 working his stills again: F1, pp. 48–49.

141 "to see who was stealing it": Interview with Annie Maud Dowdy, 6/3/99.

141 "Them niggers done that": F3, 507, 17, p. 4.

142 "he would not let me go": Ibid., p. 2.

142 took him to Moena's house: Ibid., p. 6.

142   work off his debt: F2, p. 145.
143   day after the lynching: F2, p. 142.
144   whipped him with a chain: F2, p. 42.
144   they threatened to kill him: F1, p. 40.
144   "feared no one": F1, p. 42.
146   participated in the lynching: F2, pp. 322–27.
147   not a victim of it: F2, pp. 68–69.
147   "get over to my farm": F1, p. 38.
147   delivered the news: Interview with Ruby Dorsey.
148   "you helped kill my children": F1, p. 38.

CHAPTER TWELVE

150   in the trunks of their cars: WT, 9/13/46, p. 1.
150   a half crop of cotton, maybe less: WT, 10/4/46, p. 1.
151   "paid off in savagery": "Statement to be presented to President Truman, Thursday, Sept. 19th," NAACP, II, A, 442.
151   "got to do something!": William E. Leuchtenburg, "The Conversion of Harry Truman," *American Heritage*, November 1991, p. 58.
152   "to prevent such happenings": Harry Truman to Tom Clark, 9/20/46, PSF General File, Negro folder, Harry S. Truman Library, quoted in Robert J. Donovan, *Conflict and Crisis* (New York, 1977), p. 245.
152   "how to handle the niggers": Leuchtenburg, "The Conversion," p. 58.
152   "lengths to which people would go": Harry Truman to Stephen Spingarn, 10/18/56, Oral History interview, 3/23/67, Harry S. Truman Library, p. 577.
153   "or other officials in Georgia": J. Edgar Hoover to Tom Clark, 9/19/46, File 144-02, in Elliff, "Department of Justice and Individual Rights," p. 231.
153   "enforcement by the Department": J. Edgar Hoover to Tom Clark, 9/24/46, PCCR, 220, 6, FBI folder.
153   "failed to 'solve' many cases": Ibid.
154   "infringements of a Civil Rights Statute": Hoover to Clark, 9/19/46, in Elliff, "Department of Justice and Individual Rights," p. 233.
154   "bound to exhaust the possibility": Theron Caudle to Tom Clark, 9/26/46, File 144–012, in Elliff, "Department of Justice and Individual Rights," p. 233.
155   "until we find out who did it": Tom Clark to J. Edgar Hoover, 10/7/46, in Elliff, "Department of Justice and Individual Rights," p. 234.
155   "associating with white girls": F1, p. 14.

155 "going with white women": F1, p. 145.

155 should've killed George Dorsey: F1, p. 16 .

155 "whistled at some white girls": F1, p. 148.

155 flirting with a white woman: F1, p. 11.

156 walked home and went to bed: F2, p. 62.

156 to the bus stop to meet him: Interview with Clinton Adams, 6/21/99.

157 while George Dorsey played his guitar: F2, p. 64.

157 "and find him missing": F2, p. 66.

157 had met with foul play: Interview with Robert Palmer, 2/12/99.

158 "Been dead for several hours": Coroner's report, filed 2/5/46, Walton County Clerk's Office, Monroe, Ga.

158 daughters had been "promiscuous": F1, p. 57.

159 "full of shots as would stick": F2, p. 64.

160 chief suspects: J. Edgar Hoover to Tom Clark, 10/3/46, F3, 507, 60, p. 18.

CHAPTER THIRTEEN

161 as soon as their cotton was gathered: F2, p. 141.

161 "strictly his own business": F2, p. 154.

161 "for we all need you": F3, 507, 17, p. 8.

161 "full of shots": F1, p. 47.

161 "in the integrity of Harrison": CD, 12/4/46, p. 6.

161 threatened and coached too extensively: F2, p. 155.

162 his attorney would tell him: F2, p. 146.

162 the intimidation largely worked: F1, p. 38.

162 was considering moving: Eugene Martin to Walter White, 8/24/46, NAACP, II, A, 133.

162 couldn't find her mother a place to stay: F3, 507, 17, p. 10.

163 "You know, *quietly*": Interview with Rosa Bell Ingram, 3/18/99.

163 "put a bullet in us": Interview with Gladys Taylor, 6/25/99.

163 had been done to him: E. M. Martin to Walter White, 8/24/46, NAACP, II, A, 133.

163 "means certain death": ADW, 8/4/46, p. 8.

164 "low-class blacks": Interview with Ed Jackson, 5/25/99.

164 George had a "big mouth": F1, p. 173.

165 "mighta had to kill them": Interview with Randall Whitehead, 4/10/99.

165 "that type of family": Interview with Ed Jackson, 5/25/99.

165 "back where they come from": Interview with Emma Lou Gordon, 6/3/99.

166 "more than forty people": Interview with John Pope, 1/8/99.

166 supplied by Loy Harrison via Jim Williams: Interview with Roy Jackson.

166 "call it an outlaw house": Interview with Ileane McGhee, 6/25/99.

167 "drank and fought there": Interview with Red Whitehead, 4/22/99.

167 Ruth and Effie May Adams began attending them: Roy Jackson, John Pope, and Riden Farmer say they saw Ruth and Effie May Adams at the Fanny Wright parties. Others, like Ruby Butler, say they saw them having "too close" contact with George and Charlie Boy Dorsey on the roads near the Moore's Ford Bridge. Ruth Adams denies ever attending any parties at the Fanny Wright house and denies ever having intimate contact with George or Charlie Boy Dorsey. Her younger sister, Effie May, is dead.

167 executed in Georgia's electric chair: WT, 5/26/39, p. 1.

168 "he can't do it here": Interview with Ruby Butler.

168 "a reason why George was killed": F1, p. 46.

169 Confidential Informant T-6: F1, p. 2.

170 a gray 1939 Ford: F2, p. 47.

170 second one was definitely black: F2, p. 48.

170 "a fictitious story": F1, p. 67.

170 information was false: F2, p. 49.

171 on the other side of the river: F1, p. 42.

CHAPTER FOURTEEN

173 a banker, and a retiree: AJ, 12/2/46, p. 4.

174 "of certain U.S. criminal statutes": AB, 12/2/46, p. 6.

174 "the end of my inquiry": AJ, 12/2/46, p. 4.

175 "for the discovery of evidence": Paul S. Diamond, *Federal Grand Jury Practice and Procedure*, 3rd ed. (Englewood Cliffs, N.J., 1995), p. 1.

176 "Bureau will cooperate with us": Theron Caudle to J. Edgar Hoover, 11/6/46, CRS.

177 "might be made by the Bureau's Laboratory": J. Edgar Hoover to Tom Clark, 10/3/46, F3, 507, 18.

179 He was pale and gaunt: AJ, 12/3/46, p. 1.

180 "sure of the Negroes called there to testify": ADW, 12/6/46, p. 6.

180 "if Truman said you could stay": AB, 12/5/46, p. 1.

180 "they rushed to defend": ADW, 12/6/46, p. 6.

181 since the lynching: AJ, 12/3/46, p. 1.

181 "just to please 'em": AB, 12/6/46, p. 1.

CHAPTER FIFTEEN

184 "they didn't want it stopped": Interview with Boyzie Daniels.

185 he couldn't identify them: F2, p. 56.

185 by the end of the week: Turner Smith to Theron Caudle, 12/10/46, CRS.

185 "for a Federal case": Turner Smith to Theron Caudle, 12/12/46, CRS.

186 "get him at five o'clock": F2, p. 108.

186 "mistakenly get Major Jones": Turner Smith to Theron Caudle, 12/11/46, CRS.

187 "harming him bodily": F1, p. 7.

187 "out and mob him": F1, p. 9.

189 because he was sick: Turner Smith to Theron Caudle, 12/11/46, CRS.

190 yet to appear in front of the grand jury: Turner Smith to Theron Caudle, 12/16/46, CRS.

190 several members of the Walton County sheriff's office: AC, 12/19/46, p. 12.

190 "pretty well washed out": Turner Smith to Theron Caudle, 12/16/46, CRS.

190 "civil rights statutes of the United States": Turner Smith to Theron Caudle, 12/10/46, CRS.

191 "where Negroes are the victims": Thurgood Marshall to Tom Clark, 12/27/46, NAACP, II, A, 410.

191 "no use in my saying I do": Thurgood Marshall to Walter White, 1/23/47, NAACP, II, A, 410.

191 "it is unbelievable": Testimony of Thurgood Marshall, 4/17/47, PCCR, 220, 14, p. 118.

191 "was almost unbelievable": Testimony of J. Edgar Hoover, 3/20/47, PCCR, 220, 14, p. 41.

192 "in some fashion, break them all": AC, 7/29/46, p. 6.

193 to stay with him for another year: F2, p. 154.

194 "more peaceful than small-town Monroe": Interview with Mary Alice Avery, 6/10/99.

CHAPTER SIXTEEN

195 "tell 'em down at Athens": ADW, 1/3/47, p. 1.

195 talking with Loy Harrison: F2, pp. 328–29.

196 "Take him out back": Interview with Lamar Howard, 7/31/98.

196 clouded his vision: Ibid.

197 safe through the night: ADW, 1/3/47, p. 6.

197 "could happen just like that": Interview with William Fowlkes, 2/3/99.

198 "they could not deny": Testimony of J. Edgar Hoover, 3/20/47, PCCR, 220, 14, p. 42.

198 "Can Crack Lynch Mystery": CD, 1/18/47, p. 1.

198 "dying in vain": Egerton, *Speak Now*, p. 387.

199 the evidence so overwhelming: ADW, 2/25/47, p. 1.

200 "fine white gentlemen": Ibid.

200 Verner "not guilty": Ibid., pp.1, 2.

200 running him off the road: F2, p. 324.

201 the nickname Monroe: Interview with Lamar Howard, 7/31/98.

202 "their hand to the limit": Walter White to NAACP branches, 7/30/46, NAACP, II, A, 407.

203 "civil rights of all our citizens": Harry Truman, "Address to the 38th annual conference of the NAACP," 6/28/47, OF 93, Harry S. Truman Library.

203 "prove that I do mean it": Donovan, *Conflict and Crisis*, p. 334.

203 once during the Civil War: *To Secure These Rights: The Report of the President's Committee on Civil Rights* (New York, 1947), p. 139.

204 " 'beyond hope of redemption' ": Leuchtenburg, "The Conversion," p. 62.

204 "made me sick at heart": Richard Russell to Miss Amanda Johnson, 3/1/48, Richard B. Russell Library for Political Research and Studies, University of Georgia, Box 201, Folder 4.

204 "failure will be in a good cause": Leuchtenburg, "The Conversion," p. 66.

207 "One, two, three": Arthur Gordon, *Reprisal* (New York, 1950), pp. 84–85.

CHAPTER SEVENTEEN

209 "watch them get whipped": F5, p. 43.

210 would have been proud to have: Marjorie Adams, as told to Ann Varnum, *The Secret Inside* (Webb, Ala., 1999), p. 20.

210 sounded like a fire in a canebrake: *Atlanta Journal-Constitution*, 5/31/92, p. A8.

210 heart beating in his throat: Adams and Varnum, *Secret Inside*, p. 61.

211 "paid it no attention": F5, p. 26.

211 "swallow a basketball": Interview with Clinton Adams, 6/21/99.

211 "your sister, even you": Ibid.

211   "didn't question no children": F5, p. 28.

212   "better than any white man": F5, p. 44.

212   "some people don't know that": F5, p. 15.

212   "afraid of what you might say": Adams and Varnum, *Secret Inside*, p. 7.

212   "Not if *they* have their way": Ibid., p. 1.

213   "they was watching you": F5, p. 47.

214   "haunted me over the years": F5, p. 42.

214   "This was a diversion": Interview with James Procopio, 6/18/99.

215   "That's all I want": *Dateline NBC*, 7/7/92.

215   "Don't think I will": Transcript from *The Oprah Winfrey Show*, 10/13/92, p. 11.

216   allegedly beat her son: *North Georgia News*, 6/28/89, p. 1.

216   "he wouldn't tell anything": F5, p. 28.

217   Clinton Adams wasn't visiting them: Interview with Ralph and Della Farmer.

217   Clinton Adams racing home on his horse: Interview with Frank and Gladys Taylor, 3/18/99.

218   doesn't mention Clinton Adams's name once: Interview with Special Agent Principal Mike Pearson and former special agent in charge Bill Malueg, Georgia Bureau of Investigation, Athens, 11/2/01.

218   "burned into my memory": Adams and Varnum, *Secret Inside*, p. 74.

219   surveillance Clinton Adams describes: Interview with Dr. E. M. Beck.

220   "he want to work for me?": Interview with Billy Perkins, 5/21/99.

220   " 'better talk to the FBI' ": Interview with Clinton Adams, 6/21/99.

220   "I don't dwell on it": Ibid.

220   "didn't have much associating": Ibid.

221   "I intend for that": Ibid.

221   "That is the truth": Interview with Clinton Adams, 6/21/99.

221   "black people out to be martyrs": Interview with Jamey Harrison, 9/30/99.

222   never once heard his father mention Clinton Adams: Phone interview with Barney Howard, 11/30/00.

222   "brought them to court and convicted them": Interview with Marvin Sorrells, 4/8/99.

222   "anything positive to come from it": *Atlanta Journal-Constitution*, 5/31/92, p. A9.

222   "doesn't need to be brought back out": *Dateline NBC*, 7/7/92.

CHAPTER EIGHTEEN

225 in her book that they were): Adams and Varnum, *Secret Inside*, p. 81.

226 hung, not shot, to death: Interview with Roger M. Hayes Sr., 9/18/00.

230 "where was her people?": Interview with Fannie Mooney, 4/10/99.

236 "Somebody done the work": Interview with Jack Malcom, 12/15/99.

237 "I don't think the Hesters killed anybody": Interview with Hughlon Peters, 11/30/99. The dialogue from Jack Malcom and Hughlon Peters occurred during the author's interviews with the two men. Georgia Bureau of Investigation policy prevents agents from disclosing specific information gained during their interviews. However, agents have verified that the material here is similar to that produced by their questioning of Jack Malcom and Hughlon Peters.

238 "and roughed him up": WT, 4/30/01, p. 1.

238 twelve at the time of the lynching: Interview with Special Agent Principal Mike Pearson and former special agent in charge Bill Malueg, Georgia Bureau of Investigation, Athens, 11/2/01.

238 "to find out who did this": *Athens Banner-Herald*, 7/27/01, n.p.

240 "One whore, nothing else": Interview with Mattie Louise Campbell.

240 "how much is a life worth?": Interview with Roger M. Hayes Sr., 9/18/00.

241 "I didn't go to no parties": Interview with Ruth Adams.

243 to testify at the grand jury: Interview with Ollie Hester Peters, 12/13/99.

243 "He sure did suffer": Interview with Ruby Hester, 11/30/99.

243 " 'old Roger hadn't stabbed him' ": Interview with Linda Lemonds.

AUTHOR'S NOTE

The seeds for this book were planted by the 1992 beating of Rodney King and the 1995 trial of O. J. Simpson. Both events challenged my vision of race relations in late-twentieth-century America as nothing else had, revealing that many blacks and whites fundamentally disagree about what constitutes truth—and that many blacks and whites live in different countries despite being citizens of the same nation.

In the fall of 1997, I read an article about the Moore's Ford lynching in the student newspaper at the University of Georgia, where I was then working. My first reactions were the common ones: shock and horror. But almost immediately I began to wonder if the lynching could serve as an entry point, if it would be possible to learn something about the Rodney King beating and the O.J. trial by examining an incident that had occurred more than a half century before.

I had already begun researching the Moore's Ford lynching in June 1998, when the news came that a forty-nine-year-old black man named James Byrd Jr. had been chained to the bumper of a truck and dragged to his death by three white men in Jasper, Texas. That summer, on my many drives to Walton and Oconee counties from my home in Athens, I listened to the news reports and wondered how similar Jasper, Texas, in 1998 was to Monroe, Georgia, in 1946—and how different.

Indeed, I found myself constantly shuttling between 1946 and the present during the four years I worked on this book. I'd often spend a morning reading about an event related to the lynching in a newspaper article on microfilm, and then spend the afternoon sitting on a front porch with someone who'd witnessed that same event in 1946. The combination of, and the conflicts between, the "evidence" gained from various sources allowed me not only to reconstruct the events surrounding the lynching, but to understand how those events were interpreted, believed, told, and remembered. Writing about murder is always a challenge, because the victims cannot speak. Roger and Dorothy Malcom, and George and Mae Murray Dorsey, left no diaries or letters, nothing that would explain their lives in their own words. I have tried to bring them to life (a strange phrase) in the book through information gathered from those who knew them, as well as from the FBI's report of its investigation into the lynching. Because my goal was to tell as truthful a story as possible, I did not invent scenes or dialogue, or engage in speculation that couldn't be documented.

Over the course of four years, I was able to interview more than one hundred people in Walton and Oconee counties and throughout the country. I found that reactions to my requests for interviews ran the gamut. Some people were anxious to tell what they'd heard or seen; some, in fact, seemed as though they'd been waiting for a person to knock on their front door, saying, "I'm writing a book about the Moore's Ford lynching." Others were apathetic, fearful, distrustful, duplicitous, or hostile. In general, I had far less success convincing white people to allow me to interview them than I did convincing black people. Again and again, the response from whites was "Why drag this thing up?" In asking such a question, some meant that it would be better for everyone if the lynching were relegated to the safety of the not-so-distant past. Others asked the same question, but meant: Why all this fuss over four dead black sharecroppers? Some white people were afraid to say anything about the lynching for fear they'd be labeled racist, and others simply wanted to continue hiding what they knew, as they had for more than fifty years.

My conversations with the white people who did consent to being interviewed were essential to my understanding of the lynching—less for the information they supplied than for the way they revealed how segregated the memory of the Moore's Ford lynching remains. This segregation is evident in the opposing beliefs about the lynching's victims and villains, and about its very causation. But it's evident most starkly in the differing meanings and significances attributed to the lynching. For many black people, the lynching was the most horrific thing that ever happened in Walton or Oconee counties, but for many white people, it was mainly an annoyance, an event that smudged the area's good name.

The segregated memories of the Moore's Ford lynching are the precursors to the divisive reactions to the Rodney King beating and the O.J. trial and the dragging of James Byrd Jr. And the segregated memories of the Moore's Ford lynching reveal something basic: The only way for blacks and whites to live together peacefully in America in the twenty-first century is if we begin struggling to understand and acknowledge the extent to which racism has destroyed—and continues to destroy—our ability to tell a common truth.

When I began this project, I hoped to solve the murders, hoped for prosecution of the lynchers. But now, after years of investigation, I believe we'll never know who fired the shots in the clearing near the Moore's Ford Bridge on July 25, 1946. And I wonder if that unanswered question, that hole where the center should be, isn't the truest representation of race in America.

Laura Wexler
Baltimore, Maryland

ACKNOWLEDGMENTS

I first thank Charley "Isadore" Brooks and Robert Howard, two fine Southern gents and loyal compatriots. They put their trust in me early on and stuck with me throughout the adventure. I couldn't have written this book without them.

Henry Dunow also put his trust in the project early on and stuck with me. One rainy February morning, he told me to "maximize the drama." I'm forever grateful to him for those three words and for all his wise and supportive literary counsel.

I offer a huge thanks to my talented, funny, and patient editor, Brant Rumble. He's as passionate about this story as I am, and I'm glad we got to be partners. Thanks also to Jane Rosenman, who saw the value of this project in its infancy, and to the entire team at Scribner.

I completed the research and writing of this book with the support of a grant from the Harry S. Truman Library and a residency at the MacDowell Colony. I benefited from the assistance of librarians and archivists at the Harry S. Truman Library, the University of Georgia libraries, the Auburn Avenue Research Library, the Georgia Historical Society, the Darlington County Historical Commission, and National Archives II. Thanks especially to the folks at the Library of Congress and to Nelson Hermilla, chief of the Freedom of Information/Privacy Acts Branch of the Civil Rights Division of the U.S. Justice Department.

I thank Woody Beck for his wise counsel and cheerful generosity, and Rich Rusk and the Moore's Ford Memorial Committee for their support and enthusiasm. I also offer my thanks to Louis Hutchinson, Jack Ward, Jim Procopio, Mike Pearson, and Bill Malueg; and to Wayne Ford, Ronald Finch, Wallace Warren, Hyde Post, David Garrow, Cliff Kuhn, and Lori Shaw and Susan Brenner at the University of Dayton School of Law. Thanks to Toby Thompson, Tom Lorenz, Cheryl Lester, and Patricia Hampl for their encouragement during my journey to become a writer. Thanks to Donald Antrim, for his help in finding a literary agent. And thanks to the good people at *Georgia Magazine* in Athens, Georgia, who allowed me to work part-time throughout much of the research phase of this project.

I'm profoundly grateful to those who overcame fear or suspicion to talk with me about the Moore's Ford lynching and about life in Walton and Oconee counties in the 1940s. These include: Castell Avery, Ruby Dorsey, Randall and Inez Whitehead, Ruby Butler, Elzata Brown, Frank Stancil, Larry Witcher, Boyzie Daniels, George Marshall, Lamar Howard, William Fowlkes, Frank Bolden, Ruth Adams, Burrice Gordon, Robert Bell, Marvin Sorrells, Doug and Eugene Peters, Herman and Tom Daniel, Hattie Maud Thrasher, Allene Brown, Don Garrett, Betty Foster, S.H., Lizzie Lou Vinson, Ed Jackson, Mary Alice Avery, Red Whitehead, Lugene Johnson, Portia and C. A. Scott, Anne Harrison Manders, James Barrow, Jamey Harrison, Barney Howard, Louis Cody, Patrice Dorsey, Linda Lemonds, Clinton and Marjorie Adams, Roger M. Hayes Sr., Lurie Maddox, and Tyrone Brooks. A special thank-you to Herman Robertson, who seems to know everyone in Walton and Oconee counties. In memoriam, I thank Mattie Louise Campbell, Roy Jackson, and Joe Ingram.

Thanks to Bryant Simon, Claudio Saunt, Andrew Grant-Thomas, Richard Fausset, Kristen Smith, Charlotte Stoudt, and Kimi Eisele for reading and critiquing drafts of the manuscript.

Thanks also to Kimi Eisele for being the best writer friend around. Thanks to Julie Checkoway for mapping out the book's structure on the chalkboard on a day when I needed it. Thanks to Kevin Young, Lee Thomsen, Peter Frey, Tom Payton, Pat Allen, Judy Long, Jennifer and Heather Maldonado, Deb Stanley, Rob Hilton, Melinda Weir, Pat Priest, Lew Klatt, Jenny Allen, Molly Baker, Valerie Boyd, and Heather Liszka for their friendship. Thanks to Andrea Seabrook for her enthusiasm. And thanks to Norma Wood for appearing on my front porch one day.

Thanks to my beloved parents, who supported this project even when they weren't sure why it was taking so long. Thanks especially to my father, who recognized the value of a writing office and made a generous donation that allowed me to rent one.

And thanks to Steve Lickteig, whose wisdom, wit, and love have made this book—and my life—so much better.